From Punishment to Doing Good

Family Courts and Socialized Justice in Ontario, 1880–1940

As Canada and other Western societies move from laissez-faire to welfare states, social and legal institutions have undergone dramatic transformations. Dorothy Chunn examines the nature of these changes through an in-depth analysis of developments in one such institution, the family courts system of Ontario. She explores the origins, legitimation, and impact of the court system, and addresses contentious questions about how society deals with the deviant and dependent, how social welfare reform comes about, and the consequences of such reform.

The reform impetus that produced the family court was shaped by a number of interrelated structural conditions – urbanization, industrialization, universal suffrage – which generated a sense of crisis among the urban middle classes of Toronto and other cities. At the centre of this crisis was 'the family.' Through a process of mediation, refinement, and revision, some reform proposals were selectively incorporated into policies and legislation related to deviant or marginal families.

The collective product of these reforms, including family courts, was a new 'socialized' mode for regulating and maintaining existing class and gender relations among a certain segment of the working and dependent poor. However, socialized legal coercion was not simply a uniform system of oppression conceived and used by the capitalist, patriarchal state to control marginalized groups. Rather it proved to be characterized by contradictions that had a differential impact on its clients related to social class and gender. Thus, poor families and in particular poor women were both empowered and oppressed, active and acted upon, by the new domestic relations tribunals.

Chunn makes an important contribution to the contemporary revisionist literature on social welfare reform and the moral-political regulation of marginal populations in Western market societies for the past two centuries.

DOROTHY E. CHUNN is Assistant Professor in the School of Criminology and Co-director of the Feminist Institute for Studies in Law and Society, Simon Fraser University.

DOROTHY E. CHUNN

From Punishment to Doing Good:

Family Courts and Socialized Justice in Ontario, 1880–1940

UNIVERSITY OF TORONTO PRESS
Toronto Buffalo London

© University of Toronto Press 1992
Toronto Buffalo London
Printed in Canada

ISBN 0-8020-5993-7 (cloth)
ISBN 0-8020-6927-4 (paper)

Printed on acid-free paper

Canadian Cataloguing in Publication Data

Chunn, Dorothy E. (Dorothy Ellen), 1943–
From punishment to doing good : family courts
and socialized justice in Ontario, 1880–1940

Includes index.
ISBN 0-8020-5993-7 (bound)   ISBN 0-8020-6927-4 (pbk.)

1. Domestic relations courts – Ontario – History.
2. Public welfare – Ontario – History.   I. Title.

KEO214.C58 1992   346.71301'5'0269   C91-095556-5
KF505.5.C58 1992

This book has been published with the help of a grant from the Social Science
Federation of Canada, using funds provided by the Social Sciences and
Humanities Research Council of Canada.

FOR MY PARENTS

Contents

Acknowledgments

This book reflects the collective input of many people. Professor John Beattie sparked my initial interest in the history of punishment and welfare. Dr Anthony Doob, Centre of Criminology, University of Toronto, and the School of Criminology, Simon Fraser University, gave me access to facilities that made my work easier. I am also grateful for the financial support provided at various stages of this project by the Centre of Criminology in Toronto (through funds made available by the federal Ministry of the Solicitor General), the Social Sciences and Humanities Research Council, the Social Science Federation of Canada, and the Simon Fraser University Publication Grants Committee.

A number of people facilitated the research process. Special thanks go to His Honour H.T.G. Andrews, chief judge of the Ontario Provincial Courts (Family Division), for opening doors to restricted archival materials. V. Lorne Stewart, retired senior judge of the Toronto Family Court; Mr McCann, former court administrator of the Ottawa and Carleton Family Court; and the federal Department of Justice, also provided invaluable assistance to me in obtaining data that were not publicly available. Many thanks as well to Sandra Hall at the Ottawa Municipal Archives, Tom Nesmith at the Public Archives of Canada, and Richard Ramsey and Cathy Sheppard at the Archives of Ontario, who so patiently demystified the archives for a novice; and to Roman Komar, who very generously furnished me with photocopies of relevant statutes.

Colleagues at the Centre of Criminology in Toronto and the School of Criminology at Simon Fraser University have given me much-appreciated support along the way. Discussions with Shelley Gavigan, Mary

Morton, Chris Murphy, Frank Pearce, and Gordon West were particularly helpful during the early stages of my research. Neil Boyd and Margaret Jackson have also extended ongoing encouragement. Professors Jim Giffen, Dennis Magill, and Lorna Marsden, and the two anonymous reviewers of the University of Toronto Press and the Social Science Federation of Canada provided useful commentaries on various drafts of the manuscript.

I am grateful to Virgil D. Duff, Managing Editor of the University of Toronto Press, for his enthusiasm and patience throughout this publishing venture and to Beverley Beetham Endersby for an excellent job of copy-editing the final manuscript. Thanks also to Laura Houle for compiling the book index. Chapters 7 and 8 of the book incorporate material that previously appeared in the *Canadian Journal of Family Law* 6/1 (1987): 85–102, and the *International Journal of the Sociology of Law* 16/2 (1988): 137–58.

I owe a special thank-you to Dr Richard Ericson, Centre of Criminology and Department of Sociology at the University of Toronto, who has offered unconditional support for this project over the past decade. Both his intellectual integrity and his forthright critiques of my work have been greatly appreciated.

The final acknowledgment goes to Dr Robert J. Menzies for his invaluable technical assistance and, more important, for the humour, sympathy, and love that made it easier for me to complete this book.

From Punishment to Doing Good

CHAPTER ONE

Social-Welfare Reform
and the Birth of
Socialized Justice

In brief, reform is the designation that each generation
gives to its favorite programs.

D.J. Rothman (1980: 4)

What [is] reform ... but the skilful balancing of incompat-
ibles, the ingenious expression of that middle class philosophy which believes in resisting at once the aggressions of
the rich and the pretensions of the poor?

G. Dangerfield (1961: 226)

At the most general level, this book is about social-welfare reform and
the moral-political regulation of marginal populations in Western market societies during the past two centuries.[1] The topic is a controversial
one which has fuelled an ongoing interdisciplinary debate and generated
a burgeoning revisionist literature, both historical and contemporary
(Chan & Ericson 1981; Cohen 1979, 1985; Cohen & Scull 1983; Donzelot
1979, 1980; Ericson 1987; Ericson & Baranek 1982; Foucault 1977, 1980a,
1980b; Garland 1981, 1985; Gusfield 1981; Lowman, Menzies, & Palys
1987; Rothman 1971, 1978, 1980; Scull 1977, 1981, 1983; Smart 1982,
1989). None the less, although they focus on different locales and employ divergent theoretical perspectives, researchers have found themselves grappling with the same key questions: What is social-welfare
reform? When have fundamental shifts in the modes of regulating marginal underclasses in Western market societies taken place? Why do
structures governing the deviant and dependent undergo transformation
at particular moments? How does social-welfare reform come about and
with what consequences?

I address these theoretical issues in the Canadian context through a substantive analysis of the origins, legitimation, and impact of a specific social-welfare reform – the family court. This American 'invention' made its debut in Cincinnati on the eve of the First World War (Boushy 1950; Chunn 1982), but was not instituted in Canada until the postwar era. Indeed, family courts had no official status in Canada before 1929, when the Toronto Family Court was proclaimed, and their legitimacy was definitively established only through a Supreme Court Reference in 1938.[2] However, American and Canadian advocates clearly shared a vision of the family court as a tribunal that, ideally, would exercise comprehensive jurisdiction over 'all matters concerning the family' (Hoffman 1918: 747) and operate in accordance with the principles of what Roscoe Pound described as 'corrective' or 'socialized justice' (1943a; see also 1916).[3]

The latter was both a concrete and an ideological manifestation of the 'sociological movement in law' (Hunt 1978) that signalled the emergence of welfare states in Western market societies from the 1880s to the 1940s. According to Pound (1943: 7, 9), socialized justice had three distinct features: an emphasis on individualized treatment of the deviant, dependent, and potentially marginal; a growing reliance on non-lawyer 'experts' and individualizing devices such as juvenile and domestic-relations courts to design and implement treatment; and 'a continually increasing resort to ... administrative methods.' The overall objective of socialized justice was 'to maintain the general security through prevention and maintain the individual life through rehabilitation.'

This historical study of early family-court development in Ontario is a useful addition to the existing literature on social-welfare reform and socialized justice for two reasons. First, there is a remarkable paucity of revisionist work on the origins of domestic-relations tribunals in the United States and Canada. With few exceptions (Snell 1986a), revisionist accounts of how socialized justice emerged in these societies have focused exclusively on the establishment of juvenile courts at the turn of the century (Hagan & Leon 1977, 1980; Jones & Rutman 1981; Leon 1977, 1978; Platt 1969; Rothman 1980; Ryerson 1978; Schlossman 1977; Sutherland 1976).[4] However, the family court was not simply a natural and unproblematic extension of the juvenile court. Although most Western market societies created children's courts and special arrangements for the hearing of domestic cases, only in the United States and some Canadian provinces (Canadian Corrections Assn 1960; McGrath 1976) did both juvenile and family courts emerge as distinct entities before the end of the Second World War. Thus, the latter must be analysed separately from the former.

More important, perhaps, the family court typifies the numerous sociolegal reforms that, by 1940, had collectively transformed family-welfare law and its administration in Ontario and other Western market societies. The very creation of such tribunals signified the movement towards a new mode of regulating intrafamilial relations among the working and dependent poor, which is characteristic of welfare states. Therefore, a retrospective study of Canada's pioneer family courts can tell us much about how socialized justice and the welfare state took shape in this country and about the role of such tribunals in reproducing the desired class and gender relations among a particular marginal segment of the population.

In summary, then, the family court is a concrete vehicle for addressing broader theoretical issues concerning the nature and consequences of reform. However, since there is admittedly no monolithic revisionist perspective on reform, researchers who wrestle with the same questions about social-welfare innovations and the regulation of marginality frequently come up with very different answers. As a point of departure, therefore, I outline the major agreements and disagreements among participants in the current reform debates. The overview serves as preface to a brief discussion of what my historical analysis of family courts and socialized justice in Ontario has to say about the issues in dispute. The final section of this preliminary chapter offers a general account of the transition from punishment to doing good, which marked the birth of the Canadian welfare state.

Revisionist Perspectives on Social-Welfare Reform

The plethora of literature on social-welfare reform reveals that the revisionists concur on two issues. First, they reject the conventional, and arguably still hegemonic, conception of reform as an essentially technocratic, always progressive, enterprise directed at the improvement of the status quo through 'removal or abandonment of imperfections, faults or errors' (*Concise Oxford Dictionary* 1976: 940). From that perspective, the success of any particular innovation is determined by measuring the gap between the stated objectives of the reform and its actual effect upon implementation; the smaller the cleavage between theory and practice, the more successful the reform. Negative and/or unanticipated consequences of such innovations are thus categorized as anomolies to be corrected or eradicated through further reform.

In contrast, most contemporary revisionist research is premised on a radical reconceptualization of reform as an inherently contradictory phenomenon. Unanticipated and unwanted effects are therefore an integral component of the reform process, not aberrations that can be prevented or removed through strenuous social engineering and the application of technique. Furthermore, the revisionist literature suggests that innovations are inextricably bound to a specific model of social organization and, indeed, help to maintain and reproduce it. Consequently, although they may not realize the explicitly articulated goals of their promoters and implementers, reforms can rarely be categorized as failures.

With respect to innovations aimed at the marginal, the revisionists argue that reformers always intend to do good (Gaylin et al 1978), either by improving the existing mechanisms for reproducing social order among the deviant and dependent or by introducing more humane, effective, and economical alternatives. Because their notion of 'the good' reflects a conception of social organization that is not necessarily shared by the reform targets, however, the innovations they promote will often fail to achieve stated objectives once implemented. At the same time, reforms often satisfy several inchoate agendas (Donzelot 1980; Foucault 1977, 1980a, 1980b; Garland 1985; Gusfield 1981; Platt 1969; Rothman 1980). For example, they enable moral crusaders and ascendant groups of professionals to carve out spheres of influence at specific historical junctures. In addition, social-welfare reforms almost invariably extend state control over increasing numbers of the deviant and dependent, albeit with their tacit or direct cooperation. Finally, like any other commodity in Western market societies, social-welfare innovations contain a built-in obsolescence that generates an ongoing need for new measures that will ostensibly overcome the weaknesses of previous innovations and more effectively reproduce the existing social order.

The second point of consensus among the revisionists is that a major transformation of the means used to regulate marginal populations in Western market societies accompanied the transition from laissez-faire to welfare state. Specifically, this change, which produced what has been variously described as the 'welfare sanction' (Garland 1981) and the 'tutelary complex' (Donzelot 1980), entailed a philosophical and practical shift from legal formalism, premised on the ideology of individualism and the minimal state, to socialized justice, based on the ideology of individualization and the interventionist state. Thus, a mode of regulating the deviant and dependent grounded in legal concepts of liberty, equality, responsibility, and retribution was transformed into a hybrid one as non-legal categories of determinism, inequality, non-culpability and rehabilitation were incorporated within existing welfare structures. As a result, the clear line of demarcation between the social and legal and public and private spheres in the laissez-faire state became increasingly blurred in the emergent welfare state (Garland 1981, 1985; see also Donzelot 1980; Foucault 1980a; Rothman 1978, 1980).

However, while revisionist scholars agree that such a transformation took place in most Western market societies, they diverge sharply in their accounts of when, why, and how it happened. The 'when' question – pinpointing the precise moments at which social-welfare structures in these nations have undergone fundamental change over the past two centuries – is arguably the most important and contentious one. The debate over this issue cannot be dismissed as a mere quibble because at stake is the determination of exactly when the foundations of a system that has dominated Canada and other market societies for much of the twentieth century were laid. In short, the way both the welfare state and its concomitant disciplinary apparatus – socialized justice – are explained depends on where the revolutionary juncture is located.

Revisionists split into opposing and irreconcilable camps over this question. On one side are those who argue that two key transformations in the disciplinary underpinnings of Western societies have taken place since the industrial revolution. The first, which occurred in the eighteenth and early nineteenth centuries, was characterized by the creation of 'total institutions,' particularly the penitentiary. The second, ongoing from the mid-1960s, is marked by a conspicuous expansion of the original social-welfare structures through the addition of an array of deinstitutionalized control mechanisms that 'widen the net and thin the mesh' (Cohen 1979, 1983, 1985; Donzelot 1980; Foucault 1977, 1980a, 1980b; Scull 1977, 1983).

In this view, then, the welfare state and socialized justice originated more than two hundred years ago and are only now undergoing fundamental change. Therefore, reforms effected in the social-welfare structures of market societies during the late nineteenth and early twentieth centuries, such as family courts, were not revolutionary; they merely continued the lines of development set in motion a century earlier. As Andrew Scull puts it, the sociolegal innovations instigated by American Progressives were largely rhetorical ones that supplemented 'existing arrangements' while leaving 'most of the underlying structures inherited from the nineteenth-century largely untouched' (1983: 151). Why? Because what reformers intended did not follow. Words were not translated into practices, so far as probation, parole, and socialized courts were concerned.

However, revisionist scholars on the other side of this debate (Garland 1981, 1985; Rothman 1978, 1980; Sutherland 1976) state just as unequivocally that the social-welfare structures in Western market societies have undergone three major transformations. From their perspective, the reforms implemented in the late nineteenth and early twentieth centuries did revolutionize public attitudes and contribute to 'a qualitative or structural' change, not simply 'a gradual shift of direction or emphasis' in the treatment of marginal populations (Garland 1985: 6). Thus, the transition from laissez-faire to welfare state was hardly a single, continuous line of development from the eighteenth century onward. On the contrary, the decisive movement from one form of social organization and disciplinary apparatus to another occurred during a second major period of transformation characterized by substantive changes in the treatment of the deviant and dependent. As David Rothman emphasizes (Chunn & Smandych 1982: 157), there was a huge difference between a Boston cobbler acting as a voluntary probation officer in 1869 and the personnel working in state-sanctioned probation and parole services in the early twentieth century.

Explaining why revolutionary shifts take place at particular junctures is another contentious question addressed in the revisionist literature on social-welfare reform. For example, if the late nineteenth and early twentieth centuries did indeed constitute a major period of sociolegal transformation in Western market societies, what accounted for such a momentous change? With respect to this issue, disagreements among revisionists stem primarily from their differing assessments of the relative importance of structure and culture in effecting social-welfare reforms governing the deviant and dependent, that is, whether they view ideas or material conditions as the motor force of history. David Rothman (1971, 1980) is representative of those who maintain that the former are relatively independent of and more crucial than the latter. To understand why the asylum or the juvenile court was invented and implemented, he says, one must 'turn first to the rhetoric of the reformers' (1981: 18).

At the same time, revisionists such as David Garland (1981, 1985; see also Scull 1977, 1981) insist that social-welfare reform is strongly influenced by general structural changes at particular historical moments. Through his analysis of late-Victorian Britain, for example, Garland identifies a combination of economic, political, and demographic upheavals – large-scale industrialization, universal manhood suffrage, and urbanization, among others – that challenged the stratification and divisions among the working classes so crucial to the maintenance of power by the ruling bloc and generated a profound social crisis. This crisis centred on two related issues: the proper role and function of the state with respect to the economic and social spheres and the condition and regulation of the lower classes. Between 1895 and 1914, he maintains, this dual crisis was resolved through the simultaneous birth of the welfare state and the 'welfare sanction' – social-security programs and socialized justice, respectively.

The third major point at issue in the revisionist literature on social-welfare reform – how such innovation comes about – is focused on the key question of what role human intentionality and agency play in this process. From a pluralist, instrumentalist perspective expressed as 'conscience and convenience,' Rothman (1980: 6) argues that the demands of Progressive reformers were translated into practice with the formidable support of criminal-justice and mental-health administrators who were, in fact, more favourably disposed to the proposed changes than the general public because the reforms so conveniently served their own organizational concerns. In short, he implicitly assumes there is a direct line between the intentions of particular individual- or organizational-reform advocates and the policies subsequently implemented or not implemented.

However, post-structuralists such as Foucault (1977, 1980a, 1980b) and Donzelot (1979, 1980) present the antithetical argument. They flatly assert the futility of seeking causal principles such as the 'hidden intents' or 'interests' of individuals and groups to explain social-welfare transformations. Thus, reformers may well furnish political decision makers with the rationales for more repressive and wide-ranging control strategies, but they have no direct impact on policy in the way that Rothman describes. Indeed, Foucault explicitly challenges the instrumentalist focus on the intentionality of actors with his concept of 'bio-power,' which 'dehumanizes' the explanation of social change and reform by emphasizing consequences, not causes (1980a: 143; see also Smart 1983, 1985). In the post-structuralist view, then, social change and reform are effects of practices with varied and, frequently, non-human origins (Foucault 1980b: 203, 206).

What might be called the intermediate position on the question of agency is most clearly elaborated by David Garland (1985). He maintains that reforms that coalesce to transform sociolegal structures are never the result of 'a single battle-plan, drawn up in advance.' On the contrary, they emerge through 'a complex and fragmented process of struggle, within which the calculations of individuals and agencies play a crucial, but by no means controlling, part' (ibid: 207; see also Gusfield 1981; Hall 1984). In other words, both the instrumentalist reliance on a stimulus–response model of reform and the post-structuralist dismissal of human agency are flawed. Change is not preordained because competing reform options always exist at any given time. Moreover, the process governing the selection of a particular reform proposal as the basis for policies governing the marginal is never direct. It is inevitably mediated by political bargaining, negotiation, and compromise (ibid: 208).

Not surprisingly, the conflicting revisionist positions on the role of agency in achieving reform lead to very divergent explanations of why reform invariably appears to have negative as well as positive effects. Rothman (1978, 1980) attributes unanticipated and unwanted consequences to the fact that reforms are premised on faulty assumptions, and points to the fate of Progressive innovations as a prime example of this wrong-headedness. Unlike most revisionists, therefore, he concludes that glaring gaps between ideals and practices are not necessarily inherent in the reform process itself because reform proposals based on 'sound' principles would generate the intended (positive) effects when implemented.

Predictably, the post-structuralists (Donzelot 1980; Foucault 1977, 1980a, 1980b) make precisely the opposite argument. They maintain that, since agency is irrelevant to the emergence of any particular reform program, the program inexorably takes on a power of its own. Thus, regardless of what reformers intend or expect, each new strategy for regulating the marginal that comes into play is inevitably more wide-ranging and therefore more repressive than previous ones. In sum, there is no discrepancy between its potential and its practical success.

Again, Garland occupies the theoretical middle ground on this issue. He insists that, because human agency does play a role, albeit a mediated one, in the implementation of specific reforms, there will always be some gap between the possible and actual effects of such innovations. Why is this so? According to Garland, close examination of the reform process reveals that the inevitable gap is generated by 'the operation of resistances, contradictions, limitations and failures' (1985: 257).

The Ontario Family Court as a Social-Welfare Reform

With respect to the contemporary revisionist debates about reform, my analysis of family-court development in Ontario lends the greatest support overall to Garland's theoretical position (1981, 1985).[5] On the question of when the major sociolegal transformations in Western market societies occurred, the Ontario study comes down squarely on the side of those who view the late nineteenth and early twentieth centuries as a distinctive and fundamental period of transition from laissez-faire to welfare state. Those revisionists who argue otherwise appear to have overlooked two important considerations. The first concerns the relationship between theory and practice. For example, Scull (1977) has no difficulty arguing, and correctly so, that the creation of 'total institutions' represented a major reorganization of the control structures in developing Western market societies. Yet, if we weigh the results anticipated by the eighteenth- and nineteenth-century advocates of the segregative institution – namely, deterrence and moral reform – against the actual effects of this innovation when implemented, it is obvious that what reformers intended did not follow. Thus, Scull (1983: 151) is entirely inconsistent when he denies that a major restructuring of social welfare took place from the 1880s to the 1940s simply on the grounds that the reforms instigated by American Progressives were not developed to the fullest extent.

Furthermore, because of an almost exclusive focus on segregative institutions and their persistence into the twentieth century, Scull and other revisionists in this camp ignore the notable transformation and extension of the nineteenth-century structures inspired by the American Progressives and their counterparts in other countries. Admittedly, completely unadulterated forms of social organization and disciplinary apparatus can never be found in reality since aspects of old practices and ideologies survive revolutions and become interwoven with new ones. At the same time, however, a distinctive change was effected in Ontario's sociolegal structures between 1880 and 1940, exemplified by the creation of family courts. And this movement away from an emphasis on punishment and towards a focus on 'doing good' cannot be reduced to empty rhetoric. Despite continuities between police and family courts, Magistrate George Denison's administration of family-welfare law in the Toronto Police Court in 1880 was fundamentally different from that of Family Court Judge Hawley S. Mott sixty years later (Chunn 1987, 1988b). Clearly, elements of the nineteenth-century structures survived, and continue to this day, but the foundations of the sociolegal apparatus presumably undergoing transformation now were forged during that transition period, not earlier.

On the question of why fundamental change occurs at a particular historical moment, the Ontario family-court study reveals that a conjuncture of structural conditions, similar to those identified by Garland, formed the crucial context within which English-Canadian reformers operated from the 1880s to the 1940s. During this period, Canada/ Ontario was characterized by increasing centralization and concentration of industry and finance, accelerated urbanization, and enfranchisement of the working classes and women.[6] However, there were also variations in the general trajectory of development that reflected historical circumstances unique to Canada. Although rapid social change generated apprehension and unease among middle- and upper-class Ontarians, no social crisis of the same magnitude as the one that apparently confronted their British counterparts in the late nineteenth century ensued; consequently, the issue of the proper role and function of the state was not so pressing a question in Ontario as it was in Britain. The problems generated by 'social disorganization' were resolved with no abrupt breach of the principles and ideologies governing the laissez-faire state, that is, without the implementation of the social-security programs adopted by the British between 1895 and 1914 (Guest 1980; Moscovitch & Drover 1987; Panitch 1977).

A major reason for these divergent developmental patterns seems to be that Canada never had the same type of laissez-faire state as Britain. Between 1830 and 1870 Britain arguably came the closest of any market society to approximating the ideals of individualism and the minimal state. In contrast, Canada was strongly influenced by a pre-nineteenth-century conservative paternalism right into the early twentieth century. And, while this corporatist ideology was tinged with the values of British and American liberalism, the latter, in its classic form, did not become a dominant ideology in Canada until comparatively late in history (Marchak 1981: 14). Moreover, state intervention in the economic sphere to benefit industry, the exploitation of natural resources, and the supply of public utilities have always been extensive in this country (Wallace 1950: 383–4), despite professed devotion to the principles of laissez-faire by Canadian businessmen.

At the same time, in seeming contradiction, the ideology of individualism and the minimal state acted as a bulwark against the establishment of non-means-tested social-security programs in both Canada and the United States for a longer period of time during this century than was the case in Britain and other European countries (Briggs 1961; Finkel 1977; Guest 1980; Hay 1978; Krieger 1963; Lubove 1968; Mommsen 1981; Moscovitch & Drover 1987; Panitch 1977; Struthers 1983; Tudiver 1987). The historical entrenchment of rigid and overt class divisions, characteristic of Europe, did not occur to the same extent in North

America. Consequently, upward mobility appeared to be more attainable, and the Progressive belief that the gap between classes could be bridged, that 'social control' would replace class control, seemed more convincing (Comack 1987; Hunt 1978; Pound 1942; Ross 1969; Rothman 1978, 1980, 1981; Schwendinger & Schwendinger 1974). Thus, despite considerable upheaval and unrest among the labouring classes in Canada from the 1880s to the early 1920s, and again during the 1930s, class consciousness ultimately remained subordinate to job consciousness. Until the 1940s, the threat from socialist ideologies and political parties was successfully managed without the introduction of extensive social-security measures.

The major problem facing English Canadians at the end of the nineteenth century, then, was the condition and regulation of the lower classes. Yet, even at the level of discipline, the crisis was not so severe in Canada/Ontario as it was in Britain, where the prolonged economic depression of the late nineteenth century began to erode the moral and economic divisions between large sectors of the working class that adhered to bourgeois standards – the so-called labour aristocracy – and those that did not, a division crucial to the Victorian political leadership. Unfortunately for the latter, the only legitimate response, within the ideological parameters of laissez-faire, was an increasingly ineffective one – the social exclusion and coercion of growing sectors of the population. Consequently, a poor-law amendment that denied everybody, including the 'deserving,' outdoor relief and the establishment of the Charity Organization Society (COS) to rationalize the dispensation of charity left massive numbers in large urban areas to subsist in the utmost deprivation (Garland 1985: 46–58).

By way of contrast, the crises related to the condition and regulation of Ontario's marginal populations, which erupted in the late nineteenth century and again after the First World War, were arguably more diffuse and ultimately less directly threatening to the political authorities. None the less, during both periods, the deviant and dependent posed a dual problem, in terms of who was to handle them and in what manner, that generated pressure for state rationalization of the sociolegal structures governing the underclasses. Thus, both the increased demands on charities by the urban poor, particularly women and children, and the growing case-loads in police magistrates' courts, resulting, in part, from stringent enforcement of morality laws, contributed to the implementation of substantial reforms.

However, the province had no poor law and, while both prison and workhouse were premised on the 'principle of less eligibility,' complete denial of outdoor relief was never a policy in Ontario (Guest 1980; Splane 1965). Furthermore, erosion of the divisions between rough and respectable sections of the working classes in the province did not produce the collective class consciousness that was so menacing to the established political order in Britain. And, finally, although this issue requires more in-depth investigation, it appears that the split-level nature of the Canadian state, particularly the federal-provincial division of criminal and civil powers, played an important role in preventing any abrupt change in sociolegal structures of the type that characterized Britain from 1895 to 1914.

With regard to the question of how reform is achieved, my historical analysis of the family court in Ontario does not corroborate the poststructuralist contention that agency is of negligible importance in the reform process. On the contrary, the research data provide broad support for Rothman's conception of 'conscience and convenience.' The combination of idealism and pragmatism was certainly an important factor in their development. Thus, throughout the 1920s, family-court advocates, primarily personnel in the existing juvenile courts and allied community organizations, pressed the provincial government, both formally and informally, to establish domestic-relations tribunals. However, they clearly gained strength from, and their ultimate success was due, in part, to the fact that growing numbers of legal agents – police, crown attorneys, and judges – were reluctant to administer family-welfare law and made their objections known to the provincial administration.

At the same time, Rothman takes for granted the political lens through which reform proposals are filtered and reshaped before implementation. Although he noted that the business of reform was much more complex in the early twentieth century than it had been a hundred years earlier (1980: 6–7), Rothman spent no time attempting to trace the precise ways in which the elements of a socialized justice system were forged. Had he ventured outside the confines of the social-welfare bureaucracies to examine the wider structural context in which the Progressive reformers operated, as both Scull (1977, 1981) and Garland (1981, 1985; see also Gusfield 1981) did, he would have been forced to revise his instrumentalist model of the reform process.

Despite some affinity with Rothman's findings, then, the data from the Ontario family-court research are most supportive of Garland's conclusions about how the reform process operates. On the one hand, the reorganized sociolegal structures and ideologies governing Ontario's marginal by the early 1940s were clearly the result of many ad hoc, piecemeal government policy decisions dating from the late nineteenth century rather than the outcome of a coordinated plan. On the other, the reform process in Ontario during this period followed a pattern very similar to that of Britain: reformers recurrently identified a rising incidence of problems such as desertion and delinquency among the province's working and dependent poor; they located the source of these problems in substandard family life and formulated reform programs (e.g., eugenics, social work), primarily on the basis of ideas imported from American sources, which emphasized the prevention and treatment of deviant families as the solutions to marginality; through debate, compromise, and political struggles, aspects of these programs were incorporated into the realm of official discourse as recommendations in government reports or other public documents; and eventually, modified versions of the original reform demands were reflected in state policies governing the deviant and dependent.

Thus, the demands of specific individuals and organizations were an important component of the reform process in Ontario, but not in the sense of any literal translation of this or that proposal into policy. The lack of any direct correspondence between what reformers want and what politicians and bureaucrats do becomes abundantly clear when the history of family-court development in Ontario is examined. Prior to the 1940s and in contrast to the situation in the United States (Boushy 1950; Chunn 1982), domestic-relations tribunals were created despite the absence of any unified movement demanding their establishment. As will be elaborated in subsequent chapters, both the advocates of social-work professionalism, exemplified by the Canadian Welfare Council under Charlotte Whitton, and the champions of legal professionalism, especially provincial government lawyers such as Allen Dymond, 'disowned' (Gusfield 1981) the family-court issue for much of the interwar period. Indeed, the primary basis of support for the establishment of such tribunals resided with those individuals and organizations that exerted a declining influence on political decision makers during the 1920s.

Therefore, close scrutiny reveals that, far from representing a direct government response to sustained pressure from reformers, Ontario's first family courts were essentially by-products of the attorney general's pursuit of other objectives. Similarly, when the constitutionality of socialized tribunals was challenged in the 1930s, the provincial government's request for the Reference before the Canadian Supreme Court that ultimately legitimated them stemmed from some very ad hoc, pragmatic considerations rather than from any commitment to family courts and their personnel, per se.

So far as the effects of reform are concerned, the Ontario data cast doubt on Rothman's optimistic belief that reforms based on sound principles can produce only positive results. Indeed, to a certain extent, they support the post-structuralist contention that reformers inevitably provide the legitimation for more repressive and wide-ranging control strategies. The administration of family-welfare law by juvenile and family courts between the wars was clearly the story of a burgeoning private, technocratic justice system wherein the legal rights of 'clients,' participation of legal personnel, and input from the lay public became more and more irrelevant as socialized justice took shape.

However, like Garland's findings, the Ontario data also challenge the post-structuralist assumption of a seamless relationship between theory and practice. They suggest that, during its formative years in Ontario, socialized justice developed in terms of a gap between intention and reality. Consequently, its immense potential control capability was only imperfectly realized for a variety of reasons: disagreements among social-welfare leaders outside government; divisions between and within the various provincial bureaucracies; wrangling by three levels of government about fiscal responsibility for welfare; and resistance from at least some of those who were the targets of the new form of urban policing. These are just a few of the counter-currents that operated to prevent the emergence of the omnipotent carceral apparatus that figures so dramatically in the work of both Donzelot and Foucault.

With respect to the issues being debated in the current revisionist literature on social-welfare reform, then, my analysis of early family-court development in Ontario suggests that: the late nineteenth and early twentieth centuries did constitute a period of major sociolegal change in Canada; the reform impetus was shaped by a number of interrelated structural conditions that generated a sense of crisis among the urban middle classes, a crisis centred on 'the family'; through a process of mediation, refinement, and revision, some reform proposals were selectively incorporated into policies and legislation related to the deviant and dependent; and the collective product of these reforms, including family courts, was a new mode for regulating and maintaining existing class and gender relations among a certain segment of the working and dependent poor. The enormity of this transformation in attitudes, rhetoric, and practices governing marginal populations can be grasped more clearly if the sociolegal structures that regulated the province's poor prior to 1880 are counterposed to those that were created between the late nineteenth century and the early 1940s.

From Punishment to Doing Good

A defining characteristic of the transition from laissez-faire to welfare state in Ontario, and other jurisdictions, was the creation of sociolegal structures governing the marginal that were based on the ideology of individualization and the interventionist state rather than individualism and the minimal state. Although the laissez-faire state was hardly a non-interventionist one, what changed dramatically during this period were the degree and mode of state intervention in the working-class family (Smart 1982: 130–1; see also Donzelot 1980; Poster 1978; Zaretsky 1982, 1986). For several decades prior to 1880, the province's marginal were regulated within the constraints of welfare structures premised on a parallel between economic and legal individualism. Thus, the moral-political regulation of the underclasses was achieved through the operation of distinct but very loosely coordinated spheres, which functioned on the basis of prevailing assumptions about free will and the social contract. These included segregative institutions, such as the prison, workhouse, and asylum, that were based on the 'principle of less eligibility' and, in the community, the elementary-school system and private agencies such as charities and temperance societies (Burnet 1974; Curtis 1987; Houston 1972; Rooke & Schnell 1983; Speisman 1973; Splane 1965).

Notwithstanding the relatively weak ties among them, all the components of this regulatory apparatus shared a common concern with 'moralization' of the poor (Donzelot 1980; Garland 1985), that is, with inculcating the virtues of discipline and hard work considered indispensable to the proper exercise of rationality and adherence to the social contract. However, the task of schools and private agencies was to prevent demoralization among the lower orders who were considered most susceptible to lapses of free will, and consequently to marginality, while the role of the institutions, especially the prison, was to remoralize those who had actually breached the social contract and become deviant or dependent. Reformers believed such breaches could be mended through segregation, hard labour, and moral/religious exhortation; having learned to exercise reason, the individual would not fall prey to the forces of demoralization again. Therefore, despite the admission of a few conditions that might thwart the exercise of free will, notably age and mental state, the regulation of Ontario's underclasses during the middle years of the nineteenth century remained firmly embedded within the constraints of neoclassical legal principles (ibid).

Concomitant with the emphasis on individualism was the belief in the minimal state, which was reflected in a strict differentiation between the deviant/criminal and the neglected/dependent of the province. Such a distinction between offenders and the poor was essentially one between the public and private realms.[7] With respect to this demarcation line, then, offenders were a state responsibility and could be defined only through state institutions – criminal law and criminal justice. In contrast, laissez-faire ideology dictated that the poor existed and were made poor outside state institutions in civil society. Consequently, it was felt they could and ought to be supported by the private sector – families, friends, charities – or, as a last resort, municipal governments (Guest 1980; Splane 1965).

In practice, this rigid ideological division between the state and civil society was difficult to maintain. Although workhouses and other institutions that housed the non-able-bodied poor (as well as the able-bodied who had exhausted all alternative avenues) were generally administered by the private sector, for example, government legislation, inspection, and supervision began to subvert the principle of minimal state intervention as the nineteenth century unfolded (Houston 1972; Rooke & Schnell 1983; Splane 1965). Moreover, in Canada the British North America Act of 1867 accorded powers over civil and criminal matters to both the provincial and the federal states. Thus, penitentiaries became a federal responsibility, while jails and reformatories remained a provincial one. Similarly, each level of government exercised jurisdiction over specific aspects of marriage and its dissolution.

Notwithstanding these developments, however, the neoclassical disciplinary apparatus governing the deviant and dependent in Ontario was not effectively undermined and transformed until the transition to welfare state. From the 1880s to the 1940s, particularly during the interwar years, the emergent emphasis on individualization rather than individualism signalled the ascendancy of a socialized mode for regulating the marginal of the province. Consequently, the moral-political regulation of the lower classes was increasingly accomplished through a much more integrated disciplinary mechanism organized around the principle that the deviant or dependent person, far from being a free, rational legal subject, was, in fact, a unique individual endowed with 'an uncertain degree of rationality and a character of a certain type' (Garland 1985: 31).

The growing abandonment of the nineteenth-century emphasis on formal equality (i.e., sameness) of legal subjects and the substitution of a focus on their specific and diverse characteristics inexorably changed the underlying rationale of the sociolegal structures governing the marginal from free will and contract to knowledge and expertise. A mode of regulation that relied on 'moralization' and legal prohibition/punishment was being transformed into one based on 'normalization' and social control (Foucault 1980a; Garland 1985; Smart 1982). Whereas the former was aimed at forcing people to realize their weaknesses or potential weaknesses in order that they might begin to exercise their rationality and act conventionally, the latter attempted to bring the marginal into line with normative requirements through positive techniques of intervention 'for their own good' and that of society. The onus for reform and rehabilitation thereby began to shift from the deviant and dependent to professionals with specialized knowledge and curative techniques who could not only diagnose and treat existing problems on a case-by-case basis but also proactively predict and pre-empt their development.

This fundamental reconceptualization of deviancy and dependency was reflected in a concomitant reordering of the structures governing Ontario's marginal. A disciplinary apparatus made up of loosely coordinated but distinct components started to take on the appearance of a more tightly integrated normalization grid that was formed through the extensive interpenetration of institutional and non-institutional, legal and non-legal controls. Moreover, even the segregative institutions that now marked the end-point of this regulatory grid assumed a different character from their nineteenth-century counterparts. An extended range of institutions, catering to special categories of deviant and dependent, reflected the growing twentieth-century emphasis on individualization and classification. Most notably, in the early twentieth century, for example, the mentally defective were siphoned out of existing institutional populations and placed in new institutions where they could be subject to the ministrations of mental-hygiene and other experts. And, although Scull and Foucault would likely disagree, there does appear to be a major difference between segregative institutions whose raison d'être is the determinist principle of special needs beyond the control of the individual, and those that, in keeping with laissez-faire ideology, are premised on the principle of restoring the individual's ability to exercise free will by repairing a lapse in rationality.

The heart of the emergent normalization grid, however, was not the institutions but, rather, the numerous community-based, individualized regulatory mechanisms of 'social control,' including juvenile and family courts, probation and parole, that operated in tandem with schools, private social agencies, and the police. Prior to 1918, the common concern of all those involved in normalization was the moral, physical, and mental well-being of children. During the interwar years, however, there was growing emphasis on the nuclear family as a unit of interdependent individuals (Barrett & McIntosh 1982; Poster 1978; Thorne & Yalom 1982; Zaretsky 1982, 1986). Hence, the unit itself became the focus of individualized casework.

The establishment of family courts, which grafted non-legal discourses, personnel, and methods on to the existing legal mechanisms for processing marginal populations (e.g., the lower courts), exemplified the advanced socialization of law. Internally, probation officers, non-lawyer judges, doctors, social workers, psychologists, and psychiatrists followed informal, inquisitorial procedures, applied casework methods, and spoke not only of reclamation, but also of prediction and prevention. At the same time, the family court was linked to outside organizations, including schools, social agencies, and segregative institutions. In some locales, court personnel met on a regular basis with representatives from various external groups to collaborate in the formulation of treatment plans for problem families.

Moreover, although the traditional legal personnel who had handled family-welfare cases, specifically the police and crown attorneys, were largely absent from the day-to-day operations of many juvenile and family courts, they continued to play an important role in terms of referrals and legal consultation. What this situation produced, then, was not so much a displacement as a transformation and expansion of the nineteenth-century structures for the administration of family-welfare law. By 1940, in a growing number of Ontario's urban centres, the school attendance officer, school nurse, agency social worker, court personnel, and traditional legal agents were engaged in a cooperative effort to 'normalize' marginal families, that is, to repair, reinforce, and reproduce appropriate class and gender relations among the marginal of the province. Like assembly-line workers, no one of them was responsible for the entire product, yet each contributed to the final outcome – the moral-political regulation of the working and dependent poor.

The increasing focus on individualized treatment of Ontario's underclasses from the 1880s to the 1940s was paralleled by a movement towards an interventionist state that would act to alleviate conditions causing marginality. As the relationship between the state and the marginal became less grounded in notions of individualism and contractual obligation and more focused on positive attempts to produce reform and normalization for the benefit of both, the stringent nineteenth-century ideological line of demarcation between the deviant and dependent of the province was obscured. Consequently, the analytical and practical distinction between poverty and crime was imperceptibly eroded in Ontario through the transfer of certain functions previously performed by civil (private) society – families, friends, private charity, and philanthropic organizations – to the (public) state.

Specifically, both the federal and the provincial governments began to assume a direct, paternalistic role by identifying certain categories of working and dependent poor as appropriate recipients of state protection. A spate of legislation was implemented, including a number of statutes aimed at 'normalizing' intrafamilial relations, which gave state-designated agents very extensive powers to intervene in the private realm on behalf of women, children, and the elderly. These social laws attempted to mitigate inequalities among family members, primarily by reducing the familial powers of husbands/fathers vis-à-vis their dependents, and ultimately effected a transformation of family-welfare law in Ontario (Dymond 1923; Ursel 1986; see also Brophy 1982; Brophy & Smart 1981, 1985; Gordon 1988a, 1988b; Pateman 1989b).[8] It was now an 'offence' to cause children, women, and the elderly to be poor through neglect or non-support. In addition, the federal delinquency statute made it an 'offence' for adults, especially parents and guardians, to perpetuate conditions of immorality and neglect that contributed to the criminality of a minor.

The administration of these social laws also reflected the growing presence of an interventionist state. The civil-criminal distinction became less and less clear-cut as private agencies of normalization (e.g., Children's Aid societies) were integrated with public mechanisms (e.g., socialized courts) in a state-controlled welfare structure. Moreover, a key characteristic of juvenile and family courts is a blurring of the line between crime and poverty. Thus, they administered not only the federal delinquency statute and Criminal Code sections pertaining to family maintenance and assault but also the quasi-criminal provincial laws governing child protection, illegitimacy, and desertion. Morover, court personnel increasingly tended to downplay or ignore the criminal aspects of their jurisdiction and apply family-welfare laws as if they were civil statutes. The fact that so many cases were never presented to a judge at a court hearing because they were processed informally by probation officers as so-called occurrences aided in the maintenance of this fiction.

While it would be misleading to suggest that welfare structures based on normalization (as opposed to moralization) were at more than an embryonic stage of development by 1940, there is a profound irony in the fact that reformers who wanted only to shift the emphasis from punishment to doing good in policies governing marginal populations actually helped unleash forces that ultimately effected a transition from minimal to interventionist state in Ontario. To wit, their increasing advocacy of welfare policies that were premised on the use of experts to implement and administer state-sanctioned, community-based responses to deviancy and dependency contributed to the erosion of the laissez-faire demarcation between the state and civil society in relation to *all* families, not just marginal ones, and facilitated the introduction of social-security programs based on universality, for which senior levels of government (i.e., federal and provincial) assumed direct fiscal responsibility (Guest 1980). The incipient transformation of social-welfare structures in Ontario was evident in 1893 when the government appointed a salaried official, the first superintendent of neglected and dependent children, to coordinate and supervise the work of the Children's Aid societies (Jones & Rutman 1981). Thirty-seven years later, the foundations of an emergent provincial welfare state became even more visible when, following the recommendation of the Ross Commission (Ontario 1930), Ontario established a department of public welfare with responsibility for a broad range of activities – some directly concerned with the marginal and others focused on the entire population.

By 1940, then, reformers who never repudiated the ideology of the minimal state had helped create a centralized, provincially supervised, and, to a certain extent, funded welfare system in Ontario as well as a growing number of trained social workers to run it (Guest 1980; Kirkpatrick-Strong 1930). This quasi-professional, quasi-public-welfare apparatus, which took shape particularly during the interwar years, was fundamentally different from its mid-nineteenth-century counterpart. Notwithstanding the contrary arguments of revisionists such as Foucault and Scull, the 'scientific' prevention and regulation of social failures through the medium of a state-controlled disciplinary apparatus were neither conceivable nor achievable for Western market societies in 1840. The constraints of the neoclassical legal ideology and the virtual absence of the social sciences that provided the rationale for human management delayed its emergence until a much later date. Therefore, in English Canada at least, the numerous social-welfare reforms implemented during the period from the 1880s to the 1940s, including the family court, were not inconsequential or mere supplements to existing structures. They were, quite clearly, transformative of those structures.

In subsequent chapters, I chart more fully this transformation of Ontario's disciplinary underpinnings from the 1880s to the 1940s that characterized the emergent welfare state. Chapter 2 describes the 'social disorganization' wrought by structural change that engendered a middle-class reform focus on the family as both the cause of and the solution to deviance and dependency and shows how, despite their allegiance to laissez-faire principles, social-work leaders helped create the foundations of an interventionist state. Chapters 3 to 6 track the development of family courts in Ontario and comprise the book's substantive core. I attempt to unravel the reform process itself; to trace and analyse the complex interplay of old and new social-welfare and legal ideologies and practices and the overriding political pragmatism that influenced both the creation and the ultimate legitimation of the family court and socialized justice in Ontario. In chapter 7, I assess the impact of reform by examining how and with what success the early family courts tried to reproduce desired class and gender relations among a particular marginal segment of the population vis-à-vis the traditional police courts. The concluding chapter links the past to the present through a discussion of the implications of my family-court study for contemporary social-welfare reformers.

CHAPTER TWO

Social-Welfare Reformers
and the Regulation
of Marginal Families

Every day it is becoming more evident ... that to effectively grapple with crime and vice, thought and effort must
be concentrated on the children of the poor ... A child's
education begins from its earliest infancy, and the state has
a right to insist that its training shall be such as to fit it
ultimately for the proper discharge of its duties and responsibilities.

J.J. Kelso (c. 1894; cited in Rutherford 1974: 167)

The causes pushing children into situations now are most-
ly matters of conduct and relationships of adults where relief is no real solution of the problem ... The general prac-
titioner – the family case worker – is as fundamental a
necessity in social work as in medicine.

E. King (1929)

To understand why some reform ideas enter the 'public culture' (Gusfield 1981) at a given moment and others do not, it is necessary to lo-
cate reformers and their rhetoric in a specific social context. The urban
middle classes in late nineteenth- and early twentieth-century Canada
lived during a period of enormous structural upheaval, yet no public
repudiation of laissez-faire assumptions about individualism and the
minimal state occurred prior to the 1940s. As a result, while they recurrently drew links between a spiralling incidence of social problems and
social disintegration, the 'owners' (ibid) of welfare issues exhibited continuities with their mid-Victorian counterparts in their explanations of
and proposed solutions to deviancy and dependency. Thus, they retained

a primary focus on the moral-political regulation of marginal populations through private-sector initiatives.

At the same time, middle-class reformers from the 1880s onward were clearly the harbingers of a Canadian welfare state. Their growing emphasis on the nuclear family as both the source of and the answer to social problems buttressed policies and legislation that rationalized the 'owners' of welfare issues and social work itself under state auspices and increased state supervision of family life among the marginal outside segregative institutions. By 1940, numerous piecemeal social-welfare reforms had collectively effected two major changes that signalled the ascendant ideology of individualization and the interventionist state: the development of more determinist explanations of deviancy and dependency and the creation of a new regulatory mode of socialized legal coercion that blurred the demarcation line between the public and private spheres.

Structural Change and Social Disorganization: The Context of Reform

Like their British and American counterparts, English-Canadian welfare leaders from the 1880s to the 1940s worked amid immense economic, demographic, and political changes. During this period, the predominantly agricultural Canadian economy was increasingly transformed into a corporate one based on the concentration of industry and finance (Goff & Reasons 1978; Hunter 1925; Palmer 1983; Traves 1979). However, two aspects of this development had important implications for the creation of a welfare state in Canada vis-à-vis Britain and the United States. First, the economic expansion occurred within a very compressed time span. Thus, the consolidation of what might be called the Canadian industrial revolution was not achieved until the 1880s, yet by the turn of the century corporate capitalism, with its dual emphasis on 'scientific management' and assembly-line production, had already begun to take shape (Palmer 1983: 140; see also Cohen 1988: c. 6).[1] Second, the trend towards large-scale financial and industrial enterprises was still at an embryonic stage when the economic débâcle struck in 1929 (Palmer 1983: 186; see also Clark 1942, 1968; McNaught 1982).

This economic transformation was most pronounced and clearly discernible in Ontario, where the growth of industrial establishments, the number of people employed, and the amount of capital invested in them signalled the shift from an agricultural to a corporate economy. By 1935, 43.7 per cent of goods manufactured in Canada were produced in the province (Schull 1978: 193). Toronto was at the heart of this economic activity, emerging as the province's business, financial, administrative, and distributing centre (ibid: 189). Between 1881 and 1891, for example, the total number of productive establishments in the city more than tripled, the number of workers doubled, and the capital invested increased by roughly 265 per cent (Palmer 1983: 97). Similarly, while a mere 10 per cent of Ontario's industrial workers were Toronto residents in 1881, three decades later the proportion had risen to 27 per cent. During the same period, Hamilton and London emerged as the second and third most important economic centres of the province (Schull 1978: 190–1).

Canada's rapid economic expansion was intertwined with accelerated urbanization resulting from a combination of internal migration and immigration. Between 1870 and 1900, the urban population rose from 18 to 35 per cent of the total (Palmer 1983: 96–7); by 1931, it had surpassed the 50 per cent mark (Urquhart & Buckley 1965, Series A15–19: 14). In Ontario, the creation of an industrial base was accomplished only through a massive influx of immigrants to urban settings and the growing exodus of native Ontarians from farms to cities. Between 1881 and 1941, these movements doubled the province's population and very rapidly reversed the rural/urban ratio.[2] Indeed, the urbanization rate in Ontario was two decades in advance of that for Canada as a whole, with more than 50 per cent of the population residing in urban areas by 1911 (ibid).

All the cities that established family courts during the interwar years experienced population explosions. The demographic transformation was particularly obvious in Toronto where the number of inhabitants rose from fewer than 87,000 in 1881 to almost 700,000 in 1941 (from 4.5 to 18 per cent of the provincial population).[3] However, it is important to emphasize that the province remained overwhelmingly British in character. Notwithstanding the fact that by the 1920s, 10 per cent of male workers in Hamilton were European-born and many non-English-speaking immigrants worked the mines, forests, and farms of northern Ontario, the bulk of the new arrivals came from Great Britain (Palmer 1983: 142, 146; Schull 1978: 187).

The creation of mass democracy in Canada was a third crucial development during the transition to welfare state. At the federal level, universal suffrage was achieved in 1918 when the franchise was extended to qualified women and reaffirmed through the Dominion Elections Act of 1920 (Cleverdon 1974: c. 5; see also Bacchi 1983). In Ontario the introduction of the secret ballot in the 1875 provincial election was followed, thirteen years later, by the enactment of universal manhood suffrage. The enfranchisement of women in municipal and provincial elections, a belated and grudging concession by male politicians, finally became a reality during the First World War (Cleverdon 1974: c. 2).

As in other societies, structural upheavals accompanying the emergent Canadian welfare state had significant economic and political repercussions. For example, accelerated industrialization and urbanization wrought important changes in the class structure of the country (Johnson 1972). During the 1880s and 1890s, both an industrial proletariat (Kealey 1972; Palmer 1983) and a 'new' middle class (Rutherford 1971, 1974; Sutherland 1976; see also Wiebe 1967) proliferated in Toronto and other Ontario cities. This development was increasingly perceptible in the physical organization of urban centres. By the 1930s, the nineteenth-century commercial cities with their class-integrated neighbourhoods, which survived the beginnings of industrialization (Goheen 1970), had become full-blown industrial cities with different social strata occupying specific residential areas (Taylor 1987; Weaver 1977: 404).

Politically, the implementation of universal suffrage in Ontario created two potentially formidable, albeit not mutually exclusive, electoral blocs – industrial workers and women. Now the non-middle-class populations concentrated in distinct urban neighbourhoods not only posed a potential physical threat to social order but also had the power to challenge it at the polls (Rutherford 1971: 213). Moreover, the enfranchisement of women virtually doubled the electorate, making it imperative for incumbent male politicians to consider their views more seriously, particularly in light of the warning from suffragists that political leaders ought not to assume wives would simply vote as their husbands did (Bacchi 1983; Schull 1978: 222–3). The rise of independent farmer/labour politics after the First World War as an alternative to the traditional political parties reflected, in part, the strength of an increasingly militant urban working class and of recently enfranchised women (McNaught 1982; Morton 1950; Rankin 1989). For example, the United Farmers of Ontario (UFO) gained power in 1919 primarily on the basis of the farm vote and through an alliance with the eleven Independent Labour Party (ILP) representatives elected by urban workers (Allen 1971; McNaught 1982; Morton 1950; Schull 1978). Since the agrarian population of the province was no longer in the majority at this time, it seems clear that farm women did, in fact, vote as their husbands did and that their ballots were crucial to the UFO victory (Rankin 1989).

However, despite the 'social disorganization' wrought by these unparalleled economic, demographic, and political changes, public repudiation of laissez-faire principles did not begin to coalesce in Canada until the 1940s. Notwithstanding flashes of independence and militancy, the majority of industrial workers and women remained within the fold of status-quo politics during the interwar years. Thus, while the roots of the Canadian welfare state can be located in the late nineteenth century (Wallace 1950), state-funded, non-means-tested social-security measures such as old-age pensions, family allowances, and unemployment insurance were not instituted until decades later (Bellamy 1965; Finkel 1977; Guest 1980; Herman 1971; Moscovitch & Drover 1987; Struthers 1983; Tudiver 1987).[4] Ontario shared the national indifference to comprehensive social-insurance schemes. From the 1880s to the 1940s, no provincial government of any political stripe transcended the laissez-faire ideology of individualism and the minimal state. Indeed, as J.C. McRuer later recalled, 'being a Liberal in Toronto in the twenties ... was a little like being a Communist at a later date' (Oliver 1977: 269).

Because potential threats to social order generated by structural change were managed without the adoption of universal welfare measures, reform efforts during this period were directed primarily at the moral and political regulation of the marginal, that is, those among the working and dependent poor who would not or could not adhere to middle-class norms and were therefore at risk of becoming deviant and/or dependent (ibid: 216). Among the new urban middle classes, a recurrent perception of pervasive social disorganization and crisis was articulated in overlapping discourses about rampant immorality, family breakdown, and race suicide.

Prior to the First World War, these fears fuelled a moral- and social-reform movement that was ultimately dominated by adherents of the social gospel (Allen 1971; Bacchi 1983; Kinsman 1987; McLaren 1986; Rutherford 1971, 1974; Snell 1983; Strong-Boag 1976; Sutherland 1976; Valverde 1991). As this movement crested and declined during the interwar years, reform and reformers increasingly embraced the Progressive emphasis on technocratic engineering (McLaren 1990; Rooke & Schnell 1981a, 1981b, 1987; Strong-Boag 1982, 1988). However, what characterized both pre- and postwar social-welfare leaders was the belief, first propagated in the United States (Hunt 1978; Pound 1942; Ross 1969), that capitalist societies could be reorganized around consensus and cooperation without revolutionary economic and political change. Social control would ultimately replace class conflict and control (Rooke & Schnell 1981b, 1987).

Welfare Reformers and the Rationalization of Social Work

From the 1880s to the 1940s, then, few social-welfare leaders in Canada advocated the creation of a welfare state, per se. Thus, they were not unlike the middle-class individuals who had dominated earlier reform movements concerned with the regulation of marginal populations in this and other market societies (Donzelot 1980; Fitz 1981a, 1981b; Foucault 1977, 1980a; Muncie 1981; Rothman 1971, 1980). At the same time, however, they promoted initiatives aimed at rationalizing social-welfare work within the constraints of a laissez-faire state that ultimately fostered the development of a new form of social organization. The increasing professionalization, secularization, and institutionalization of welfare reformers, particularly during the interwar years, effected a qualitative transformation of both the 'owners' (Gusfield 1981) of welfare issues and the practice of social work. Over a sixty-year period, the part-time volunteers associated with private, church-based or -influenced organizations who dominated the social-welfare arena during the late nineteenth century were displaced, to a visible extent, by full-time, paid, professional personnel working in secular, state-coordinated and/or -funded agencies and bureaucracies.

In Canada, the First World War marked a great divide in this process. Despite its roots in the late nineteenth century, the push towards rationalization and bureaucratization of social welfare can be most clearly traced during the interwar years (Rooke & Schnell 1981a, 1981b, 1987; Schnell 1987; Strong-Boag 1979, 1982, 1988; Struthers 1983). Thus, whereas many American social-welfare leaders were full-time, paid professionals by 1918 (Lubove 1965; Woodroofe 1962), their Canadian counterparts had moved only slightly in that direction (Pitsula 1979; Sutherland 1976). None the less, a small corps of self-professed social-service experts, some trained in the United States and all integrally linked to a series of developing international professional communities, did emerge before the 1920s (Sutherland 1976: 26; see also Allen 1968, 1971; Hareven 1969; Rutherford 1971, 1974).

The same period also marked the advent of national umbrella organizations concerned with social-welfare issues. These church-based or -influenced groups included the National Council of Women (1893), the Canadian Conference of Charities and Corrections (1898), and the Moral and Social Reform Council of Canada (1907), which became the more broadly based Social Service Council of Canada (1913) (Allen 1971; Crysdale 1961; Guest 1980: 32–4; Hareven 1969: 86; Morrison 1976; Strong-Boag 1976). Arguably the first national social-work organization in the country, the Social Service Council of Canada (SSCC), established branches in several provinces, including Ontario, and held its first conference on the eve of the First World War (Allen 1971; see also Guest 1980: 32–4; Held 1959: 3).

John Joseph Kelso exemplified the social reformer in Ontario prior to 1918 (Jones & Rutman 1981; Sutherland 1976). An immigrant with no university education, he became a child-welfare advocate through his work as a Toronto journalist and embarked on a career in the field within the context of urban reform during the 1880s. Later, staunch religious convictions and overt moralism steered him in the direction of the social gospel and to eventual membership in the Social Service Council of Canada (Allen 1971: 21). A part-time volunteer who was the driving force behind the creation of various private welfare organizations, most notably the Children's Aid Society of Toronto, Kelso subsequently became a state employee when he was appointed the first superintendent of neglected and dependent children for the province in 1893. While he placed great stress on 'moral commitment as well as intellectual ability' in social workers (Jones & Rutman 1981: 132), Kelso also helped launch Canada's first school of social service at the University of Toronto in 1914 (Pitsula 1979: 40–1; see also Jones & Rutman 1981: 132). Kelso and his counterparts were thus transitional figures, setting the stage for the advocates of professional social work who became the primary definers of social-welfare issues during the interwar years.[5]

The accelerated trend towards professionalization and specialization of social-welfare leaders and personnel after the Great War began under the aegis of the church-influenced Social Service Council of Canada when the pre-war moral- and social-reform movement was approaching its zenith. By 1918 the SSCC – a federation comprising fourteen dominion-wide affiliates and eleven provincial units (Allen 1971: 64) – had emerged as the dominant organization in the welfare field. That same year the national body hired Dr J.G. Shearer as full-time general secretary, and the provincial councils took on a total of fourteen full-time, salaried personnel (ibid), including the Reverend Gilbert Agar, a Methodist minister, who became the first paid secretary of the Social Service Council of Ontario. Seven years later, the SSCO acquired the Reverend David B. Harkness as its full-time educational director (Held 1959: 7). Formerly a Winnipeg juvenile-court judge and secretary general of the Social Service Council of Manitoba (Allen 1971: 243), Harkness emerged as one of Ontario's major welfare leaders in the later 1920s.

The Social Service Councils did not enjoy their monopoly over the definition of social-welfare issues very long, however. Despite an emphasis on professionalization, they were plagued by a number of serious problems, one of the most troubling being the growing tension between church-based and secular social work. Although comprising both secular and religious affiliates, the councils operated on the same assumption as did the social-service departments of the various Protestant churches: namely, that 'the direct impetus of religious motivation [was] essential to the effective practice of social work' and thus the 'prominence, if not dominance, of religious institutions' was necessary (Allen 1971: 284). They were not entirely averse to the new trends in social welfare evident in the United States, but 'that those developments should be fully secular was quite outside the standpoint of the progressive social gospel' (ibid: 285).

Unfortunately, dwindling numbers of social-welfare leaders agreed with this stance and, by the mid-1920s, the councils were in decline. Secular, professionally oriented organizations, which, ironically, they helped to create, were assuming control of the social-welfare arena (Allen 1971: 286–7; Schnell 1987). The most important of these new groups was the Canadian Council on Child Welfare (1920), which, under the stewardship of Charlotte Whitton, became the pre-eminent 'owner' of social-welfare issues in the country. Whitton launched her social-work career in 1918 as the assistant to Dr Shearer at the Social Service Council of Canada. However, two years later, Whitton also became honorary secretary to the fledgling Canadian Council on Child Welfare (CCCW), a position that, by 1926, she had successfully converted into a full-time paid appointment that continued until her resignation in 1941 (Rooke & Schnell 1981a: 491, 1987: 46–8; Schnell 1987; see also Canadian Welfare Council 1941–2). Holding an honorary MA in history from Queen's University, she was representative of a new breed of social-welfare leader: university-educated and imbued with the ideology of secular, professional social work, but not specifically trained as a social worker.

The ascendancy of the secular professionalizers as the primary definers of social-welfare issues was not simply the result of individual will, however, but rather a consequence of the long-term decline of the social gospel during the interwar years. As Social Service councils suffered more and more from neglect by the Protestant churches, the withdrawal of secular affiliates, and the adoption of secular social work by former social-gospellers, Charlotte Whitton was able to move the Canadian Council on Child Welfare, and herself, to the fore through a number of astute manoeuvres (Allen 1971: 287).[6] First, by the early 1930s, the Child Welfare Council had absorbed and assumed the functions of several rival organizations, beginning with the Social Service Council of Canada. The turning-point for the SSCC came in 1928 when its annual meeting attracted only 32 delegates as opposed to the 710 who registered for the secular Canadian Conference of Social Work (Allen 1971: 288). Having recognized the impossibility of maintaining its research responsibilities and leadership in the social-welfare arena, and after much deliberation, the SSCC simply transferred them to the Canadian Council on Child Welfare (Hareven 1969: 95).

Two other potential rivals absorbed by the CCCW were the Child Welfare Division of the federal Department of Health (later resurrected) and the Canadian Association of Child Protection Officers (CACPO).[7] The latter, which corresponded to the National Probation Association (NPA) in the United States, was dominated by individuals and groups imbued with the pre-war conception of church-based social service (Schnell 1987). However, unlike its American counterpart, the CACPO was always a weak organization. Throughout the 1920s, Whitton categorically rejected a recurrent proposal that the group take over the CCCW division on crime and delinquency, and ultimately the CACPO was assimilated by the council in 1935. Its demise was of particular significance because, in the United States, the NPA had emerged as the umbrella organization that defined family courts as an issue and acted as the coordinator of the early family-court movement (Boushy 1950; Chunn 1982).

Under Whitton, the CCCW also gained a pre-eminent position in the social-welfare field through its control over the infant Canadian Association of Social Workers (CASW 1926a: 103; see also 1926b: 284–6; Walker 1943) and the Canadian Conference of Social Work, founded in 1926 and 1928, respectively. Whitton, in fact, initially resisted the efforts of organizers to involve the CCCW in the latter endeavour. However, upon discovering that David Harkness hoped to turn the Social Service Council of Ontario into the national organization for the development of professional social work, she moved swiftly and successfully to pre-empt him.[8] Whitton was able to impose her particular definitions of social-welfare issues on both groups, particularly after her appointment as the convener of the CASW Recruitment and Training Committee in 1930 and her forging of direct links between the CCCW and the schools of social work at the University of Toronto and McGill.[9]

Whitton's most important move in promoting the ascendancy of the Child Welfare Council, however, was to create a network of social workers who agreed with her definitions of social-welfare issues. Increasingly, she managed to ensconce hand-picked choices in pivotal positions in social-work agencies and government departments and to link them to the council through executive and committee positions. The result was a fairly tight control over social work across Canada (Rooke & Schnell 1981a: 491–2 and 495–6, 1987). During the late 1920s, Whitton was particularly successful in luring key people away from allegiance to the Social Service Council of Ontario. The co-opted, all directors of major social agencies, were kindred spirits – university-educated and imbued with the ideology of secular, professional social work, but not trained social workers.[10] Like J.J. Kelso and other pre-war reformers, then, Charlotte Whitton and her allies were transitional figures, preparing the way for the professionally educated social workers who became the 'owners' (Gusfield 1981) of social-welfare issues in the 1940s as the welfare state developed.

Professionalization and secularization of social-work leaders during the interwar years were accompanied by a movement towards the institutionalization of welfare reform and reformers. The latter became creatures of the state as governments began to consult routinely specific individuals and organizations on questions related to the marginal. A major consequence of this trend was the generation of state-sanctioned reform constituencies that could be integrally involved in the formulation of legislation and policy governing the marginal without fear that they would advocate changes which governments did not want to implement and/or could not turn to their own ends (Guest 1980; Rooke & Schnell 1987; Struthers 1983; see also Gusfield 1981). Until the late 1930s, reformers who fell outside the implicit parameters of laissez-faire acceptability – for example, those who advocated socialist policies or even the creation of a full-fledged welfare state – could be, and were, safely ignored.

In Ontario, the institutionalization of welfare reformers and reform after the Great War was characterized by two developments. First, as J.J. Kelso discovered, government bureaucrats could no longer be reform activists. Before the war, he had been free to advocate publicly policies that the provincial government did not support, despite his civil-service position as superintendent of neglected and dependent children. However, in 1918, when Kelso began to spearhead the rejuvenated movement for mothers' allowances, a major pre-war reform demand placed on hold during the conflict, the provincial secretary quickly informed him that 'it was no longer acceptable for government officials to dissent publicly from official policy' (Jones & Rutman 1981: 154). Thereafter, until his 1934 retirement, Kelso was forced to operate completely within the constraints of his role as a state employee.

Second, the welfare leaders and organizations that received the government seal of approval as consultants were ideologically and politically compatible ones. After the 1919 provincial election, for example, the Social Service Council of Ontario quickly established itself as a consultant to the United Farmers of Ontario on social-welfare questions. This success was due in no small part to the fact that Premier Drury, Attorney General Raney, and several other government members had played an active role in the pre-war moral- and social-reform movement and were infused with the philosophy of the social gospel, particularly in relation to the prohibition issue (Allen 1971: 202; Oliver 1975: 12, 1977: 93). Drury directly involved the SSCO in the drafting of postwar social legislation (Splane 1951). And, although the Conservatives swept the UFO out of office in 1923, the council remained the principal consultant to the provincial government on social-welfare issues during the tenure of the prohibitionist attorney general, W.F. Nickle (Held 1959: 7).

Ultimately, however, the failure of prohibition and subsequent resignation of Nickle undermined the privileged position of the fiercely pro-temperance council (Oliver 1977: 278; Schull 1978: 276–7). The advocates of secular, professional social work in particular rapidly gained credence as government consultants on social-welfare questions. Robert E. Mills, director of the Toronto Children's Aid Society and ally of Charlotte Whitton, was one of the rising stars. Asked for his views on a number of issues, Mills responded with a confidential memorandum to the provincial secretary, Lincoln Goldie, in which he criticized J.J. Kelso and, by implication, the pre-war approach to welfare concerns: 'It is only fair to the government to say that Mr. Kelso has not of late years given the leadership that these various [child-welfare] activities require. His standards of social work have not always been up to the level recognized by social workers and his general "laissez-faire" attitude has lost for him the confidence of progressive people in social work.'[11]

Charlotte Whitton shared this assessment of Kelso and church-based social work.[12] One of her major goals was to entrench the Canadian Council on Child Welfare – 'a voluntary agency, supported by federal subsidies' – as the primary adviser to *all* levels of government about social-welfare issues. Thus, she worked tirelessly to fulfil the mandate of the CCCW, which was 'to serve as a national clearing house for child welfare, to issue professional guidance materials, to inform public opinion, and to formulate briefs for legislation' (Hareven 1969: 92; see also Anon. 1935: 1–2; 1949: 42–3; Schnell 1987). When the Social Service Council of Ontario's consulting monopoly foundered on the rock of prohibition, Whitton, who was a lifelong Tory, had an opportunity to entrench the Child Welfare Council as an alternative consultant to the Conservative government on social-welfare issues.

However, she could not fully exploit the growing weakness of the SSCO at mid-decade. For one thing, Whitton herself was a staunch prohibitionist who had also established friendly relations with the temperance-minded Attorney General Nickle during the early 1920s. Furthermore, after he resigned to protest the government's legalization of alcohol, Whitton did nothing to endear the CCCW to the Ferguson government by announcing that all her free time would be devoted to defeating them in the next election (Oliver 1977: 269). None the less, the increasing problems faced by the Social Service Council of Ontario together with Whitton's ability to forge links with key Toronto people such as Robert E. Mills meant that, by the early 1930s, the Canadian Council on Child and Family Welfare (as it became in 1929) had become an established consultant to the Ontario government on welfare issues and the recipient of small provincial grants. In contrast, David Harkness resigned from the SSCO in 1932 because the council had no money (Held 1959).

The transfer of leadership from the Ontario Social Service Council to the Child and Family Welfare Council was obvious in the report of the Royal Commission on Public Welfare in Ontario (Ontario 1930). Whitton's views were solicited and frequently cited verbatim by the commission (ibid: 8). Thus, although few had expected the CCCW to fulfil its original mandate, by 1935 the council was the repository of secular, professional social work in the country and enjoyed a virtual monopoly over the definition of social-welfare issues. The token agency had been transformed into 'the moral watch-dog over all aspects of child and family life' (Rooke & Schnell 1981a: 491; see also CWC 1935).[13]

Overall, then, Canadian social-welfare leaders from the 1880s to the 1940s made no decisive break with laissez-faire assumptions, yet they promoted policies that led to that eventuality. Thus, J.J. Kelso was personally disposed towards voluntary, private-sector social work, exemplified by the CAS initiatives, yet through his government position he helped construct a state-run public-welfare department in Ontario, which was ultimately staffed by full-time, paid professionals. Similarly, Charlotte Whitton's vision of university-educated persons, like herself, directing social work in private agencies with government coordination and funding failed to recognize that, unlike those of law and medicine, the profession of social work was a creature of the welfare state and its expansion depended upon the establishment of public-welfare bureaucracies. By 1940, the path was cleared for the graduates of university social-work programs who would people those bureaucracies and act as consultants to governments in the decades to come.

Problem Families and Social Problems

The 'owners' of social-welfare issues in Canada/Ontario from the 1880s to the 1940s were similarly contradictory with respect to explanations of deviancy and dependency. On the one hand, reformers during this period never totally abandoned the social-Darwinist emphasis on individual moral failings as the cause of marginality. On the other, unlike most of their Victorian counterparts, welfare leaders from the late nineteenth century onward focused much more explicitly on the family as the chief incubator of social problems. Indeed, they increasingly made a direct link between deviation from the middle-class or bourgeois family model and social problems (Ariès 1962; Fitz 1981a, 1981b; Muncie 1981; Parr 1982; Rooke & Schnell 1982).

This model has always been less a reality than an ideological construct based on several key assumptions: first, that the natural, inevitable, and highest form of the family is a particular type of household arrangement – a nuclear unit comprising two adults in a monogamous, heterosexual, legal marriage, and their dependent children; second, that the family is premised on the biological or sexual division of labour that gives each member a different, but complementary, role with attendant obligations; third, that the family is a private haven that operates on the basis of consensus as opposed to the public sphere of the market-place where competition and conflict prevail (Barrett 1988; Barrett & McIntosh 1982; Dahl & Snare 1978; Eichler 1985, 1988; Gavigan 1988; Lasch 1979; O'Donovan 1985; Poster 1978; Thorne & Yalom 1982).

Because there are no inherent conflicts of interest between its members, the 'normal' family is thus a harmonious family where each individual fulfils the duties and responsibilities attached to his or her role. Women's 'proper' sphere is the home because, as child-bearers, they are biologically predisposed to be care-givers, monogamous wives, and housekeepers. In contrast, men's 'proper' domain is the public arena because they are equipped by nature to act as providers and protectors. And children exist in a 'natural' state of subordination to adults, including parents, and engage in behaviour befitting their dependent status (Donzelot 1980; Fitz 1981a, 1981b; Foucault 1980a; Houston 1982; Muncie 1981; Weeks 1986).

Given the equation of the bourgeois family model and normality, then, reformers very early on began to explain social problems and intrafamilial conflict in terms of deviation from it. By the mid-nineteenth century, for example, some middle-class professionals, intellectuals, and philanthropists were defining the 'true state' of childhood as one of dependency, requiring the provision of moral and physical well-being within the nuclear family – biological or surrogate – and talking about 'delinquency' and other social ills as products of 'deficiencies in working-class family life and social organization' (Fitz 1981b: 37, 39; Muncie 1981: 17; see also Houston 1972; May 1973; Parr 1982; Rooke & Schnell 1983). This was the first step towards causal explanations of such problems as juvenile crime and poverty, which emphasized individual differences.

However, it was the welfare leaders from the 1880s to the 1940s who marked the passage from an individualistic era that forgot the individual to an era of 'socialized individualism' that explored the potential of the individual (Allen 1971: 290; see also Stapleford 1938). They began to espouse ideas about social and individual pathology that are central to the determinist theories of deviancy and dependency that prevail in welfare states. Thus, reformers may have embraced the same general conceptions of childhood and family as did some of their mid-nineteenth-century counterparts but the precise *content* of the constructions changed markedly during the transition from laissez-faire to welfare state in Canada and other market societies as the production and dissemination of knowledge about social-welfare problems underwent increasing rationalization.

To a growing extent, university-based and/or -trained 'experts' provided the 'close, detailed' knowledge used by the 'owners' of social-welfare issues to legitimate their reform proposals, including the 'factual' basis for middle-class conceptions of childhood and family (Gusfield 1981: 37). This transformation of knowledge production and dissemination had two major consequences: first, fewer and fewer individuals and organizations possessed the credentials to be sources of authoritative knowledge about child and family life; and, second, the discourses of 'child-saving' (Platt 1969) became more and more secular, professional, and technocratic.

Between 1886 and 1900, a large number of middle-class city dwellers, especially in Toronto, began to express, debate, and elaborate systematically the notion that childhood was a special stage of 'institutionalized dependency' (Houston 1982: 131) in the life cycle for all children in which school attendance and supervised leisure replaced gainful employment (Sutherland 1976: 10). Social Darwinism was tempered by the emergence of new philosophies, particularly the social gospel and the romanticism of Friedrich Froebel, which emphasized how important environmental influences were in shaping behaviour. Froebel was enormously influential in legitimating the conception of childhood as a distinct stage of life and, by 1895, Froebel societies were flourishing in Ottawa, Toronto, and London (ibid: 18).

Rejecting conventional wisdom, Froebel argued that the child was not an immutable object but, rather, a seed requiring the most careful nurture and tending. Childhood was a period of innocence, 'easily corrupted'; of 'incipient waywardness' requiring control; of dependence, which made the young more malleable but also protected them from the 'brutalities of the adult world'; and of subordination owed by youth to 'its natural superiors' (Fitz, 1981b: 39; see also Muncie 1981; Rothman 1980; Sutherland 1976). In short, *all* children could be evil as well as innocent, dangerous as well as endangered (Fitz 1981b: 37, 38; see also Donzelot 1980: 82, 96; May 1973; Platt 1969). Thus, it was of crucial importance to provide a firm but loving and protective family environment that would ensure the harmonious development of a child's threefold nature – mental, physical, and moral (Sutherland 1976: 18).

In the twentieth century, these beliefs were reshaped through the infusion of specialized, 'scientific' knowledge, and child-care experts imbued with the 'relativism of the modern social sciences' became increasingly important (Strong-Boag 1982: 166, 1988). The new professionals, typified by Dr William Blatz, who dominated a Toronto-based Canadian child-study movement during the interwar years, rejected Froebel's romantic essentialism, arguing that behaviour was intrinsically neither good nor bad. Thus, children could be 'adapted to their social environment' through persistent affirmation of certain conduct (Strong-Boag 1982: 166, 1988). The image of child as machine began to supplant the image of child as flower.

This behaviourist emphasis on the mutability of the child in response to environmental stimuli, together with the psychoanalytic insights of Freud about the long-term significance of early childhood and the parent–child relationship, shifted reformers' attention from school-age children to pre-schoolers. They still believed that the deprivation of adequate physical and moral sustenance created problems, but the accumulating knowledge of child-care experts increasingly convinced them that the quality of emotional services provided within the family during children's early years was crucial to their normal development. Adopting a more psychological orientation, welfare leaders began to focus on the relationship between husband and wife as the potential source of social problems (Lasch 1979: 37–43). More and more, they drew causal links between marital tensions and discord, which were presumably more pervasive in non-middle-class families, and domestic violence, delinquency, and child neglect.

By the 1940s, then, the normal childhood was to a large extent the one defined by numerous child psychologists and psychiatrists from G. Stanley Hall and William Healey (Rothman 1980: 207–8, 211, 212) to John Watson (Miller 1982; Strong-Boag 1982, 1988), to Sigmund Freud and his followers (Donzelot 1980; Muncie 1981: 20). It was not only a separate period of life, but also a series of distinct and complex psycho-sexual stages, including early childhood and adolescence. Similarly, the normal family was increasingly the one constituted by social psychologists and sociologists: a 'unity of interacting personalities,' performing indispensable emotional services rather than economic functions (Lasch 1979: 31). Consequently, motherhood, parenthood, and spousal relationships were not simply a product of biological instinct; they were momentous undertakings requiring the most specialized knowledge and training (ibid; see also Strong-Boag 1982, 1988).

As the constructs of childhood and family were reformulated from the 1880s to the 1940s, developing industrial cities provided further corroboration for the prevailing belief among welfare leaders that there was a direct link between 'deformed' families (Lasch 1979: 15) and social problems. With the various classes and social strata increasingly segregated in clearly demarcated residential areas, discrepancies between the child-rearing practices and family life of middle-class and non-middle-class people became very visible (Houston 1982: 131). During the late nineteenth century, for example, urban reformers in Ontario only had to look around them to see that the nuclear family with a small number of dependent children was more a middle-class reality than anything else. Non-middle-class populations continued to embrace the conception of children as miniature adults and economic assets and to rely on extended forms of family organization (Houston 1982; Jones & Rutman 1981; McConnachie 1983; Parr 1982, 1990; Rooke & Schnell 1983; Sutherland 1976; Ursel 1986; see also Fitz 1981a, 1981b; Gillis 1975; Muncie 1981).

Indeed, many non-middle-class immigrants and migrants from rural areas of Ontario who poured into the burgeoning cities quickly realized the necessity of adopting 'a collective strategy' for survival. Thus, most first-generation urban children grew up in households that included distant relatives, frequently interacted with nearby kin, and experienced periods when they were more materially dependent on extended- than on immediate-family members (Parr 1982: 13–14, 1990). Moreover, there was a veritable population explosion among the lower orders, whereas the birth rate among middle-class families was steadily declining (McConnachie 1983; McLaren & McLaren 1986; Snell 1983; see also Leacy 1983: Series A248-253 and Series A254-259).

It is hardly surprising, then, that during the transition to welfare state in Canada, social-work leaders recurrently identified crises of the family that coincided with the periods of greatest dissonance between their child-rearing practices and family life and those of non-middle-class children and parents. At these junctures, reformers perceived an immediate danger to the nuclear family and an ultimate threat to the foundations of social order (Morrison 1976). The first major crisis of the family in Ontario occurred amid the social disorganization wrought by urbanization, industrialization, and immigration during the 1880s and 1890s (Allen 1971; Rutherford 1974; see also Lasch 1979). These structural changes exerted a marked and differential impact on families across social strata that was manifested by a marked increase in mother-headed households and the 'feminization of poverty' (Gordon 1988b; Pateman 1989b). Moreover, the discrepant lived experience of middle- and non-middle-class families was paralleled by reformers' perceptions of an alarming increase in social problems among non-middle-class populations, particularly delinquency (Houston 1982; Jones & Rutman 1981; Morrison 1976; Sutherland 1976; see also Fitz 1981b; Muncie 1981).

Welfare leaders were thus confronted with an obvious question. Since *all* youth were potential delinquents because of their 'incipient waywardness,' why was delinquency so obviously the monopoly of non-middle-class children (Fitz 1981b: 39; see also Donzelot 1980; May 1973; Muncie 1981; Platt 1969; Rothman 1980; Sutherland 1976)? Almost inevitably, reformers began to develop ecological explanations. They concluded that 'pathological' families, which were concentrated among the lower classes residing in specific urban areas, must be the main cause of deviancy and dependency. Adequate child training was impossible in homes where children were allowed to behave like adults; parents engaged in vice, drunkenness, and immorality; husbands/fathers failed to maintain their dependants; mothers engaged in paid employment; and/or parents were divorced or separated.

In the twentieth century, reformers identified a similar crisis of the family during and after the Great War when many families, particularly among the non-middle classes, deviated from the nuclear form of organization. Fathers were missing through death, desertion, or physical and mental incapacitation; mothers worked outside the home, leaving children untended and unsupervised; and children in both rural and urban working-class families continued to be economic assets, often contributing substantially to the family income (Held 1959; Parr 1982: 14–15; Ramkhalawansingh 1974; Strong-Boag 1979, 1982; Sutherland 1976). As they had in the late nineteenth century, reformers attributed the apparently soaring rates of postwar juvenile crime, illegitimacy, child neglect, desertion and divorce to such deviant families (Strong-Boag 1979, 1982; see also Fitz 1981b; Lasch 1979). Moreover, statistical evidence provided increasing support for ecological explanations of deviance and dependency during the interwar years. For example, the authors of a report on Ontario's reformatory system were not at all surprised to find that virtually every child committed to industrial and training schools and to Children's Aid societies between 1929 and 1933 was from a specific non-middle-class residential area of Toronto, Hamilton, Ottawa, or London (Ontario 1935: 8).

Reproducing the Middle-Class Family among Marginal Populations

The way marginality is explained has obvious implications for policies aimed at treatment and prevention. Thus, it is entirely consistent that reformers who pinpoint the family as the source of social problems also see it as the solution to them. Even in the mid-nineteenth century, some reformers advocated state-sanctioned educative, philanthropic, and legal strategies to inculcate bourgeois norms of childhood and family life among non-middle-class populations. To this end, they launched campaigns to enforce the dependency of children and the sanctity of marriage (Curtis 1987; Houston 1972; Rooke & Schnell 1983; Splane 1965; see also Donzelot 1980; Foucault 1977, 1980a; Muncie 1981).

None the less, the prevailing ideology of individualism and the minimal state and the underdevelopment of the social sciences set limits on the publicly acceptable responses to social problems at this time. Thus, the idea that the state should act directly to normalize and maintain marginal families in the community was, for most people, inconceivable, particularly in the context of a predominantly rural society such as Canada's. On the contrary, social-welfare leaders emphasized the use of private-sector initiatives, particularly segregative institutions, to moralize and remoralize the marginal. Moreover, although they viewed bad family conditions as the root cause of social problems, reformers advocated policies that actually facilitated the dismemberment of families. For example, the creation of 'family-like' residential facilities – orphanages, homes, and reform and industrial schools – to differentiate deviant and/ or dependent children from their adult counterparts meant that indigent mothers and their children were often committed to different segregative institutions (Komar 1975: 156–7; Rooke & Schnell 1983).

Consequently, in 1880, the experience of childhood as a stage of dependency in a nuclear family was primarily confined to urban, middle-class Canadian children. The conception of children as property to be used as family (economic) assets was still embraced by the majority of parents and employers and also upheld in law (Katz, Stern, & Doucet 1982; Parr 1982; Ursel 1986; see also Fitz 1981b: 13). For example, Canada had no prohibitions on child labour, and many children were employed in factories, mines, agriculture, and domestic service. Schooling remained under parental control and was often informal, sporadic, and dependent upon the exigencies of the family economy. The leisure time of non-middle-class youth was largely unsupervised and, in urban areas, frequently centred on street activities. And, despite the progressive legal differentiation of children from adults in the courts and segregative institutions, many children continued to be subject to adult procedures and sanctions.

During the transition to welfare state in Canada, however, the moral-political regulation of the marginal under conditions of industrialization, urbanization, and mass democracy became a burning issue. Although reformers initially retained a faith in segregative institutions as the antidote to the pathological family life that produced deviancy and dependency,[14] by the late 1880s they saw the growing ineffectiveness of such a policy. The private sector simply could not finance enough institutions to accommodate all the marginal individuals now residing in urban centres. At the same time, a declining birth rate meant that the middle classes were increasingly outnumbered. Thus, reformers began to perceive an urgent need to devise new strategies for 'policing' industrial cities.

Like their counterparts in other jurisdictions, they came to view the nuclear family as the key element in the social reorganization of Canadian society. Reformers began to lobby for state policies that would induce non-middle-class populations to embrace and adhere to alien standards of child-rearing and family life associated with the bourgeois family model (Barrett 1988; Donzelot 1980; Lasch 1979; Lewis 1986; Poster 1978: c. 7; Sutherland 1976; Zaretsky 1976, 1982, 1986). Consequently, while the publicly accepted and acceptable antidotes for social-welfare problems continued to hinge on assumptions about individual responsibility and the minimal state, marked changes in the response to marginality did occur between 1880 and 1940. Solutions to social-welfare problems started to take the form of state-sponsored and/or -financed, community-based, family-centred policies and programs aimed at entrenching the conception of childhood as 'forced dependency' and 'forced obligation' and of the family as nuclear (Fitz 1981b: 20).

These initiatives were phenomenally successful. In Canada/Ontario, middle-class conceptions of childhood and family became more and more hegemonic *within* the middle class itself, and *across* social classes, from the 1880s to the 1940s. Moreover, success was achieved primarily through non-coercive strategies for upgrading standards of family life. These included public-health campaigns to reduce infant mortality; the introduction of domestic-science programs in the schools; the implementation of supervised leisure through the construction of playgrounds and the formation of youth organizations (e.g., Scouts, Guides, Brownies, YMCA, YWCA) aimed at instilling middle-class values through the provision of appropriate role models and activities; the mass dissemination of prenatal and postnatal advice literature; the establishment of nursery schools predicated on the tenets of the child-study movement and 'scientific' child-rearing; and media portrayals, especially in films, popular magazines, and advertising, of middle-class images of childhood and family life (Arnup 1986; McLaren & McLaren 1986: c. 5; Snell 1986b; Strong-Boag 1982, 1988; Sutherland 1976).

Central to the effectiveness of all these non-coercive initiatives was the widespread acceptance among girls and women of the 'separate spheres' ideology (O'Donovan 1985; Pateman 1989a). The media, churches, schools, clinics, and other forums disseminated a common image of mothers as guardians of the future welfare of society and reinforced reform efforts to direct girls to motherhood as the most important career (Morrison 1976; Roberts 1979; Strong-Boag 1976, 1982, 1988; Sutherland 1976; Vipond 1977). As a result, women of all classes increasingly accepted the idea that the onus for maintaining the 'proper' standards of child-rearing and family life should fall on the mother since, ideally, she did not work outside the home and could devote her entire time to domestic duties. Indeed, the domestic-role ideology was so seductive that even feminist and socialist women were among its staunchest adherents (Bacchi 1983; Roberts 1979; Sangster 1989; Strong-Boag 1976). Thus, women's suffrage produced 'no real repudiation of tradition'; the 'occasional talk of companionate marriage and professional employment for women foundered before the insistence that being a mother was "the highest of all professions"' (Strong-Boag 1982: 161–2, 1988).

When ideology failed, the recalcitrant – individuals who would not or could not voluntarily adhere to middle-class norms of child-rearing and family life – were subject to legal coercion (Houston 1982; Muncie 1981; Sutherland 1976; Ursel 1986). During the late nineteenth and early twentieth centuries, federal and provincial governments enacted a spate of criminal and quasi-criminal legislation that was ostensibly applicable to all children and all families but, in effect, targeted the non–middle classes. Some laws and by-laws regulating labour, education, leisure, and sexuality restricted the activities of children and women in extrafamilial sites. Other statutes governing child welfare and spousal maintenance regulated intrafamilial relations.

While all these laws had obvious continuities with earlier ones, they were also qualitatively different from them in two major respects: the degree and mode of state intervention. The legislation enacted to regulate state–family and intrafamilial relations during the transition to welfare state in Canada sanctioned unprecedented intervention into deviant, or potentially deviant, families. At the same time, the new statutes emphasized the deinstitutionalized treatment of the deviant and dependent, which fostered a growing reliance on social work to repair and maintain nuclear family units in the community. The result was a breakdown of the rigid demarcation line between the civil and criminal and social and legal spheres.

With respect to extrafamilial sites, Ontario enacted statutes that reduced parents' powers over their offspring outside the family and restricted women's access to the public sphere, thereby enforcing the conceptions of children's 'natural' dependency and of women's 'proper' sphere. Between 1880 and 1914, the province implemented legislation governing factories, shops, and mines, prohibiting child labour and excluding or restricting female labour (Cohen 1988; Ursel 1986). At the municipal level, Toronto and other urban centres also banned street trading, which became an alternative source of family income after factory work was banned (Houston 1982; Jones & Rutman 1981; Stewart 1971; Ursel 1986; see also Muncie 1981: 20). Compulsory-education laws required parents to surrender their children to a systematic regime of full-time schooling in which a small number of middle-class adults had the authority to assist, control, and even dictate a child's social and intellectual development (Fitz 1981b: 37). Finally, curfew laws and regulations governing entertainment venues, such as theatres and dance and pool halls, held parents responsible for monitoring the leisure activities of their children outside the family (Jones & Rutman 1981; Sutherland 1976; see also Gillis 1975).

However, the provincial and federal legislation regulating intrafamilial relations was most central to the work of socialized courts. New family-welfare laws reflected the increasingly direct role of governments in sanctioning and facilitating the appropriation of patriarchal and parental rights by authorized state agents when it was deemed to be in the 'best interests' of the deviant and dependent (Splane 1953–4; Sutherland 1976). Between 1880 and 1940, then, the social statutes enacted in response to perceived crises of the family collectively contributed to a reform of welfare law that had profound implications for the families of the working and dependent poor.

Prior to 1914, the major social statutes that sharply circumscribed parental rights over their children were those related to child protection and juvenile delinquency. Reformers representing churches, women's groups, Children's Aid societies, and charity organizations, particularly Toronto-based ones, argued that, when one or both parents consistently failed to provide the 'proper' environment for the physical, mental, and moral growth of their children, the state had both a right and an obligation to rescue and save children at risk in bad surroundings. As one prominent reformer put it: 'The rights of parents are sacred and ought not to be lightly interfered with but they may be forfeited by abuse' (Scott 1908: 893–4, 1938a; see also Dymond 1923; Jones & Rutman 1981; Leon 1977, 1978; Sutherland 1976).

The Children's Protection Act, 1888 (S.O., 1888, c. 40) reflected the new interventionist attitude towards marginal families. Despite a continued emphasis on the use of segregative institutions, the statute was a trail-blazer in the state delimitation of parental rights. For the first time in Ontario, police magistrates were empowered to remove children from the care of their parents or guardians and place them in industrial schools when they felt it was necessary for the children's welfare. Reformers quickly found the 1888 legislation too restrictive, however. In 1891, after the Royal Commission on the Prison and Reformatory System issued a report (Ontario 1891) that advocated increased state regulation of child-rearing and domestic life, the newly organized Children's Aid Society of Toronto (CASOT), led by J.J. Kelso, began to campaign for a more comprehensive statute that would specify exactly who constituted a dependent or neglected child, and who might act as a state agent and their powers in such cases, and emphasize community-based rather than institutional care of children at risk.

The Children's Protection Act, 1893 (S.O., 1893, c. 45), met many of their demands. It made parental cruelty to children an offence, provided a very broad definition of neglected children, and granted 'any duly authorized Children's Aid Society' potentially Draconian powers of intervention in family life. For example, CAS agents were empowered to apprehend any children deemed to be at risk and detain them in special shelters prior to a legal hearing. The societies could also exercise guardianship rights over children committed to their care by court order, including placement in foster homes selected and supervised by them and committal to institutions, until either the child turned twenty-one or the parents were deemed fit and able to have the child returned to them. The courts, too, were accorded expansive powers under the statute. For the first time, justices of the peace and police magistrates were empowered to make guardianship decisions in neglect cases.

Fifteen years later, the federal Juvenile Delinquents Act, 1908 (S.C., 1908, c. 40), added another potentially coercive edge to state powers of intervention in family life among the working and dependent poor. By creating the offence of delinquency and mandating the establishment of special socialized children's courts, the state enlarged its parental role and powers. For the first time, a child could be sanctioned – albeit it in a kindly, parental manner – for non-criminal behaviours such as truancy, wandering, and loitering, and for engaging in adult practices, particularly gambling, drinking, smoking, and sex. Moreover, even without a formal hearing, a juvenile could be committed to a probation officer, Children's Aid Society, or any person deemed suitable by the court, or to an institution or his or her family, which would be monitored by the court. At the same time, adults who contributed to the commission of any delinquent acts were now subject to criminal penalties under the rules of summary conviction that allowed a maximum sentence of a $500 fine and/or imprisonment for one year (Stewart 1971; Sutherland 1976; see also Fitz 1981a, 1981b; Rothman 1980).

The enactment of a delinquency statute distinct from existing child-protection legislation ostensibly allowed the courts and Children's Aid societies to differentiate between neglected and dependent children and juveniles who committed criminal and status offences. However, this distinction was not obvious in practice. Both categories of children were commonly lumped together in the CAS shelters and the courts. As a result, the two major children's laws progressively facilitated state penetration of family life and the erosion of parental rights among non-middle-class populations by increasing the categories and numbers of children covered by the legislation; the number of adults, particularly parents, who could be charged with contributing to dependency, neglect, and delinquency; and the powers of the Children's Aid societies and the lower courts.[15]

The social law that was instrumental in delimiting the rights of husbands within the families of the working and dependent poor was the Married Women (Maintenance in Case of Desertion) Act (S.O., 1888, c. 23). In the late nineteenth century, charity organizations and municipal governments found it increasingly difficult to cope with demands from deserted women for financial assistance (Dymond 1923). At the same time, maintaining families deserted by the male breadwinner was of mounting concern to many welfare leaders who were beginning to draw a causal link between 'broken' homes and delinquency (Houston 1982; Morrison 1976; Strong-Boag 1976; Sutherland 1976).

Like the 1886 English legislation it emulated, the Ontario law incorporated a conception of desertion as 'the poor man's [sic] divorce' and, in effect, provided a cheaper alimony procedure for impoverished women. Previously, they had to use the higher courts to bring errant husbands to justice, a process that entailed court costs and lawyers' fees that few could afford. Those who could not obtain help from family and friends ended up as charity cases and/or in workhouses. What the 1888 statute did was provide a summary procedure that allowed a deserted woman to appear before a police magistrate or two justices of the peace who, upon a finding of desertion, would summons the delinquent husband, issue a maintenance order (regardless of whether the husband appeared at the hearing), and enforce the order with criminal sanctions, if necessary, including a jail sentence.

The unstated assumption underlying the desertion law was a paternalistic one. Because women were not equal to their husbands in law, the latter had an obligation to support them, and the province had an obligation to protect the 'best interests' of the dependent by enforcing the man's legal responsibility to his wife. Thus, the statute acknowledged for the first time that the state had a duty to assist 'deserving' women to maintain themselves, and, indirectly, any children, as a family in the community. It thus marked the beginning of a transition from institutional to community-based treatment of the marginal poor (Dymond 1923).[16]

At the same time, the limits on state benevolence were clear: only morally deserving women were entitled to state assistance. Every version of the deserted wives' statute contained the explicit proviso that no maintenance order would be issued by the court if it were proven that a wife had committed 'uncondoned adultery.' An order could also be

rescinded on the same grounds. In contrast, not until 1934 was 'uncondoned adultery' by the husband accepted as a reason for a finding of
desertion.

Following the Great War, another crisis of 'the family' generated demands from social workers, churches, and women's organizations, including the women's branch of the United Farmers of Ontario (Splane
1951: 9), for amendments to existing social legislation and the enactment
of new laws to strengthen and prevent the breakdown of the nuclear
family (Clark 1942; Dymond 1923; Guest 1980; Strong-Boag 1979: 25,
1982). However, the view of pre-war reformers that the state should
intervene in family life only with respect to individual children or deserted wives now seemed too narrow and ineffective, given 'the casual-
ties appearing before probation officers' (Strong-Boag 1982: 160). Social-
welfare leaders began to focus on the family as a unit of interdependent
members in which relations between adults as well as those between
adults and children were of equal importance and concern (Balharrie
1929; Bryce 1922; Canadian Welfare Council 1940; Clarke 1928; Friedman 1927; Held 1927; Hill 1920; King 1929; McPhedran 1919; Stewart-
Hay 1931; Vernon 1929). As had occurred earlier in the United States
(Chunn 1982), social agencies and churches in Ontario began to emphasize family casework and to establish special committees on the family.
Many agencies also created special family divisions, including the Canadian Council on Child Welfare, which, in 1929, became the Canadian Council on Child and Family Welfare.[17]

In the immediate postwar period, the apparently dramatic increase
in family desertion directed the attention of workers in social-service
agencies and administrators of municipal institutions and charity organizations to the desertion statute, which was only directly applicable to
wives. Reformers proposed that the law be revised to specifically include
children, 'owing to the number of children found to be wholly or par-
tially neglected by their natural protector' (Dymond 1923: 39). Subsequent amendments to the Deserted Wives' Maintenance Act (DWMA)
during the interwar years successively augmented the state's power of
intervention in family life, and simultaneously reduced the domestic
rights of husbands and fathers, by increasing the number of persons
covered by the law; the powers of those with jurisdiction under the statute; the numbers of people able to lay complaints; the grounds for a
finding of desertion; and the maximum weekly amount payable by husbands and fathers.

Reformers' efforts to expand the scope of the DWMA coincided with
and were supplemented by an ongoing, somewhat successful, movement

to obtain legislation for the reciprocal enforcement of maintenance orders among the various Canadian provinces and with the United States and Britain. As the ascendant leader in the social-welfare arena, the Canadian Council on Child Welfare under Charlotte Whitton was at the forefront of this struggle. The council drafted model statutes and worked hard to generate support for such laws among the commissioners on the uniformity of legislation, the provincial attorneys general and public welfare ministers, and the federal justice department.[18]

Between 1920 and 1922, the Drury government in Ontario also enacted a number of new social laws, including statutes pertaining to adoption, illegitimacy, and parents' maintenance, which reflected the growing postwar emphasis on the nuclear family unit (Dymond 1923; Kirkpatrick-Strong 1930; Spettigue 1957).[19] This legislation, particularly the Children of Unmarried Parents Act (CUPA), was the result of extensive provincial government consultation with social-work organizations. The latter had produced 'scientific' studies of the social and legal aspects of the illegitimacy problem that supported the conclusion that inadequate laws made it easy for the putative father to escape responsibility (Mohr 1920: 20; Neighbourhood Workers' Association 1920).

Like the pre-war desertion and child-protection statutes, the new social laws sanctioned the use of state power to help those who 'through no fault of their own suffer for the mistakes of others' (Dymond 1923: 76), either by forcing a man who did not live with his dependent children and/or parents to provide for them or by placing children in suitable adoptive families. Under the CUPA, for example, the provincial officer acted as a statutory protector and guardian for mother and child. He was required to take such action as might seem to him advisable in the interests of both and had the authority to intervene at any time (ibid: 68). In brief, he assumed the role of parent in the absence of the child's biological father and forced the latter to meet his moral and financial obligations.

It is important to emphasize, however, that most of the social legislation enacted prior to 1940 did not directly challenge the ideological basis of the minimal state. What was different about the new welfare statutes, relative to earlier ones governing women and children, was an explicit provision for the use of state power to enforce the privatization of the costs of social reproduction (Ursel 1986). For example, the Children's Protection Act, 1893, essentially sanctioned 'a marriage between public authority and a community-centred, privately administered child welfare agency' (Hareven 1969: 88), in short, state-backed voluntary social work. The province assumed the direction, supervision, and control through the creation of a central office and the appointment of a full-time official, the superintendent of neglected and dependent children, but 'the whole system was organized around the local government unit which retained primary financial and organizational responsibility' (Oliver 1977: 215).

Thus, while all the legislation that facilitated direct state intervention in domestic life and imposed middle-class definitions of childhood and family on non-middle-class recipients was justified in terms of humanitarian rhetoric, the Ontario government was probably moved primarily by monetary considerations. Both municipalities and the province were better off if individual husbands and fathers were compelled to support their families since there would be a corresponding decrease in the number of charges on municipal relief rolls and in poorhouses, which received government grants.

At the same time, reform leaders from the 1880s to the 1940s were not entirely consistent about adhering to the laissez-faire principle of individual and local responsibility for welfare. Many were strong advocates of the Mothers' Allowances Act (S.O., 1920, c. 89) – a postwar social statute that signalled a move away from the minimal state. Viewed as an antidote to the infant mortality and juvenile delinquency that so often destroyed mother-headed families, the legislation sanctioned state financial assistance to families lacking a male provider because of his physical or mental incapacitation, death, or (following a 1921 amendment) desertion (Guest 1980; Strong-Boag 1979). The mother thus became a state employee, with the province and local governments each assuming half the cost of her 'salary,' and was subject to supervision and disqualification if she failed to do a competent job. While such assistance was means-tested, the 1920 statute was ground-breaking because, for the first time, the Ontario government assumed direct financial responsibility for maintaining the dependent poor outside institutions.

Ultimately, then, the reform emphasis on community-based treatment of deviant families, which characterized the social legislation enacted from the 1880s to the 1940s in Ontario (and other provinces), fostered a reconceptualization of deviancy and dependency and thereby helped to undermine the ideology of individualism and the minimal state. Welfare reformers' concomitant advocacy of decriminalized, informal mechanisms for enforcing these statutes contributed to a parallel transformation of the traditional structures for the administration of family-welfare law in Ontario. The following chapters present an analysis of how that transformation came about by tracing the political and legal history of one reform – the family court.

CHAPTER THREE

Social Workers,
Lawyers, and
Socialized Courts

The movement in favour of so-called Courts of Domestic
Relations is simply a further evidence of the humanizing
and socializing tendency in modern thinking.

D.B. Harkness (1924: 2)

A first class [crown attorney] will do much more good in
checking the activities of an over zealous non professional Juvenile Court Judge than he will do harm by introducing Police Court methods more or less.

E. Bayly (1921)

Because old ideologies and practices do not simply disappear as new
ones emerge, reform is never a linear, unproblematic process. The debates in Canada/Ontario from the 1880s to the 1940s about how family-welfare law ought to be administered clearly reveal the operation of
conflicting and competing legal philosophies. On the one hand, the
ascendancy of socialized justice, which is a defining feature of welfare
states, was increasingly evident as non-legal personnel, discourses, and
procedures began to infiltrate the existing legal structures governing
marginal families. On the other, legal formalism, the prevailing legal
philosophy in the laissez-faire state, remained strong throughout this
period.

Moreover, although Ontario had a rudimentary system of socialized
justice by 1918, the socialization process during the interwar years was
further impeded by ideological splits among social-welfare leaders and
among government lawyers and bureaucrats. Lack of consensus about
who should administer family-welfare law and in what manner effective-

ly pre-empted the emergence of the unified support for socialized courts among social workers and lawyers that is a prerequisite for their widespread development. Thus, an organized, national movement for the creation of family courts failed to materialize in Canada before the 1940s. Indeed, Ontario governments implemented several policies during the 1920s that suggested that there would be no expansion of socialized justice in the province.

Towards the Socialized Administration of Family-Welfare Law in Ontario, 1888–1918

Although Canada's first family courts were not established until the interwar years, reforms implemented in Ontario's magisterial system before 1918 had already begun to undermine nineteenth-century legal structures and practices. As previous discussion revealed (see chapter 2), urban, middle-class reformers responded to a perceived crisis of 'the family' in the 1890s with demands for legislation aimed at enforcing bourgeois standards of domestic life among resistant, non-middle-class populations. At the same time, their other concern – that the courts administering the social laws be accessible to the poor – was met when the government assigned jurisdiction over family-welfare statutes to the police courts. The administration of the Deserted Wives' Maintenance Act (S.O., 1888, c. 23; S.O., 1897, c. 167), the Children's Protection Act (S.O., 1888, c. 40; S.O., 1893, c. 45), and other related statutes by the lower courts opened the way for the increasing incorporation of non-legal personnel, methods, and discourses by these tribunals. For example, Children's Aid Society agents were rarely professionally educated social workers or lawyers, yet they were accorded extensive powers to apprehend neglected children and their negligent guardians, to remove children from their parents, and to generally oversee the upbringing of young people.

Social-welfare reformers in the late nineteenth century were not content, however, to leave the administration of social legislation to the traditional police courts, in their open, adversarial form. They lobbied hard for private, separate hearings of cases pertaining to the family life of children among the working and dependent poor. This emphasis on inquisitorial procedures in the processing of such matters buttressed the drive to establish a distinct juvenile-justice system in Ontario, organized around the use of probation. Because children were the primary targets of reform efforts at this time, Canadian welfare leaders expressed little of the concern about extending socialized procedures such as probation to adults exhibited by their American counterparts prior to the First World War (Oliver & Whittingham 1987; Rothman 1980: c. 3).

The demands of social-welfare reformers in the late nineteenth century coincided with a crisis in the provincial magisterial system – court congestion – that had two major causes: the marked acceleration of industrialization and urbanization during the 1880s and the adoption of the first Criminal Code by the federal government in 1892. The former effected marked demographic shifts in Ontario that concentrated people in urban centres throughout the province (see chapter 2) and generated vastly increased case-loads for police magistrates in those areas. Thus, the administration of lower-court justice became increasingly chaotic and untenable, particularly in the larger cities such as Toronto.

The enactment of the Criminal Code exacerbated this situation because it accorded considerably more authority to police magistrates. Suddenly, a police magistrate, with the consent of the accused, exercised as much jurisdiction over criminal matters in his locale as a county- or district-court judge (Denison 1920: 3; Ontario 1921: 3–4). In addition, he had authority over all cases related to disorderly houses, all non-indictable offences, all breaches of municipal by-laws, and all cases where penalties were imposed by provincial legislation, including the family-welfare statutes enacted to that time (Ontario 1921: 4).

Police magistrates adopted two strategies aimed at improving lower-court efficiency that had important implications for the socialization of law. The first was a growing reliance on assembly-line justice. For much of the nineteenth century, the administration of criminal justice in Ontario was officially governed by the ideology of legal formalism based on individual rights and procedural guarantees (Banks 1983; Craven 1983). However, summary justice meted out in the police magistrates' courts increasingly became the reality, particularly after 1875, and by the end of the First World War, criminal justice in Ontario *was* summary justice. The old system of preliminary hearings before police magistrates and committal for trial at the sessions or assizes had been superseded in 90 per cent of the cases by summary trial before a police magistrate, who might well not have legal training. Of the 7,904 persons convicted and sentenced during 1919 in Ontario, for example, 7,033 were sentenced by justices of the peace and magistrates (Ontario 1921: 4). Clearly, legal formalism had been subverted in practice, if not in the ideological sense, when the police courts emerged as the backbone of the province's criminal-justice system.

Nowhere was this trend more pronounced than in the Toronto Police Court, which evolved as the principal criminal court of the province during the tenure of Colonel George Denison. While on the bench from 1877 to his retirement in 1921, Denison single-handedly disposed of more than 650,000 cases (Denison 1920: vi). Moreover, he handled 83 per cent of all indictable cases in Toronto during that time (ibid; see also Craven 1983; Homel 1981; Ontario 1921). Indeed, Denison was renowned for his reliance on assembly-line justice as a means of combating court congestion: 'His goal was to render justice and quickly. Usually a moment or two sufficed. It was not uncommon for [him] to deal with 250 cases in 180 minutes' (Homel 1981: 173; see also Craven 1983).

The second strategy employed by police magistrates trying to cope with vastly expanded case-loads was the creation of specialized court divisions, each of which handled a specific type of case. Here was a timely coincidence of interests between social-welfare reformers who advocated the separate, private hearing of cases involving women and children on humanitarian grounds and police magistrates who were desperately trying to maintain case flow. Again, the Toronto Police Court was at the forefront of this trend. In 1892, at the urging of child-welfare reformers and with no legislative authority, Colonel Denison established a so-called children's division within the city's police court, where he tried children who were charged with provincial offences and violations of municipal by-laws (Denison 1920: 24; see also Stewart 1971: 5–6). Given their primary focus on children prior to 1918, reformers did not launch a drive for separate, private hearings of women's cases until the turn of the century. None the less, in 1913, a women's court with jurisdiction over domestic-relations and morals cases was created as a division of the Toronto Police Court, following a three-year campaign by the Toronto Local Council of Women (Gordon 1980: 7, 1984; see also Chunn 1988a).

The most important step in the direction of socialized justice before 1918, however, was the mandate to establish a separate system of juvenile justice provided by the Juvenile Delinquents Act, 1908 (JDA). The federal statute, which accorded juvenile courts exclusive jurisdiction over all children under age sixteen who were charged with any crime, provincial offence, or violation of a municipal by-law, promoted the use of non-legal personnel and informal, inquisitorial procedures in cases of juvenile deviance and/or dependency. Two years later, the Ontario Juvenile Courts Act (S.O., 1910, c. 96, s. 1, s. 3) facilitated the further incorporation of non-legal personnel and methods by the lower courts of the province. The legislation stipulated that, in any area where the JDA had been proclaimed, police magistrates could also act as juvenile-court commissioners, and Children's Aid Society agents would act as probation officers for such a court.

Significantly, while most of the new juvenile courts were simply special divisions of existing police magistrates' courts, the Toronto and Ottawa children's courts were created as distinct entities, separate from and independent of the police courts in their respective cities. Moreover, the emphasis on socialized justice for children was reinforced with the extensive revision of the Juvenile Courts Act in 1916. The revamped statute was a product of complaints about and dissatisfaction with the operations of the existing juvenile courts, particularly the Toronto court. Following discussions with a number of people working in the children's tribunals and in various social agencies, A.N. Middleton, a solicitor in the attorney general's department, concluded that 'the chief trouble [was] in the lack of machinery for carrying out of the work.'[1] Consequently, the 1916 legislation explicitly assigned the superintendent of neglected and dependent children responsibility for administering the statute, 'subject to the directions of the Attorney General' (S.O., 1916, c. 54, s. 18). Assigning this task to a non-lawyer provided an obvious opportunity for the expansion of socialized justice within the lower courts of the province.

Despite certain parallels between the juvenile-court movements in Canada and the United States, however, there was no Canadian equivalent to the identifiable family-court movement, which had coalesced in the United States under the aegis of the National Probation Association before 1918 (Boushy 1950; Chunn 1982; Snell 1986a). Many of the individuals and organizations involved in the Canadian campaign for the establishment of juvenile courts and probation, including Children's Aid societies, women's groups, and charity associations, were extremely concerned with the issues of desertion and non-support, but all pre-war efforts to achieve the creation of domestic-relations courts proved to be abortive. For example, while federal politicians enacted a 1912 Criminal Code amendment, drafted by W.L. Scott, making it mandatory for the head of a family to provide 'necessaries' for his wife and any children under age sixteen or be held criminally responsible, they did not implement his suggestion about how the legislation ought to be enforced.

Scott had proposed that, wherever the Juvenile Delinquents Act was in force, the juvenile court should be accorded 'exclusive jurisdiction to deal with offences under this [Criminal Code] section'; it would thus serve 'as a Court of Domestic Relations.' He also suggested a rudimentary type of adult-probation system requiring delinquent family breadwinners to make regular court appearances to pay support monies, and police on the beat to oversee the particular family.² In 1914, a bid by the Montreal Charity Organization Society to persuade that city to establish a domestic-relations court failed as well (Harkness 1924: 7). Ultimately, with the onset of the First World War, reformers dropped the idea of pressing for the creation of such tribunals. As J.J. Kelso stated in a letter to Scott: '[with] the appalling European situation I fear nothing more can be done until matters have again settled down.'³

Overall, the socialization of lower-court justice in Ontario prior to 1918 was a slow and contradictory process. On the one hand, police magistrates were not particular or conscious advocates of an inquisitorial approach to justice administration. Colonel Denison not only created special arrangements for hearing the cases involving children and women squarely 'within the shell of traditional methods' (Homel 1981: 180), but also fought against the establishment of a Toronto children's court in 1911, which was distinct from the city's police court and administered by a non-lawyer (Leon 1978). In many ways, he was constrained by the ideology of legal formalism. Thus, the origins or causes of conduct were of no interest to him and 'the notion of discharging prisoners for "failure" to meet certain standards of fitness was hardly conceivable' (Homel 1981: 182). Denison's primary concern remained the overt criminal act and its immediate effects. Similarly, the early juvenile courts represented only a tentative step in the direction of socialized justice. A mere seven such tribunals had been established by 1918, and most were part-time enterprises.

On the other hand, significant changes in the administration of lower-court justice occurred before the war's end. For example, Denison's paternalistic style of decision making pointed towards the individualization characteristic of socialized justice. He felt no compunction to assume a neutral stance, and his preconceptions about certain types of defendants were strongly and publicly expressed. Similarly, although he was a trained lawyer, Denison declined to follow or be bound by legal precedent and decided upon guilt or innocence intuitively rather than on the evidence (Homel 1981: 174). Moreover, the speed with which he adjudicated cases and his self-professed goal of administering 'substantive justice' led him to simply ignore 'legal technicalities and rules' if he felt that 'close adherence to them would result in injustice' (Denison 1920: 9), or, presumably, if close adherence to them would contribute to court congestion.

Staffed mainly by workers from the voluntary social-work tradition exemplified by the Children's Aid societies, juvenile courts also pointed towards individualization and a de-emphasis on lawyers. For example, the first commissioner of the Toronto Juvenile Court, the Reverend J.E. Starr, had previously served as the first full-time secretary of the Toronto CAS (Jones & Rutman 1981: 71, 118). Moreover, despite a growing focus on professional education prior to 1918, good character and personality were still considered more pivotal qualifications for court personnel than formal training (Scott 1908: 898; Toronto Family Court 1912). Thus, while ideally a juvenile-court judge would have some legal training, 'he' [*sic*] absolutely had to be 'optimistic and philanthropic, a student of social problems and a lover of children' (Kelso 1908: 165). Personality was even more crucial than education for probation officers whose task was to restore children 'to good living' through example (ibid; see also Kelso 1907). It was also important that probation officers 'be chosen from the best class' and, as W.L. Scott argued, because 'a better class of women than of men can frequently be got for the money available,' perhaps the best arrangement would be 'to have the chief probation officer a man, and most, if not all, of his assistants, women' (1908: 896).

By the end of the Great War, then, Ontario had created the rudiments of a socialized justice system in some locales: private, separate hearings of cases involving children and the adults responsible for them and, to a more limited extent, cases involving women; an increasing reliance on inquisitorial rather than adversarial procedures; and a certain blurring of the civil–criminal distinction. The beliefs that police courts, as well as the higher courts, ought to exercise jurisdiction over child- and family-welfare legislation and that children and the adults responsible for them ought to be dealt with on an individualized basis by non-lawyer specialists had achieved some acceptance, at least in principle.

A Toronto newspaper story about the twenty-fifth anniversary of the Children's Protection Act, 1893, illustrates how the ideology of socialized justice, the assumption that 'doing good' should take precedence over legal rights in the administration of family-welfare law, was beginning to take hold. Noting that the future of a child was frequently fixed 'by a Juvenile Court at a session lasting only a few moments of time, or at a brief meeting of a Children's Aid Society,' the article went on to acknowledge that, given 'the almost unlimited power' of the CAS 'the machinery if improperly used, might easily become a tyranny.' Yet, the account concluded with a vote of confidence in the benign intentions of the decision makers. Everything depended on 'the character of the persons who dominate the organizations,' it said, and in Canada 'few injustices occurred.'[4]

Social-Welfare Leaders and Family Courts

Agreement in Principle

Thus, in the immediate aftermath of the First World War, social-welfare leaders confronted seemingly optimum conditions for expanding the new system through the extension of probation and socialized methods to adult offenders, especially those involved in domestic cases. A family-court movement spearheaded by Canadian social-work organizations was a distinct possibility, given that no one seemed to oppose the idea in theory. Indeed, as desertion statistics soared and maintenance of nuclear family units in the community emerged as a social-work focus, the issue of domestic-relations courts, set aside in 1914, once more became a concern to those working in the social-welfare arena.

The church-based Social Service councils, pre-war leaders in the welfare arena; the Councils of Women; and personnel in the existing juvenile courts were among the first to talk about the need to establish domestic-relations courts as a means of coping with the effects of desertion and non-support. The Reverend Peter Bryce, a Methodist minister and first chair of the Mothers' Pensions Board in Ontario, was typical of the individuals and organizations who viewed the creation of family courts as an integral part of the solution to these problems. In an address to the annual meeting of the Social Service Council of Ontario in 1921, he said: 'We know enough of the problem to state that a Domestic Relations Court should be established in all large cities; that money should be appropriated for the purpose of locating family deserters and bringing them back to their respective cities or towns for trial; and that the sentence should be hard labour of a productive character and the wages earned paid to the family' (1922: 82).

At the national level, the Social Service Council of Canada also emerged as a proponent of family courts in the postwar period. During her Toronto sojourn as assistant secretary of the SSCC from 1918 to 1922, Charlotte Whitton was a member of a council subcommittee on 'disintegrating forces in family life' (Rooke & Schnell 1987: 17–21). As a result, she became 'particularly interested in Courts of Domestic Relations' and had correspondence 'with several centres in the United States' about this subject.[5] Subsequently, the council's Committee on the Family prepared a special report on courts of domestic relations because the need for such tribunals was becoming 'more and more keenly felt' as time went on (Social Service Council of Canada [SSCC] 1923: 103). This early

SSCC interest in the question of domestic courts did not diminish over time. Nearly a decade later, for example, the Vancouver committee prepared a statement on such tribunals for the Dominion Council Meeting at the express request of the national organization (United Church of Canada 1931: 22).

In the aftermath of the First World War, the Councils of Women, which had played an important role in the creation of juvenile courts and were the driving force behind the establishment of the Toronto Women's Court, also began to emphasize the need for domestic-relations courts. Throughout the interwar years, desertion and divorce were perennial concerns of the maternal feminist councils (Strong-Boag 1976), and family courts were seemingly viewed as one possible mechanism for resolving these problems. At its annual meeting in 1922, for example, the National Council of Women adopted a resolution advocating the establishment of domestic-relations courts 'in every large city' (Parsons 1922: 4; see also Strong-Boag 1976). Seven years later, with no trace of irony, the outgoing president of the Ontario Provincial Council of Women, Mrs R.G. Smyth, urged the development of both domestic-relations and divorce courts in all cities.[6] Whether she was thinking of divorce courts for the rich and domestic-relations courts for the poor is unclear.

As was the case earlier in the United States, personnel in the existing juvenile courts and in the social agencies with the closest court ties also formed a strong core of support for the creation of domestic-relations courts during the early 1920s. Many of them had been active participants in the pre-war campaign to establish children's courts as part of the magisterial system and were now members of the Canadian Association of Child Protection Officers (CACPO). At the 1923 Canadian Conference on Child Welfare, jointly sponsored by the Canadian Council on Child Welfare and the CACPO, Edmonton police magistrate and juvenile-court judge Emily Murphy, spoke passionately about the need for family courts. She lamented the fact that the only domestic-relations court in Canada was an unofficial one operated by the Ottawa police magistrate; in her own capacity as a juvenile-court judge, 'domestic troubles' often came to her attention. To remedy the situation, Mrs Murphy proposed 'a vigorous campaign' for the implementation of more domestic-relations courts throughout Canada, arguing that 'the best way to have better children is to have better parents' and that with knowledge comes interest and with interest comes action.[7]

As a result of proselytizing by Murphy and other CACPO members, the conference's Resolutions Committee prepared a resolution, subsequently adopted by the delegates: 'That this conference urge the establishment of Courts of Domestic Relations in various centres throughout the Dominion for the purpose of adjusting family disputes, and of encouraging reconciliation between husband and wife before the situations between them shall have reached the acute stage usually represented by the act of family desertion.'[8]

The ascendant postwar leader in the welfare arena – the Canadian Council on Child Welfare – also seemed amenable to the idea of domestic-relations courts during the early 1920s. For example, Charlotte Whitton, whose interest in such tribunals developed through her earlier work for the Social Service Council of Canada, was a member of the committee that drafted the resolution adopted by the 1923 Child Welfare Conference cited above. However, the CCCW had devoted no particular attention to this issue until Whitton received a request earlier that year for sample legislation on the constitution of domestic-relations courts. The request came from the Reverend David B. Harkness, still a Winnipeg juvenile-court judge and not yet the formidable adversary of Whitton he was to become later in the decade (see chapter 2). As a member of the Winnipeg Board of Welfare Supervision, Harkness wished to impress upon other board members 'the necessity for some provision along this line' with a view to keeping welfare rolls low.[9]

The letter from Harkness was not the first request for information about family courts received by the council. Whitton acknowledged that she was 'continually getting questions' on the topic, but the CCCW had no model legislation or other information for distribution. To fill the gap, Whitton asked Harkness to prepare a pamphlet. 'There will,' she said, 'be no more needed or popular subject in our list.'[10]

Published in 1924, the pamphlet, written by Harkness in consultation with Whitton and W.L. Scott, now honorary counsel to the CCCW, delineated the council's initial, albeit unofficial, position on domestic-relations courts. Harkness (1924) supported the establishment of such tribunals, citing approvingly the writings of family-court advocates in the United States, but insisted that domestic-relations courts had to be accommodated within Canadian legal and constitutional structures, which were quite different from the American ones. Six years later, the CCCW, now the Canadian Council on Child and Family Welfare (CCCFW), issued a second publication on the topic of family courts, written by a sitting family-court judge (Hosking 1930). Apparently, the council was still receiving 'many inquiries on the subject,' and Whitton was anxious to produce a pamphlet that was 'as extensive and direct in its appeal' as possible.[11]

Following American precedent, then, Canadian social-welfare leaders in the post–First World War period supported the idea of establishing special courts to process family cases involving adults. But what was the rationale for creating such tribunals? The existing juvenile courts already exercised considerable control over adults under the 'contributing' clauses of the Juvenile Delinquents Act, and police magistrates were empowered to address the issues of desertion and non-support through the Deserted Wives' Maintenance Act as well as the relevant Criminal Code sections. Moreover, amendments to the JDA in the early 1920s and its extensive revision in 1929 awarded the courts unparalleled jurisdiction over children. Seemingly, the proponents of domestic-relations courts were increasingly convinced, as their American precursors had been, that the processing of *all* family matters ought to be decriminalized. In Canada, however, decriminalization was impossible unless the use of the ordinary police courts for domestic hearings was abandoned and a new type of socialized adaptation implemented.

To achieve that end, reformers needed to present a convincing case that special domestic-relations courts would be an improvement on the traditional police courts in terms of their ability to resolve family problems and help the working and dependent poor to cope with the strains of urban life. They did so by echoing the time-honoured reform arguments about humaneness, effectiveness, and economy that had been espoused so convincingly by the pre-war American family-court advocates (Chunn 1982; see also Boushy 1950). From a humanitarian point of view, asserted Canadian proponents of domestic-relations courts, it was cruel to expose women and children to a police-court environment with its embarrassing publicity and adversarial proceedings. Indeed, many women were being deprived of deserved assistance because they refused to appear in such an arena (County of York, Special Committee on Juvenile and Domestic Relations Courts 1931: 81; SSCC 1923: 106). Family problems were much too personal for public airing: 'All too long, we have flaunted the unfortunate victims of family troubles before the public, making them appear as ludicrous actors with the home as a state to be held up to ridicule by a curious and thrill-seeking public. We all believe in the privacy of family life. Let us respect it' (Hosking 1930: 2). Furthermore, it was unfeeling to force respectable women to appear in the same court as 'vagrants, petty criminals of all classes and prostitutes' (Harkness 1924: 5) and dangerous to expose the pure to possible moral contamination (Hosking 1930: 2).

In addition, legal advocacy in a police court merely exacerbated domestic conflict, making it impossible to mend ruptured relationships.

Family disputes required a 'social' approach, which police magistrates were rarely willing or able to apply because they devoted most of their time to criminal cases and procedures. The solution, then, was to create a special court in a separate building away from both police and other criminal courts. Socialized tribunals where magistrates were empowered to relax the usual rules of evidence and make judgments 'in accordance with the social needs of the family' (Stewart-Hay 1931: 87) and where trained workers could mediate out-of-court settlements would be far more conducive to domestic reconciliation than litigious hearings.[12] Some family-court advocates even felt that it 'would be advantageous from every point of view if all courts would engage the services of trained social workers' for this purpose (Williams 1928: 49–52).

Domestic-relations courts predicated on the use of socialized procedures and expert personnel would also, it was maintained, be more efficient, and therefore more effective, than the existing patchwork system for tackling judicial questions involving the family. Such tribunals would approach the problem family as a unit, thus allowing for a comprehensive treatment plan, rather than focusing on each individual family member (Hosking 1930: 3). In particular, the centralization of resources and personnel in one place would prevent overlap and allow for the speedier disposal of cases (SSCC 1923: 106). More important, domestic-relations courts would provide individualized treatment through the scientific and exhaustive investigation of all circumstances surrounding family cases before they came to court, through the utilization of nonlegal sciences (e.g., psychiatry, medicine, social work), and by the reliance on court workers who specialized in family matters. As one proponent of family courts put it: 'Too often [in the current context] unorganized, inexperienced and unskilled workers only "meddle and tinker" with the lives of other people' (Hosking 1930: 3).

Adoption of a 'scientific' approach might also, it was asserted, ultimately uncover a cure for delinquency and dependency. For example, one analysis of welfare department cases involving deserted families had revealed 'the preponderance of personality and temperament factors and the almost negligible number of cases in which economic conditions [were] found to be the basic factors' (Harkness 1924: 6). Probation officers would be in a position to discover, and perhaps check, problems since they would be in fairly close touch with homes where trouble had occurred and might erupt again (SSCC 1923: 106). And, finally, domestic-relations courts could coordinate work with social-work agencies in the community, government departments, and other organizations: 'Family problems are very intricate and difficult ... Nothing but the cooperative effort of all the resources of the community will ever solve them' (Hosking 1930: 3).

For those who remained unmoved by arguments about humaneness and effectiveness, reformers could offer a more pragmatic one. Domestic-relations courts, they maintained, would save money: 'The cost of maintaining the court is a bagatelle to the economic loss to a city and province in allowing the home to be broken up and the children to run upon the streets' (Harkness 1924: 7). The additional expense of trained probation officers or other social workers would be more than offset 'by the decrease in the work of the Juvenile Court with child offenders and the decrease in the work of the Police Court and welfare organizations dealing with families and children,' and as well lessen 'the necessity and expense of our hospitals and of our jails and reformatories' (ibid).

Moreover, deserted wives and children would be relieved of court costs and lawyers' fees since, in non-support cases, the complainant would not require counsel and there would be no costs or occasion for pleadings (SSCC 1923: 107). And, most significantly, both family and state would gain from the implementation of a method for collecting support payments that eliminated the self-defeating practice of incarcerating defaulters whose dependants subsequently became a drain on the community. Whereas under the old system the burden of collecting lay with the complainant, the probation department of a domestic-relations court would accept and distribute maintenance payments and assume responsibility for tracking down defaulters. At the same time, a socialized court could try to effect reconciliation, or at least an agreement to pay, outside of court. Official hearings and the use of jail as a disposition would thus be a last, as opposed to a first, resort (Williams 1928: 49–52).

Disagreement on Specifics

Since the social-welfare constituency across English-speaking Canada apparently accepted the desirability of domestic-relations courts in principle, why was there no concerted campaign for the establishment of such courts during the interwar years? Analysis of the American family-court movement suggests that the development of such tribunals requires solid organizational backing from both lawyers and social workers (Boushy 1950; Chunn 1982). In Canada, this support was forthcoming only from social-work and bar associations after the Second World War (Dingman 1948).[13] The failure of social-welfare leaders to mount a unified family-court campaign during the 1920s and 1930s was largely attributable to a lack of consensus about how such tribunals ought to be constituted. They had divergent answers to some key questions: Should family courts be part of the lower-court system? Should they be administered by legal professionals? Should they incorporate social services?

Following the Great War, the main impetus for a family-court campaign came from members of the volunteer, church-based social-work organizations and personnel in the existing children's courts, most of whom had been part of the pre-war juvenile-court movement. They soon emerged as the most zealous advocates for the implementation of what would, in essence, have constituted a system of comprehensive domestic-relations courts in each province. Reformers proposed that provincial governments establish juvenile courts on a province-wide basis and extend their jurisdiction to cover all matters pertaining to child and family welfare. This emphasis on obtaining province-wide proclamation of the Juvenile Delinquents Act and a corresponding system of children's courts with expanded powers was apparently endorsed by the 1923 meeting of the Canadian Child Welfare Conference. In addition to the resolution supporting the establishment of domestic-relations courts, cited earlier, the conference adopted a resolution sponsored by the Canadian Association of Child Protection Officers (CACPO) that the JDA be 'made applicable to all parts of all the Provinces.'[14]

At the provincial level, the Social Service Council of Ontario was still the dominant social-welfare organization in the early 1920s and it emerged as the leading force in the quest for province-wide proclamation of the JDA, particularly after David Harkness became the educational secretary in 1925. Almost immediately, Harkness assumed the role of consultant to the provincial government on social-welfare issues and began to press for the further development of socialized justice. Three years later, the entire Child Welfare Committee of the council met with Premier Ferguson to discuss the 'extension of Juvenile Courts and child guidance service generally' and the possibility of having the JDA proclaimed throughout Ontario.[15] The Social Service Council also received some support from the Ontario Association of Children's Aid Societies on this particular issue. At least six petitions from local CASs were presented to the attorney general, together with a resolution passed unanimously at the 1925 annual conference of the association, which exhorted the government to make the JDA applicable to all parts of the province.[16]

By the late 1920s, David Harkness had also displaced J.J. Kelso as the attorney general's representative with respect to the establishment of juvenile courts, travelling extensively to cities and towns throughout Ontario and attempting to gauge the extent of local interest in such tribunals. After each trip, he submitted his observations to the attorney general, together with recommendations about the possibilities for creating juvenile courts in various centres. In 1929, for example, Harkness sent W.H. Price a very comprehensive memorandum detailing his discussions with people in a number of locales and reported on a conference in Parry Sound about the possible establishment of a juvenile court there, a conference that had been suggested by the attorney general's department. In a concluding comment, Harkness revealed his close government ties: 'As these matters have been discussed on many occasions with you and you have suggested that you would like to be kept informed as to what is doing I have thought it well to send you this bare outline.'[17]

The Social Service Council of Ontario clearly envisaged domestic-relations courts as extensions of the existing juvenile courts. In the early 1920s, when the council was involved not only in determining the content of family-welfare statutes such as the Children of Unmarried Parents Act and the Adoption Act, but also in suggesting how they should be administered, a joint committee of the council and the Toronto Neighbourhood Workers' Association (NWA) argued vociferously that the provincial government should empower juvenile-court judges under the new laws as well as the county- and district-court judges. The joint committee emphasized that the children's courts already had 'machinery and officers ... charged with matters related to this type of work' and would be 'especially qualified by experience' to have jurisdiction in these matters: 'Everywhere there is a tendency of juvenile courts to become courts of domestic relations as in dealing with the child domestic matters are so largely concerned. The interest of the child is, we presume, the first interest and juvenile courts are concerned with the social history of the child and the social problems surrounding him.'[18]

This position was reiterated during the revision of provincial laws in 1927. Following an invitation from Attorney General Nickle, who said the government was 'anxious to cooperate with those interested in the social work of the province' (Held 1959: 10), an inter-organizational committee on the revision of child-welfare legislation was created to study and make recommendations about the proposed revision of welfare statutes. Dominated by the Social Service Council of Ontario under the Reverend Harkness, the committee proposed the continued and expanded administration of the Children's Protection Act and other family-welfare statutes in the lower courts. Emphasizing that the county-court judges were 'too busy to give much time to this work,' the committee went on to underline the advantages of using the magisterial system to regulate the family relations of the working and dependent poor: 'The old days when two JPs constituted the Court are gone ... A larger percentage of our Magistrates are now men trained in the law and accustomed to formation of judgment. Juvenile Court Judges are of comparatively recent appointment but such Judges are already handling these matters in a number of the larger centres. It is to be hoped that their number will be increased.'[19]

These efforts by the Social Service Council and its allies to expand the juvenile-court system in Ontario throughout the 1920s were supplemented by the demands for extended jurisdiction emanating from children's-court personnel and their social-work supporters, particularly in the two key centres of Toronto and Ottawa. Early in the decade, the courts in both cities were placed under the direction of new, non-lawyer 'judges' who were strongly oriented towards the ideology of socialized justice and an inquisitorial approach to family-welfare law. Hawley S. Mott, a former school principal, replaced presiding Commissioner Boyd in 1920 after a bitter struggle involving the attorney general, the Toronto City Council, and various social agencies and church groups.[20] Almost immediately, Mott launched initiatives aimed at enlarging the scope of his court.

Part of that effort was the ongoing attempt to acquire extended jurisdiction, both territorial and legislative. With respect to the former, he began to lobby for an expansion of his authority beyond the city limits into York County. When the attorney general contacted Mott in December 1920 about his needs for the coming year, for example, the judge quickly seized the opportunity to request the extension of his jurisdiction to cover 'that part of the City just outside the border so that children who come to our City and commit delinquencies might have their homes placed under the supervision of the Court.'[21]

Judge Mott was equally tenacious in his pursuit of enlarged authority both under the existing social laws of the province and through the enactment of new statutes. Most of his efforts centred on the intertwined issues of support and custody. In 1920, he turned his attention to the former and pressed the attorney general either to implement a new law, similar to the Deserted Wives' Maintenance Act (DWMA), which would make child maintenance compulsory, or to amend the DWMA to cover children. As it stood, Mott said, the act sent deserting husbands to jail or fined them but did not force them to support their children, and, while fathers were in jail, children were 'suffering,' However, if the suggested changes were implemented, he concluded, 'I think our hands could be greatly strengthened in the care of deserted children.'[22]

Two years later, Mott sought an amendment that would expand his powers under the Children of Unmarried Parents Act (CUPA). Again the issue was child support. As the statute was worded, most maintenance agreements with putative fathers were subject only to the approval of the superintendent of neglected and dependent children, who had the overall responsibility for supervising the administration of the CUPA. Judge Mott strongly disagreed with this assignment of authority and so informed the assistant provincial secretary, F.V. Johns. All agreements should be subject to judicial approval, he said, and, furthermore, there should be ways of arresting men who try to leave the municipality or country before trial after receiving notice of the proceedings.[23]

In 1923, Mott turned his attention to the custody question. To eliminate cases where he felt compelled to institutionalize children for their own protection, he sought an amendment to the Children's Protection Act that would give the court authority to remove children from their parents where one or both were judged by two competent doctors to be mentally unfit.[24] The judge also wanted the power to decide 'to a certain degree' the custody of children in support cases. Quite frequently, Mott argued, a father or mother appearing before him could not afford the cost of applying to the Ontario Supreme Court for a custody determination. This situation forced Mott either to make the father support his children in the custody of an unfit mother or to let the father go free, leaving the children 'without adequate supply.' If the juvenile court could assign a child to a Children's Aid Society, Mott continued, it ought to have the same power to make custody decisions. The more so, he concluded, because the juvenile court 'has the machinery to determine fit and proper homes through the Probation Department, and to supervise the home after the children are in it; no other Court has this machinery.'[25]

The strongest support for Mott's expansionist endeavours came from the Big Brother Movement (BBM) of Toronto, the social agency most closely linked to the juvenile court. From its inception in 1912, the BBM had provided volunteer probation officers for the court and, later, even shared the same premises (Brett 1953). Given the primary concern of the organization with the treatment and prevention of male delinquency, it is not surprising that agency personnel became more and more convinced during the 1920s that the extension of juvenile-court jurisdiction would be of immense help in their work. In 1928, Frank Sharpe, general secretary of the BBM, wrote to Attorney General Price with the suggestion that the juvenile court be granted the power to intervene in homes with delinquency-breeding conditions: 'If Juvenile Courts were given authority to deal with adults along such lines, I think we would be taking a big step forward in the correction of many things responsible for delinquency. In so many cases the boy's trouble is directly the result of some domestic difficulty which might be smoothed out at the same time as the boy appears in Court.'[26]

While Judge Mott and his allies sought to expand the powers of the Toronto juvenile court, the judges of the children's court in Ottawa pursued a similar strategy throughout the 1920s. At the beginning of the decade, Judge Archibald requested the 'direct approval' of Attorney General Raney to make changes in the work of the court, which would have increased its reliance on non-legal personnel and socialized methods. Although he thought a recent suggestion (see Coatsworth 1920) that juvenile courts be attached to the higher criminal courts was a good one that 'would probably give us a better status,' what he really wanted was 'a more intelligent and thorough system of studying the boys and girls deemed delinquent in our various communities.'[27] In a subsequent memorandum, Archibald specified more precisely what was required to implement a more scientific approach to delinquency. He needed full-time probation officers with 'certain qualifications and some expertice [sic] in their work through technical knowledge'; as it was, the only officer he had worked two-thirds of his time for one of the city departments.[28]

When Archibald died suddenly in 1922, his replacement, John F. McKinley, became the first full-time judge of the Ottawa Juvenile Court (McKnight 1963). Some women's groups opposed McKinley's appointment because he was a young, unmarried man, but it was generally well-supported by City Council, the media, and other individuals and organizations.[29] Although not a trained lawyer or social worker, McKinley was thoroughly imbued with the notion of 'doing good' and, like Judge Mott in Toronto, he moved quickly to consolidate and expand his powers, particularly through the acquisition of jurisdiction under social legislation other than the Juvenile Delinquents Act. In 1923, for example, he specifically requested authority under the Children of Unmarried Parents Act and the Adoption Act.[30]

Viewed retrospectively, then, the core of support for the development of family courts after the First World War resided with those individuals and groups who wanted the Ontario government to establish juvenile courts with extended jurisdiction on a province-wide basis and as an integral part of the magisterial system. Such tribunals were not conceptualized as essentially legal in orientation but, rather, as socialized courts predicated on the incorporation of extensive social services. Thus, court workers did not necessarily have to be professionally trained; they did, however, need to be humanitarians who would act in the 'best interests' of their clients. The main concern was that family courts have comprehensive jurisdiction over all domestic matters, which was characteristic of the 'best' courts in the United States (SSCC 1923; Hosking 1930, 1932; Stewart-Hay 1931). There was some disagreement about the matter of divorce jurisdiction, however. Although a few advocates (Stewart-Hay 1931: 87) envisaged the domestic-relations court as having authority over the issuing of marriage licences and over all divorce and alimony cases, the majority felt strongly that granting family courts authority in those areas was 'a grave mistake' since the raison d'être of such a court was to 'build up and strengthen the family' (Hosking 1932: 24; see also Harkness 1924: 3).

However, the 'owners' of the family-court issue in Ontario during the interwar years enjoyed meagre success in achieving their objective. A province-wide system of socialized courts with comprehensive jurisdiction did not materialize. This failure was due, in part, to lack of active support from the major women's organizations and, more important, from the Canadian Council on Child Welfare under Charlotte Whitton, which had quite different visions of how domestic-relations tribunals ought to be organized.

The absence of strong backing from the Councils of Women was surprising, given their enthusiastic participation in the pre-war juvenile-court movement, acting in tandem with the church-based social-work organizations. The councils did concur with the advocates of expanded juvenile-court jurisdiction that domestic-relations tribunals ought to be part of the lower-court system and hence not necessarily administered by legal professionals and/or other professionally trained personnel. However, they favoured the creation of juvenile and domestic-relations courts as separate, socialized divisions within the existing police magistrates' courts. The former would handle child-welfare issues, whereas the latter would deal with husband–wife problems and thus operate much like some of the early domestic-relations courts in the United States, such as the Buffalo (New York) court, which opened in 1910 (Boushy 1950).

This orientation of the leading women's organizations probably stemmed from their support for Dr Margaret Patterson, who became the first woman magistrate in eastern Canada when the United Farmers of Ontario assigned her to preside over the Toronto Women's Court in 1922 (Chunn 1988a; Gordon 1980, 1984). Patterson's appointment was a long-overdue victory for maternal feminists, especially the city's Local Council of Women, who had fought for it when the women's court was created in 1913 but were not able to achieve their objective until years later, after prolonged agitation. Once on the Bench, however, Dr Patterson quickly set up a domestic-relations division within the women's court and devoted a large proportion of her time to the adjudication and resolution of domestic cases, particularly in relation to desertion and non-support. Therefore, given the implications for Dr Patterson's court, the councils were hardly likely to advocate that family courts be developed by extending the jurisdiction of the existing juvenile courts (see chapter 4).

During the early 1920s, the Canadian Council on Child Welfare under Charlotte Whitton also showed little interest in actively promoting family courts and had no formal policy on this issue. However, like the women's organizations, albeit for different reasons, the CCCW unofficially favoured the separate development of juvenile and domestic-relations courts. This stance reflected the council's primary and ongoing emphasis on child–parent as opposed to husband–wife relationships.

Thus, echoing reservations expressed earlier by some American juvenile-court personnel, the first CCCW pamphlet on domestic-relations courts stated flatly that the creation of family courts with comprehensive jurisdiction, like the one in Cincinnati under Judge Hoffman, was not 'a course to be desired' (Harkness 1924: 5) because a tribunal that attempted to combine the functions of both juvenile and domestic-relations courts 'would tend to lower the standards of work for Juveniles by associating the treatment of adult delinquency more closely with that of the treatment of children.'[31] For maximum effectiveness, the juvenile court had to 'stand as a distinct entity rendering its service to the child and placing emphasis upon the duty of the State to see that its young are protected, nourished and trained in the principles of useful and self-respecting citizenship.'[32] Therefore, such courts required jurisdiction over all matters related to children – delinquency, neglect, non-support, dependency, adoption, and unmarried parenthood (Scott 1927: 39). However, the primary purpose of domestic-relations courts was to resolve family problems involving adults such as desertion, difficulties between man and wife, and non-support (Harkness 1924: 3).

While the CCCW concurred with the women's organizations that domestic-relations courts ought to be constituted separately from children's tribunals and not through the extension of juvenile-court jurisdiction, the council did not particularly endorse the idea of establishing such courts through provincial enactment as socialized divisions of the police magistrates' courts. In his 1924 pamphlet, Judge Harkness reviewed several possible ways through which domestic-relations courts might be implemented in Canada but gave strongest support to the notion of a new federal statute similar to the Juvenile Delinquents Act or, alternatively, an amendment of the JDA (1924: 11–16). A federal statute was viewed as the most desirable option because inconsistencies would 'result inevitably' from a series of provincial enactments (ibid: 14). Moreover, if domestic-relations courts were federal creations presided over by federal appointees, they might be more likely to function primarily as judicial tribunals administered by lawyer-judges. Although this point is not spelled out in the 1924 publication, both W.L. Scott and Charlotte Whitton were convinced that juvenile and family courts ought to be courts of justice as opposed to social agencies (see chapters 5 and 6).

This position, of course, reflected Whitton's particular conception of professional social work, which was increasingly ascendant during the 1920s (see chapter 2). It was not that she opposed the utilization of socialized methods by non-legal personnel but, rather, that she sought to build up a network of community social services under the direction of professional social workers to be used *by* the courts. Thus, the CCCW opposed the creation of juvenile and family courts when it appeared that such tribunals would become administrative social agencies under the direction of individuals who were not trained legal professionals. For example, while approving in principle the resolution of the 1923 Canadian Child Welfare Conference that the Juvenile Delinquents Act be generally proclaimed in every province, the council did not extend the same blanket approval to the corollary that called for the province-wide establishment of juvenile courts.[33] Under Whitton's leadership, then, the CCCW consistently argued that such courts ought not to be created without the guarantee of specific, professional (i.e., judicial) standards of operation and of adequate, professionally run ancillary social-work services in the community.

The council's apathy on the question of domestic-relations courts was one of the crucial stumbling-blocks to the formation of a unified family-court movement in Ontario prior to the 1940s. In effect, the ascendant leader in the social-welfare arena between the wars 'disowned' the issue. Thus, the support for such tribunals was concentrated primarily among individuals and groups associated with the pre–First World War tradition of social-welfare and social work that was declining throughout this period. The increasing ability of the CCCW to define which social-welfare issues were important and which were not, including the family court, became obvious during the 1929 conference that was organized to discuss proposed revisions to the Juvenile Delinquents Act. The closed meeting with the federal minister of justice had been jointly requested by the council and the Canadian Association of Child Protection Officers (Stewart 1971: 22). A weak counterpart of the National Probation Association in the United States (see chapter 2), the CACPO was keenly interested in the development of domestic-relations courts and viewed the 1929 conference as a chance to further that objective.

However, Charlotte Whitton and W.L. Scott, now a spokesman for the CCCW in his capacity as honorary counsel, determined the course of the deliberations. Prior to the meeting, various CACPO members submitted suggestions to Whitton and Scott about revising the JDA to provide for the creation of domestic-relations courts. Ethel MacLachlan, a Regina Juvenile Court judge and the secretary-treasurer of the CACPO, wanted the delinquency statute revamped in such a way that it would apply to adults in all domestic situations. Similarly, in a pre-conference letter to Whitton, the Toronto Juvenile Court judge, Hawley Mott, raised the question of whether the federal government could enlarge the jurisdiction of the juvenile court. Like MacLachlan, he seems to have been thinking about the possibility of revising the JDA so that family courts could be created through the extension of juvenile-court authority.[34]

Responding to these proposals, W.L. Scott argued that they were legally untenable. He told MacLachlan it was highly improbable that the federal Parliament would amend the JDA to make juvenile-court judges *ex officio* justices of the peace, which it would have to do if the judges were to be empowered to deal with adult domestic cases. Parliament would balk, he continued, because such a move would give juvenile-court judges, who were frequently non-lawyers, 'certain jurisdiction with regard to criminal offences committed by adults and unconnected with children.'[35] Scott and Whitton ultimately prevailed at the 1929 conference, thus demonstrating the growing influence of the CCCW and the increasing weakness of the CACPO. The council's reluctance to push the family-court issue proved to be the death-knell for any concerted family-court campaign by social workers during the interwar years.

Government Bureaucrats and Socialized Courts: J.J. Kelso versus the Lawyers

The lack of unity on the question of socialized courts was not unique to social-work leaders in the community. The issue of who should be accorded jurisdiction over family-welfare legislation also created divisions among Ontario government bureaucrats during the 1920s. On the one hand, the superintendent of neglected and dependent children, J.J. Kelso, was a keen advocate for creating a province-wide juvenile-court system and extending the powers of socialized tribunals. On the other hand, solicitors in the attorney general's department were staunch adherents of legal professionalism, as evidenced by their oft-stated view that judges should be lawyers, and thus they vociferously resisted the fundamental reordering of the legal structures governing the marginal that was already observable in 1918. Consequently, the 1920s were characterized by a certain government schizophrenia with respect to the administration of family-welfare law. While Kelso pressed his superiors for the establishment of more socialized courts in the magisterial system, the lawyers attempted to prevent the further erosion of legal formalism in the adjudication of domestic cases.

Kelso had been one of the most important Canadian social-welfare leaders before the Great War. Thus, it is not surprising that he concurred with those segments of the postwar social-welfare constituency that were pushing for a province-wide proclamation of the Juvenile Delinquents Act and the establishment of socialized courts in every area of Ontario. He seemed to envisage a centralized system of children's courts operating as essentially non-criminal administrative tribunals under his direction. This vision was clearly compatible with a growing reliance on non-legal personnel and methods characteristic of socialized justice.

At the same time, in contrast to those who increasingly emphasized the importance of staffing socialized tribunals with social-work and/or legal professionals, Kelso continued to put his faith in volunteers. For example, he believed that school principals, women, and 'others acting without salary' would make the best administrators of juvenile courts and strongly opposed the provincial government's 1920 decision to retitle the existing juvenile-court commissioners as judges: 'To give all these people the title of Judge would seem to me almost an absurdity.'[36]

Following the war, with the United Farmers of Ontario in power, Kelso seemed to be in a position to provide strong support inside the government for the creation of a province-wide juvenile-justice system within the lower courts. As superintendent of neglected and dependent children, he exercised considerable power within the provincial secretary's department, which was responsible for child welfare prior to the formation of the public welfare department in 1930, particularly through his role as administrator of the Children's Protection Act. In addition, under the Juvenile Courts Act, Kelso was responsible for the supervision of all juvenile courts in the province.

At the beginning of the decade, then, he began to lobby inside the government for the expansion and consolidation of socialized justice in Ontario. One of Kelso's first requests was for a clarification of his po-

sition as supervisor of juvenile courts. In 1920, he sent a letter to the
attorney general, W.E. Raney, explaining the unsatisfactory state of
affairs and hinting at a solution. The primary reason for the fact that
there were only seven such tribunals in the entire province, Kelso said,
was the lack of necessary support from past attorneys general: 'The
condition of the Juvenile Court movement in Ontario is somewhat chaotic at present and I do not feel that I am personally responsible for its
efficient administration. I have not had either the authority or the
money.'[37]

Three years later, Kelso suggested another reason for the 'difficulty
in securing Juvenile Courts' – the many police magistrates who were
'practically doing the work without waiting for this special law [JDA]'
(Ontario 1924: 8). Consequently, although Kelso's primary objective was
the establishment of a system of children's tribunals, distinct from the
police courts, he consistently pressed for the empowerment of both juvenile-court judges and police magistrates under all the provincial family-welfare statutes, including the postwar legislation. For example, when
the UFO government drafted the Children of Unmarried Parents Act in
1921, Kelso wanted a provision in the new law for the designation of
lower-court officials.

In stark contrast to Kelso, the law clerks and solicitors attached to the
attorney general's department during the early 1920s were imbued with
the ideologies of legal professionalism and legal formalism. Since the
attorney general's department was ultimately responsible for overseeing
all the courts of the province, it is important to examine in more detail
the attitudes of the lawyers who drafted many of the social statutes. In
general, they were entirely supportive of the welfare legislation, aimed
at assisting and protecting women and children, that had been enacted. As the chief law clerk, Allen Dymond, said: '[It is] a case of the
[Christian] state assisting in the maintenance and education of children
which are its greatest asset and ... [setting] an example of practical
Christianity' (1923: 110). However, like many lawyers at this time, Dymond and his government colleagues did not believe that family-welfare
legislation should be administered by juvenile-court judges or magistrates
who lacked legal training, and they deplored the growing number of
non-professionals receiving such appointments (Chunn 1988a).[38]

Not surprisingly, then, they were totally opposed to the prospect of
a province-wide system of children's courts administered by non-lawyers
who would employ socialized, inquisitorial procedures and exercise jurisdiction under the welfare laws over questions, such as guardianship,
that had traditionally been handled by the higher courts. Consequent-

ly, Dymond and his lawyer colleagues in the attorney general's department consistently resisted efforts by the Social Service Council of Ontario, some CASs, juvenile-court personnel such as Judge Mott of Toronto, and other individuals and groups to extend the jurisdiction of children's courts and increase their number through a general proclamation of the JDA. For example, in 1921, when the Joint Committee of the SSCO and the Toronto Neighbourhood Workers' Association proposed that juvenile-court judges be granted authority under the new Adoption and Children of Unmarried Parents acts, Dymond and the other law clerks protested that giving all juvenile court judges such jurisdiction would be 'objectionable' on several grounds.

For one thing, they said, virtually all such children's-court commissioners or 'judges' were laymen and lacked professional training. Therefore, the county judge, who had to be a qualified, experienced lawyer to receive a judicial appointment, was 'a much more suitable person' to handle such matters.[39] Second, adoption cases were not restricted to Children's Aid Society wards, the offspring of the poor. Thus, in view of the interests that might be affected, adoption ought to remain 'a judicial proceeding and of record.'[40] And, finally, they emphasized, 'Juvenile Courts are still in an experimental state and it has not yet been demonstrated that they are an absolute success.'[41]

Dymond reiterated the same position in response to the requests from Judge Mott during the early 1920s for an extension of his powers. When Mott first asked Attorney General Raney for legislation that would allow him to help children deserted by their fathers, the attorney general was apparently amenable and he instructed Dymond to draft 'whatever amendment you may think necessary.'[42] No legislation was forthcoming, however, and Mott raised the issue again in 1921 and 1922, emphasizing each time that an amendment to the Deserted Wives' Maintenance Act to include children 'would be of real service to us in this work.'[43] Faced with Mott's persistence, the law clerks strongly recommended that the attorney general reintroduce a 1921 bill on the maintenance of deserted women and children, which had been withdrawn, 'probably owing to the lateness of its introduction.'[44] However, the bill amending the DWMA in 1922 made no provision for juvenile-court judges to exercise jurisdiction.[45] Clearly, Dymond and his colleagues remained unconvinced by Judge Mott's argument that, through his probation staff, he was 'in closer touch with this work' than other judges since the home in question might already be under supervision.[46]

Similarly, Mott's request for extended power to determine custody matters in certain instances received a cool reception from the chief law clerk. Dymond informed the new Conservative attorney general, W.F. Nickle, that he was 'doubtful as to the expediency of making any change in the law in the direction desired by Judge Mott,' which would give lower-court judges powers traditionally restricted to high-court judges. In the first place, said Dymond, social workers had learned that, if children were removed from a mother following separation from her husband, she sank 'lower and lower into dissoluteness.' Moreover, in such cases, the father would probably be unable to care for the children, and they would end up in the charge of strangers anyway. Finally, not all juvenile-court judges had as much 'common sense' as Mott. Therefore, if the law were changed, Dymond advised the attorney general to keep the question of technical guardianship 'out of sight' and to make the juvenile-court judge's order 'entirely subject to the jurisdiction of the Supreme Court and Surrogate Court under the *Infants' Act*.'[47]

The ideological differences between J.J. Kelso and the lawyers in the attorney general's department were very evident during a dispute that erupted in 1924 over the issue of who was to administer the Children of Unmarried Parents Act in several northern Ontario locales. Should the county-court and high-court judges, who were legal professionals, exercise sole jurisdiction under the statute or should magistrates and juvenile-court judges, who were often non-lawyers, also be accorded general jurisdiction under the legislation? The dispute arose in August of that year when the county judge in Parry Sound refused to travel to the east side of his district to hear cases under the CUPA. He suggested shifting the burden either to one of the police magistrates in the area or to one of the county judges in an adjacent district.[48]

Predictably, the response of the solicitors in the attorney general's department was a legalistic one: unequivocal opposition to transferring the judicial authority, under statutes that dealt with important questions like paternity, to the lower courts. Departmental lawyer A.N. Middleton set out in an internal memorandum, what was to become the initial position of the attorney general: 'the District Judge should try all these cases and has plenty of time to do so.'[49] With this response, the attorney general's department began a protracted struggle with the recalcitrant county judge in Parry Sound to make him resume his responsibilities under the CUPA.

At the same time, Judge Powell's reluctance to adjudicate CUPA cases outside the town of Parry Sound provided J.J. Kelso with a long-awaited opportunity to expand the scope of socialized justice in Ontario. He stepped up his own internal campaign to secure the empowerment of juvenile-court judges and police magistrates under the CUPA and other provincial welfare laws. In September 1924, Kelso informed the provincial secretary, Lincoln Goldie, about the difficulties being experienced by Children's Aid Society agents in northern Ontario in arranging hearings of CUPA cases before the district judges. Using district judges involved time, expense, and delay, he explained, which meant that only 'the most urgent cases' were being heard, and after such long delays that the outcomes were not satisfactory. Stressing the 'urgent requests' he had received for the appointment of local police magistrates and juvenile-court judges under the Act, Kelso specifically recommended the speedy designation of three police magistrates and one juvenile-court judge.[50]

However, when the provincial secretary forwarded Kelso's letter to the attorney general for comment, A.N. Middleton reiterated his previous position that the district judges ought to process the cases under the CUPA. He added the further suggestion that, if judicial expenses were a concern in such proceedings, the provincial secretary's department might well assume them, as it would still be cheaper for the government than paying for the parties involved in paternity cases to travel to the judge.[51] Knowing that Kelso had a vested interest in the expansion of juvenile- and police-court powers, Middleton also contacted the district judges in two of the areas where Kelso wanted police magistrates designated under the CUPA. Both replied that they had no objection to handling all the cases under the statute in their respective jurisdictions, and one of them – Judge Hewson of the Manitoulin District – explicitly emphasized that he saw no reason to designate a 'non-professional' police magistrate. Responding to Judge Hewson, Middleton noted that 'the situation is about what I imagined it was.' Therefore, he intended to inform the provincial secretary's department 'that the difficulty in the matter [was] really the fault of their own Officer [J.J. Kelso].'[52]

Upholding Legal Formalism

Clearly, those social-welfare leaders in the early 1920s who pressed the Ontario government to create a province-wide system of socialized courts as part of the magisterial system received little or no support from the increasingly influential adherents of social work and legal professionalism exemplified by Charlotte Whitton and Allen Dymond. Although their motives varied, Whitton and Dymond were adamant that the administration of family-welfare law should be restricted to lawyer-judges presiding over judicial rather than administrative tribunals. To that end, government lawyers consistently urged their political masters to adopt policies that would stem, or even reverse, the obvious trend from the late nineteenth century onward to assign jurisdiction over family-welfare law to the lower, provincially constituted, courts, where non-legal personnel and procedures were more and more the norm. Beset by the advocates of two contradictory perspectives on socialized justice, successive attorneys general seemed to find the arguments about the need for professionally trained judges and judicial due process more compelling. They implemented a number of policies during the 1920s that reduced the role of non-lawyers and provincial courts in the administration of family-welfare legislation and pointed towards the restoration of legal formalism.

One important policy change was the curtailment of lower-court jurisdiction over new social statutes. When such laws were enacted prior to 1918, the police magistrates' and/or juvenile courts had been automatically empowered to administer them; that is, the presiding officials in those tribunals did not have to be individually designated. Thus, all Ontario magistrates exercised authority under the two major pieces of provincial welfare legislation adopted in the late nineteenth century – the Children's Protection and the Deserted Wives' Maintenance acts. Indeed, magistrates were actually accorded exclusive jurisdiction under the DWMA. Similarly, when juvenile courts were established after the turn of the century, the presiding officials in those tribunals were granted general authority to administer the CPA in addition to their jurisdiction under the JDA.

After the Great War, the same policy continued to apply if changes were made to existing legislation. Thus, during the early 1920s, when the DWMA was amended to include children, all police magistrates (S.O., 1922, c. 57, s. 2, ss. 1) and, a year later, all juvenile-court judges (S.O., 1923, c. 32, s. 2) were empowered to administer the new sections pertaining to child maintenance. However, family-welfare legislation enacted after the First World War no longer gave lower-court judges automatic authority. For example, although J.J. Kelso was charged with the overall administration of the Adoption and Children of Unmarried Parents acts passed in 1921, only designated juvenile-court judges could administer the former statute, and police magistrates could not be designated at all. Similarly, the CUPA specified that both juvenile-court judges and police magistrates had to be individually authorized before they could process cases under the new law.

Admittedly, the provision for the designation of particular individuals was a compromise position adopted by the attorney general, W.E. Raney. On the one hand, his law clerks and departmental solicitors fought to restrict jurisdiction over the two new pieces of legislation to the county, district, and supreme courts, and their draft statutes did just that. On the other hand, the joint committee of the Social Service Council of Ontario and the Toronto Neighbourhood Workers' Association, which was integrally involved in the preparation of the statutes at Raney's request, recommended that all juvenile-court judges be granted authority under the acts (1921). After considering the arguments from both lawyers and social workers, Raney did amend the exclusionary draft statutes prepared by his law clerks to allow the special designation of juvenile-court judges under both laws and police magistrates under the CUPA.[53] None the less, compared with their pre-war counterparts, attorneys general during the 1920s assumed a more restrictive, legalistic stance on the issue of who should administer family-welfare legislation.

The Ontario Statute Law Revision, completed in 1927, generated policies that continued this trend. Two years earlier, the Conservative government had appointed a commission headed by W.G. Middleton, a provincial Supreme Court judge, to examine all existing legislation and make recommendations for reform. That the commissioners were staunch adherents of both legal formalism and the federal-provincial division of powers under the British North America Act was evident in their proposed revisions of the existing family-welfare legislation, particularly the four major statutes – the Children's Protection Act, the Deserted Wives' and Children's Maintenance Act, the Children of Unmarried Parents Act, and the Adoption Act. Like the attorney general's chief law clerk, Allen Dymond (1923), the commissioners were 'entirely in sympathy with ... the underlying principle' of such statutes but they were concerned, from a 'rule of law' perspective, with two issues.[54]

The first was the obvious erosion of due process that resulted from the provisions and administration of the existing social legislation. The commission was alarmed about the fact that an accused could be processed as a criminal and subjected to penal sanctions under the welfare laws without being accorded the right to procedural guarantees. Thus, many men were at the mercy of discretionary decision making by state-authorized personnel, such as Children's Aid Society officers and/or lower-court judges, who often had no legal training. More important, particularly in relation to the DWCMA and the CUPA, the commissioners felt it was wrong to regard 'the liability of the father ... as criminal in its nature' and to enforce it 'through the criminal or quasi criminal machinery of the magistrates' courts, police courts, etc., instead of through the civil courts presided over by the County Judges who [were] ... much more capable and efficient men than justices of the peace, or even Police Magistrates.'[55]

Furthermore, since liability under the social laws was essentially a civil one, the commissioners felt it was hardly appropriate that a man 'who may sometimes be wrongfully accused' should be arrested and kept in pre-trial detention 'on the fiction that he is being held as a material witness' or that a convicted man should be imprisoned if he were unable to give security for 'payment of what may be in the aggregate an exceedingly large sum compared with the possible ability to pay.'[56] The commissioners noted disapprovingly that the latter power had been used in the past to force friends and relatives of a convicted man to 'pay money for which they [were] not in any sense liable' and that 'in some cases it [was] hard to refrain from regarding it as legalized blackmail.'[57]

The second general issue of concern to the commission was whether the provincial government had 'the power to pass legislation which is in its nature quasi criminal, and which looks like an expansion of the provisions of the Criminal Code which are deemed to be inadequate.'[58] The commissioners feared that the reorganization of magisterial justice in Ontario, which included the enactment of social laws carrying 'drastic penal sanction,' breached the so-called 1867 rule governing the federal-provincial division of powers. In their view, the province was overstepping its jurisdiction not only by passing quasi-criminal statutes, but also by granting what were essentially high-court powers to inferior, administrative tribunals, particularly in the areas of custody and alimony. Under the Children's Protection Act, for example, Children's Aid societies were frequently granted permanent wardship of boys and girls. Similarly, under the Deserted Wives' and Children's Maintenance Act, a police magistrate could order payment 'of what is in effect an alimentary allowance' of up to twenty dollars, a week, which might conceivably continue over a lifetime.[59]

In revising the family-welfare statutes, then, the Law Commission aimed to restore judicial due process to their administration. To do so entailed the redrafting of the substantive provisions in the existing social laws to protect the rights of those subject to them. At the same time, it required moving jurisdiction over such legislation out of the lower courts altogether, in the case of the statutes governing adoption, illegitimacy, and child protection, and implementing legal guarantees, in the case of the DWCMA, particularly a provision for a non-criminal appeal court.

Perhaps surprisingly, the commissioners met total resistance from social-welfare leaders. Despite the inevitable internal clashes between David Harkness and Charlotte Whitton, who represented the Social Service Council of Ontario and the Canadian Council on Child Welfare, respectively, the Inter-Organizational Committee on the Revision of Child Welfare Legislation presented a unanimous submission to the Law Revision Commission at a special meeting in February 1926.[60] Most of its recommendations concerned the welfare statutes governing illegitimacy, adoption, and child protection. And, while they did so for different reasons, every member of the Inter-Organizational Committee strongly rejected the Law Commission's stated intention not only to transfer power from the social-work agencies, particularly the Children's Aid societies, to the courts but also to strip the magistrates' and juvenile courts of their jurisdiction over the child-welfare statutes.

Ultimately, the revised welfare legislation represented a compromise between the views of the law commissioners and the social workers, but it was a compromise that veered in the direction of legal formalism. On the one hand, although the commission advocated the removal of all jurisdiction exercised by lower-court officials under the child-welfare laws, the amendments to the Children of Unmarried Parents and Adoption acts maintained the status quo, whereby designated police magistrates could administer the CUPA and designated juvenile-court judges could administer both statutes.

On the other hand, the Adoption Act was completely remodelled along the lines of a 1927 English statute that was much more legalistic in emphasis than the original Ontario legislation. Of even greater significance was the fact that magistrates and juvenile-court judges were no longer automatically accorded jurisdiction over the Children's Protection Act; they now had to be individually authorized. The revised CPA also restricted the power of Children's Aid societies vis-à-vis the courts with respect to decisions about the disposition of neglected children. And, finally, the revised Children of Unmarried Parents and Deserted Wives' and Children's Maintenance acts stipulated that enforcement of maintenance orders against husbands and fathers could now be done through the division courts as well as the criminal courts and that the latter could not impose a prison term of more than three months on convicted defaulters.

A third policy decision that pointed towards the restoration of legal formalism in the lower courts during the 1920s concerned the supervision of juvenile courts in Ontario. After the superintendent of neglected and dependent children was given responsibility for overseeing these tribunals in 1916, J.J. Kelso visited municipalities that expressed interest in a children's court and then presented recommendations to the attorney general about whether a juvenile court ought to be established in a particular locale. Thus, in practice, although the attorney general appointed the personnel for new courts, Kelso essentially determined which jurisdictions should have courts and, once established, whether the courts were being administered satisfactorily.

As Kelso's influence in the provincial government and among social-welfare leaders declined during the postwar period, however, Ontario attorneys general increasingly relied on the services of outside consultants, particularly David Harkness of the Social Service Council of Ontario, to provide information about the juvenile courts. Ultimately, the attorney general decided to end the superintendent's legislated supervisory control of children's courts. In 1928, Kelso was completely stripped of his power through an amendment to the Juvenile Courts Act (S.O., 1928, c. 48, s. 4) that placed these tribunals under the sole administration of the attorney general's department, and, specifically, of the inspector of legal offices, who was a lawyer.

The adherents of legal professionalism, particularly the government law clerks and solicitors, were undoubtedly delighted with this decision, as were many social workers. Indeed, the Inter-Organizational Committee on the Revision of Child Welfare Legislation, perhaps united by their contempt for Kelso, sent the attorney general an express statement of approval.[61] Obviously, the government decision to transfer supervisory power over socialized courts from the child-welfare superintendent to a lawyer was a death blow to Kelso's hopes for creating a province-wide system of non-criminal courts under the direction of lay volunteers who would employ inquisitorial procedures. It also illustrated the renewed emphasis on legal formalism in the administration of family-welfare law that emerged in Ontario during the 1920s.

From a retrospective vantage point, then, it seems clear that, while the development of socialized justice was well launched in Ontario's lower courts by 1918, there was a strong countervailing trend throughout the 1920s towards the restoration and reinforcement of the procedural guarantees associated with legal formalism in the administration of family-welfare law. The potential for organizing a broadly based family-court drive, similar to the pre-war juvenile-court movement, was thwarted by the conviction of people like Charlotte Whitton and Allen Dymond that family-welfare law ought to be administered in the higher courts by lawyer-judges. Thus, the 'owners' of the family-court issue during the 1920s were the very social-welfare leaders whose influence was declining throughout the interwar period. At the same time, J.J.

Kelso's dwindling prestige increased that of the lawyers in the attorney general's department. None the less, although the proponents of legal professionalism and judicial process in the resolution of domestic cases won a few battles, they ultimately lost the war. Notwithstanding their concerns, the Ontario government established several family courts in the province's lower court system prior to 1940.

CHAPTER FOUR

Conscience, Convenience, and Family Courts

The view of the provincial government is that the responsibility for the care of its citizens rests primarily with the municipality.

H. Ferguson (1925, cited in Oliver 1977: 225)

The Attorney General is deeply interested in the successful operation of [Family] Courts ... and the Government is to be commended for its sympathetic interest in the Social-welfare of the people.

J.J. Kelso (n.d. [c. 1929])

There will be a great increase in these Juvenile Courts and Domestic-relations Courts within the next ten years.

W.H. Price (1933)

Despite the implementation of policies that reinforced legal formalism in the administration of family-welfare law, Ontario governments also facilitated the continued expansion of socialized justice within the provincial magisterial system during the interwar years, including the establishment of Canada's first official family courts. Because family courts represent the advanced socialization of law, the government decision to sanction the creation of these tribunals in the absence of unified support from either lawyers or social workers raises a number of questions: What motivated a Conservative government to proclaim several domestic-relations courts between 1929 and 1931? Why were they located within the magisterial system as opposed to the higher courts? Why were the juvenile courts in Toronto and Ottawa singled out for family-court status?

What the evidence suggests is that the creation of family courts in Ontario prior to the 1940s followed a pattern of 'conscience and convenience' similar to that characterizing the rise of socialized justice in the United States (Rothman 1980); that is, the government took up the rhetoric and proposals of family-court advocates when it became advantageous to do so and filtered them through the lens of political pragmatism. Thus, the attorney general's decision to implement family courts was neither a direct response to nor a literal translation into policy of reformers' demands. On the contrary, a careful analysis of the political process reveals that Ontario's pioneer family courts were actually by-products of a more general government effort to rationalize the magisterial system of the province as economically as possible.

Why Family Courts?

The Official Explanation: Helping the Poor

At first glance, it seems rather incongruous that Ontario's first official family court was established by the 'mossback' Tory government of Howard Ferguson (Oliver 1977). However, in 1928, Attorney General William H. Price decided to extend the powers of the Toronto Juvenile Court and thereby convert it into a domestic-relations tribunal. Enabling legislation was passed in March of the following year, and the new court opened on 19 June 1929.[1] Subsequently, three more family courts were officially proclaimed during the interwar years: in Ottawa (1931), the County of York (1931), and Hamilton (1936).

Once the attorney general had resolved to create the Toronto court, he began making the rounds of social-work agencies to explain the government's apparent policy shift. Whenever he discussed the impetus for his decision to create a family court, Mr Price echoed the rhetoric of reform, bathing his actions in the most humanitarian of motives – concern for the poor. In January 1929, he addressed the annual meeting of the Toronto Big Brother Movement on the topic of wife desertion and its treatment, a meeting chaired by Richard S. Hosking, then chief probation officer of the Toronto Juvenile Court.[2] Later that year, the general secretary of the BBM, Frank Sharpe, played a pivotal role in the launching of the Toronto Family Court.[3] Sharpe, of course, was among the long-time advocates of such a move.[4]

At another meeting, in April 1929, the attorney general explained to his audience that the Conservatives had concentrated, first, on the economic situation in the province, so the public would have confidence and financiers would invest in northern Ontario and other developments, but that, now, the government was in a position to focus on the social-welfare sphere: 'It remains ... to see that the average citizen in our midst realizes his responsibility to the less fortunate in our midst.' If 10 per cent of people were poorly housed and lacked proper means of subsistence, he continued, the children in such families would eventually break the law.[5] Ironically, given his opposition to granting non-lawyers judicial powers (see chapter 3), Allen Dymond, the chief law clerk, represented Price at the annual conference of the Ontario Association of Children's Aid Societies the following month. Emphasizing that police courts were 'horrible ... for decent people' and that such 'condition of things should not exist,' Dymond explained the recently enacted Magistrates' Jurisdiction Act (S.O., 1929, c. 36), which allowed magistrates to deal privately with adults and children, 'not to try the case but to simply enquire into certain circumstances.'[6]

The government emphasis on its humanitarian concern for the poor was also clearly evident at the official openings of the Toronto and Ottawa family courts. On both occasions, the attorney general's remarks were suffused in the rhetoric of socialized justice. The creation of the Toronto court was an 'epochal event,' Price said, that would relieve congestion in the ordinary criminal courts, provide an entirely new atmosphere for handling domestic cases with an emphasis on rehabilitation and keeping the home intact, and save 'a very considerable sum of money,' since probation staff would be able to collect money for deserted wives and children and also keep 'in closer touch as to how the moneys [were] expended.'[7]

Two years later, Price announced that Judge McKinley was subsequently going to handle 'all cases falling within the classification of family matters' in seven counties, using the machinery he had 'developed so highly and satisfactorily in Ottawa.' This was an 'experiment,' said the attorney general: 'We are grouping a number of counties to see if the work of a juvenile court cannot be carried out over an area instead of only a city benefitting [sic].'[8]

Without denying the attorney general's humanitarian concern for poor families, an examination of how family courts were created during the interwar years in Ontario reveals that the government had absolutely no consistent, articulated policy for implementing these tribunals. What should the new courts be called?[9] Should they be separate from or divisions of the police courts? Should they exercise exclusive jurisdiction over family-welfare law or not? The government seemed to follow a different course of action with each new court.

On the question of the relationship between police courts and family courts, for example, the attorney general decided that, in Toronto, the two types of tribunal ought to be physically and operationally independent. Mr Price explicitly emphasized to Mayor McBride how 'very anxious' he was to establish the family court and that, 'for best success,' it should be in a different building from the police court.[10] However, this was merely an official stamp of approval for the status quo since the Toronto Juvenile Court was always autonomous of and located in quarters separate from the police magistrates' court. Moreover, when providing larger premises to accommodate the juvenile court, the probation officers, Big Sisters and Big Brothers, 'as well as the Domestic Relations Court,' appeared to entail too much expense, Price had no compunction about instructing the mayor that the new family court would have to be ensconced in the basement of a building then occupied by several city departments.[11] In Ottawa, the juvenile court was also separate from the magistrates' court, but it had been housed in the police department building since 1925 (McKnight 1963). This accommodation did not change with the opening of the family court in 1931.

However, the Hamilton and County of York family courts were both created as divisions of the existing police court in their respective locales, which, in Hamilton, was the police department building, until 1966 (Torrance 1967: 78). In York County, the attorney general seemed to leap from one strategy to another in creating the family court. Initially, he contemplated extending the authority of Toronto's juvenile-court judge to cover the county, as that judge had suggested, rather than setting up a second court. Failing that, Price attempted to obtain space for a domestic-relations court when the county renovated its police court and offices in 1929. Informed that there was no room for a domestic-relations tribunal at the new premises, the attorney general opted to follow the suggestion of his departmental solicitor, A.N. Middleton, that they proceed with 'present plans' and take up the matter of a family court again later, 'if necessary.'[12] Given his antipathy to extending the jurisdiction of non-lawyers (see chapter 3), Middleton was undoubtedly relieved that the county was unable to accommodate the government.

In Hamilton, the development of both the juvenile and domestic-relations courts was shaped by the attorney general's consistent refusal to entertain suggestions that a full-time juvenile-court judge be appointed. The Hamilton Children's Aid Society so recommended in a 1929 Report, which also advocated that the Magistrates' Jurisdiction Act, 1929, be used 'for the constitution of hearings on Domestic-relations problems in closest cooperation with the Juvenile Court' (1929: 42). Similarly, the Social Service Council of Ontario pressed for the creation of a juvenile court in Hamilton that would be dissociated from the police court and exercise jurisdiction in the County of Wentworth as well as the city.[13] Notwithstanding this advice and contrary to his earlier statements about the Toronto Family Court, Mr Price hinted to Magistrate Burbidge that he would like to see a domestic-relations court established as a division of the Hamilton Police Court.[14] Indeed, the attorney general issued this hint almost simultaneously with his proclamation of the Toronto Family Court.

Part of the explanation probably relates to the fact that Henry Burbidge had just received a magisterial appointment in 1929 as a Conservative government protégé, and Mr Price wanted to enhance rather than diminish his powers. For example, it is noteworthy that even officials inside the attorney general's department who proposed the establishment of a juvenile court in Hamilton that would be distinct from the police court met with the same rebuff experienced by the social-service organizations. The inspector of legal offices, now the supervisor of children's courts for the attorney general, was a keen advocate of appointing a new juvenile-court judge because he felt that police magistrates were not appropriate persons to handle juvenile matters in a city the size of Hamilton. However, the inspector was quickly informed that Magistrate Burbidge *was* the juvenile-court judge for Hamilton and that nobody had complained about his work before.[15] In the end, Burbidge simply operated an unofficial domestic-relations division within the city's police court, an arrangement that was later legitimated when a juvenile and family court was created in the County of Wentworth under his administration.[16]

If the attorney general was inconsistent in his approach to the constitution of family courts, he was equally eclectic about the allocation of exclusive jurisdiction to the judges of these tribunals. The judge and deputy judge of the Toronto Family Court were granted exclusive and joint authority under a number of provincial family-welfare statutes, the Juvenile Delinquents Act, and several Criminal Code sections related to family matters. However, Mr Price was loath to follow the same policy with the other family courts (Hosking 1930: 1, 1932; see also this volume, appendices B and C).[17] Judge McKinley of the Ottawa court, for example, was accorded jurisdiction over the same legislation as his Toronto counterparts but it was not absolute. Thus, the city's police magistrate also had authority under some of the statutes, such as the Deserted Wives' and Children's Maintenance Act, at least in theory.[18]

The decision not to grant McKinley exclusive jurisdiction over family-welfare legislation seems to have been a deliberate one, based on the belief that such a specification was unnecessary. When he sent Mr Price a copy of the order-in-council, Deputy Attorney general Israel A. Humphries indicated as much in an attached memorandum: 'This practically establishes the same Court as we have in Toronto ... [and] will clean the Ottawa situation up nicely.'[19]

Moreover, the inspector of legal offices, Joseph Sedgwick, failed when he attempted to intercede with the attorney general's department on McKinley's behalf. Sedgwick pointed out in a letter to Deputy Attorney general Humphries that Judge McKinley was already empowered to hear cases under the statutes listed in the order-in-council. What McKinley needed, therefore, was exclusive authority: 'The object of the *Magistrates' Jurisdiction Act 1929* was to take certain matters out of the regular Police Court, giving them to the Juvenile or Family Court Judge who would have absolute jurisdiction.' This procedure had been implemented in Toronto, and Sedgwick felt that all 'the regularly established Courts, namely those in Toronto, London and Ottawa, [were] intended to have exclusive jurisdiction over their particular types of offences.'[20]

The attorney general obviously did not agree. When Henry Burbidge was appointed as the Hamilton Police Court magistrate, he was not granted absolute authority over specified statutes either. Mr Price apparently concurred with the opinion of his solicitor, A.N. Middleton: 'It will not be necessary to designate Mr. Burbidge as having exclusive jurisdiction in Domestic Relations matters under the new *Act* passed last Session,' because he is the only police magistrate in Hamilton and can simply 'segregate the classes of cases to be heard before him.'[21]

Initially, the attorney general followed the same policy in York County when he acted on the recommendation of a special municipal committee that a domestic-relations tribunal be established. However, although the committee's report attributed the success of the Toronto Family Court to 'the wide powers placed in the hands of the Judge and his staff' and urged that Magistrate William Keith be appointed 'with exclusive authority to hear and dispose of juvenile and domestic cases' in York County (County of York, Special Committee on Juvenile and Domestic Relations Courts 1931: 82), Mr Price did not immediately comply with this request. It was only several months later when another magistrate was accorded joint jurisdiction with Keith in the Township of Georgina that the latter received 'exclusive jurisdiction in what is commonly known as the Domestic or Family Court.'[22]

The Unofficial Explanation: The Rationalization of Magisterial Justice

The inconsistency that characterized the establishment of family courts during the interwar years in Ontario reflected the reality that the provincial government was not concerned with these tribunals, per se. Although some government decision makers may well have been imbued with the ideology of socialized justice, it is difficult to avoid the conclusion that the first domestic-relations courts were merely by-products of a more general overhaul of the province's magisterial system between 1920 and 1940. On the one hand, this reform generated policies that pushed towards the restoration and reinforcement of legal formalism in the lower courts (see chapter 3). On the other, however, the rationalization of magisterial justice in the 1920s created the conditions for the further socialization of the traditional legal structures. In short, during the interwar period, the attorney general's department adopted a position on the administration of family-welfare law in Ontario that mirrored the growing conflict between the prevailing ideology of legal formalism and the ascendant ideology of socialized justice, but was not a direct response to the proponents of either perspective.

Although there had been previous complaints about the province's police courts, criticism and demands for reform of the lower courts became more clamorous and insistent in the immediate aftermath of the First World War. While solicitors inside the government fought to uphold legal professionalism (see chapter 3), lawyers, media representatives, and members of the general public pressed for a reorganization of the magistrates' courts aimed at restoring equality, openness, and other characteristics of legal formalism to their operation. There were two foci of concern. The first involved the endemic conflicts of interest for personnel in the existing system: most police magistrates and crown attorneys received compensation through the fee system and were paid only if a conviction were obtained; the majority were 'engaged in active business callings or in professional life,' including the practice of law; police magistrates sat on boards of police commissioners and 'took a leading part in making the appointments and promotions'; many police courts were located in the same buildings as police departments; and magistrates frequently conducted both the pre-trial proceedings and the court hearings for the same cases (Ontario 1921: 5, 7, 12).

The second concern of reformers centred on the problems of the criminal accused who were processed through the magisterial system. They feared that the assembly-line justice characteristic of the larger urban centres was quite possibly injustice. Moreover, the absence of state provision for defence counsel or court interpreters left many accused open to shameless exploitation. Consequently, the majority of defendants in the cities were 'foreign with little or no knowledge of our laws or our language' and few financial resources; they were thus easy prey for 'unscrupulous lawyers' and court interpreters (Ontario 1921: 13).

The Toronto Police Court emerged as the main target of reform efforts. Voices of discontent, which throughout Magistrate Denison's career had lamented his celebrated pace, disregard of evidence, and abbreviated working hours, grew louder after 1918 (Homel 1981: 173). The Drury government came under intense pressure from diverse sources to make changes and to replace Denison's traditional methods with efficient, legal standards (ibid: 181). In 1920, Toronto City Council asked the government 'to conduct a thorough investigation into the administration of the Toronto Police Court and institute such reforms as may be necessary' to give the city 'impartial, modern and progressive Police Court administration.'[23] Lawyers (Popple 1921, 1927) also pressed for police-court reform. And, when Denison finally retired in 1921, a *Toronto Daily Star* editorial demanded a complete overhaul of the city's police court, arguing that, while Denison's good character had guaranteed criminal defendants protection from gross injustices, his successors might not possess the same sterling qualities (Homel 1981).

Typically, the Ontario government responded to reform demands by appointing a royal commission to study the administration of justice in the province and by dispatching Emerson Coatsworth, the senior county-court judge in York County, to conduct an inquiry into the administration of justice in New York and Chicago. The reports from these investigations are significant because they both acknowledged that, by 1920, most justice administered in Ontario *was* summary justice; that it was not feasible to try turning back the clock, if only because it was so much cheaper to try criminal cases in the police courts (Ontario 1921: 9); and that the government should therefore rationalize and professionalize the magisterial system.

However, the reports contained divergent proposals for achieving the last-named objective. The royal commission was strongly oriented towards the British tradition of justice. Thus, the recommendations in its interim report on police magistrates, which drew on submissions from many magistrates, judges, crown attorneys, and practising lawyers, were essentially directed at rationalizing the operations of the lower courts within the constraints of legal formalism (Ontario 1921: 13–14). At the same time, the commissioners were evidently influenced by the English practice of appointing lay magistrates because, while they agreed that inferior-court judges required some legal training, they did not feel that such officials needed to be professionally educated lawyers (ibid: 10, 13).

Emerson Coatsworth's report (1920) was heavily coloured by the American practices he had observed. Indeed, the judge had unilaterally expanded his mandate to include a visit to Detroit because of a recent reorganization of that city's criminal courts. In addition, he examined the Toronto criminal courts to see how they compared with their U.S. counterparts (ibid: 3). Coatsworth's recommendations that police magistrates be experienced members of the bar and that the Toronto Juvenile Court be affiliated with the higher criminal courts (ibid: 4) clearly reflect the influence of the American model of professional legal education. However, he made a number of other suggestions that pointed in the direction of socialized justice for adult offenders. For example, he proposed the routine creation of special divisions within the police courts to handle specific types of cases, including traffic, alcohol, and domestic-relations cases.

More significantly, Judge Coatsworth expressed enthusiastic support for both adult-probation and mental-health facilities to determine whether offenders were 'of unsound or unbalanced mind' (1920: 13). He specifically recommended the creation of an adult-probation bureau in the County of York, to be modelled on those in the American cities he had visited (ibid: 21). Coatsworth lamented the absence of any probation officers in the criminal courts of the county and 'the disadvantage of dealing with convicted prisoners without the reports and recommendations' of such officials, who should, he emphasized, be 'selected purely on merit and after a very strict examination and with proper conditions as to age limit' (ibid: 21, 4).

So far as the mental assessment of offenders was concerned, Coatsworth proposed that Ontario develop a psychopathic laboratory along the lines of the one he had observed in the Chicago Municipal Court. He had been most impressed with the statement of the Chicago chief justice that mental evaluations could be completed 'within an hour,' using the Binet tests. Thus, mentally disordered offenders could quickly be identified and placed 'in a home where they may be useful and not dangerous' (1920: 13).

After the First World War, it became more and more apparent that the Ontario government had to do something about the police courts. The magisterial system was increasingly paralysed by court congestion, generated primarily by the concerted efforts to enforce stringently the Ontario Temperance Act (Oliver 1975: 80–1; Schull 1978: 250–4). For example, despite Magistrate Denison's best efforts, the Toronto Police Court was in a state of crisis by 1919 because the four magistrates now attached to the court shared the same court-room. Consequently, none of the four could spend more than about one-quarter of his time each day processing cases (Coatsworth 1920: 20).[24]

Thus, in the early 1920s, there was a coincidence of interests between court-reform advocates who were concerned about the erosion of legal formalism in the lower courts and Attorney General Raney who wanted to make the police-court enforcement of the prohibition laws more efficient. However, the reform process initiated by Raney was an ongoing one during the interwar years. By 1940, through the piecemeal enactment of legislation, successive provincial administrations had effectively reorganized Ontario's magisterial system.[25] Although the English legal tradition continued to exert a strong influence on policy during this period, officials in the attorney general's department also implemented reforms that facilitated, albeit unwittingly, the development of socialized justice in the lower courts.

One important step in that direction was the replacement of magistrates who died or retired with individuals, not necessarily trained in the law, who were receptive to modern methods of judicial administration and also sympathetic to the ideology of socialized justice. Such appointments were made in several key urban centres through the 1920s. On 4 January 1922, Attorney General Raney assigned Dr Margaret Patterson, a former medical missionary, to preside over the Toronto Women's Court. Long an active member of the Local and National Councils of Women, Dr Patterson had been among those who successfully lobbied for creation of the women's court in 1913 (see chapter 3). Immediately following her magisterial appointment, she swore allegiance to the gospel of individualized justice: 'If possible ... I want a quiet room where I can take every case, and, before forming any opinion, inquire into all the circumstances that led to the misdemeanour, the home life, the state of the physical health, for without thorough investigation, we can never do our best for our patients.'[26] Not surprisingly, Magistrate Patterson became a vocal proselytizer for socialized police court work (Chunn 1988a; Gordon 1980, 1984).

Three years later, a Conservative attorney general ensconced Emerson Coatsworth as senior police magistrate in the Toronto Police Court after his retirement as the senior county judge in York County.[27] He was thus Patterson's superior and, like her, receptive to socialized justice. Throughout his magisterial career, Coatsworth continually sought to educate lawyers as well as the general public about the need for extensive socialization of the law. As he told one audience: 'The legal profession ought to be at work on the reduction of the cancer of crime ... but I believe that the medical profession will beat us out.'[28]

At the end of the decade, new magistrates were also installed in the County of York and the City of Hamilton. William Keith replaced the deceased Magistrate Brunton in January 1929. A non-lawyer, Keith was a strong advocate of rationalized justice administration and had been 'long identified with the work of the County.'[29] Six months later, in June 1929, Henry A. Burbidge, KC, replaced the presiding Hamilton magistrate, George Jelfs, after the latter was forced to resign by the attorney general's department. In a lengthy statement, Attorney General Price cited the unsatisfactory disposition of cases as one reason for his decision to request Jelf's resignation.[30]

Another reform implemented by the Ontario government that had important implications for the development of socialized justice in the province was the establishment of a rudimentary adult-probation system in 1922. This turn of events was rather unexpected. Extending the application of individualized-justice principles to adult criminals was never a serious objective for pre-war reformers, and the situation did not change markedly after 1918. Adult probation remained very much a non-issue among Ontarians (McFarlane, Sumpter, & Coughlan 1966; Oliver & Whittingham 1987), despite Judge Coatsworth's positive recommendation in 1920 and the support of the Canadian Bar Association and the Social Service Council of Canada for the creation of adult-probation systems in all the provinces (SSCC 1923: 1).

However, at least two developments may have motivated the United Farmers' government to confront the question of adult probation. One was the 1921 Criminal Code amendment (S.C., 1921, c. 25, s. 1081, ss. 5) that provided for suspended sentence and probation, with supervision under any officer designated by the court, for first offenders. Although a previous Code revision sanctioned the use of the suspended sentence in adult cases, the 1921 amendment now made probation supervision mandatory and persons convicted of offences punishable by more than two years' imprisonment eligible for probation consideration, with the concurrence of the crown attorney (McFarlane, Sumpter, & Coughlan 1966: 25). A second pressure on the Drury administration was the dramatic increase in criminal offenders created by intensified enforcement of the temperance laws. Thus, the Probation Act (S.O., 1922, c. 103) can be interpreted as a forced response by the Ontario government both to the federal law reform and to the growing number of convicted criminals who could not all be sent to jail or prison.

Seemingly pushed to develop an adult-probation system, the provincial government was determined to do so with the least expenditure. An initial bill, drafted in collaboration with County Court Judge Emerson Coatsworth, and Toronto Juvenile Court Judge Hawley S. Mott, attempted to foist financial responsibility for adult probation onto the municipalities (McFarlane, Sumpter, & Coughlan 1966: 25). However, strong opposition to the proposed bill produced an amendment stipulating that adult-probation officers would be paid out of the province's Consolidated Revenue Fund (ibid: 28–9).

Given this turn of events, the UFO government elected to implement adult probation on a selective rather than a province-wide basis, beginning in York County, including Toronto. The new system was officially launched on 22 November 1922, with Judge Mott as the chief probation officer and one probation officer being attached to each of the four courts handling criminal cases.[31] Mott's appointment placed him in an obvious conflict-of-interest position and contradicted the growing government emphasis on rationalizing the magisterial system. At the same time, the attorney general's decision made economic sense because the municipality assumed most of the costs of the Toronto Juvenile Court, including the salaries of probation officers who supervised juvenile offenders. Thus, the province could create an instant adult-probation department with minimal expenditure, simply by appointing and remunerating a small number of so-called adult-probation officers.

Through another twist of fate, the first facility for the mental assessment of adult offenders in Ontario was also located in the Toronto Juvenile Court. Six months after the appointment of Judge Mott, in January 1920, a clinic opened under the directorship of the court psychiatrist, Dr George Anderson (Toronto Family Court 1920: 2). Since funding was provided by the Rockefeller Foundation, the clinic was created at no cost to either the city or the province. Later, after adult probation was implemented in York County, the clinic, which had dealt almost exclusively with children to that point, also began to assess and treat adult offenders. Judge Mott explicitly emphasized the close links between the two: 'The present plan of operation is secured by extending the Juvenile Court probation system, adding sufficient new officers and endeavouring to co-ordinate the two Departments, *using where possible the same officers* [my emphasis]. This means that records will be co-ordinated, and also that the Adult Courts will have the service, when required, of the psychiatrist of the Juvenile Court, and a home report of the person charged' (Toronto Family Court 1922).

Clearly, then, politicians were guided by pragmatic motives, quite apart from any desire to expand or retard the development of socialized justice, in their reform of Ontario's magisterial system during the interwar period. They were not responding directly to demands from either the family-court proponents or the legal professionals, yet they unintentionally facilitated the selective incorporation of non-legal personnel and methods by the adult criminal courts of the province. Thus, while the ideology of legal formalism remained strong throughout these years, adult offenders were increasingly governed by practices that reflected the ascendancy of socialized justice.

The early family courts were created within the same context of tension between old and new legal philosophies and exemplify the same shift towards the latter. Indeed, the establishment of such courts was premised on the reform idea that adults involved in domestic disputes could be best 'rehabilitated' using inquisitorial methods (see chapter 3). Therefore, although many people concerned about social legislation and its administration opposed the move to treat adult family members without procedural due process, the early family courts, especially those in Toronto and Ottawa, subjected increasing numbers of children *and* adults to socialized personnel, discourses, and methods and exercised extended jurisdiction over the various family-welfare statutes and relevant Criminal Code sections (see chapter 7).

Locating Ontario's first family courts within the magisterial system was also significant. The new tribunals were either special divisions of the existing police courts, as was the case in York County and Hamilton, or spin-offs from them, as in Toronto and Ottawa. Thus, Canada had no equivalents of some American family courts, such as the one in Cincinnati under Judge Hoffman, which were part of the higher-court system. At least two major factors account for this developmental pattern in Ontario: the perennial reluctance of the province to assume financial responsibility for social welfare and the growing unwillingness of police, prosecutors, and county-court judges to process domestic cases.

Family Courts as Magistrates' Courts

Government Tight-Fistedness and Socialized Justice

It seems clear that the overriding consideration for politicians with respect to the development or non-development of socialized justice in Ontario during the interwar years was the fiscal one. Thus, while members of the UFO government might have been more personally and philosophically amenable to socialized justice, and welfare programs in general, than the Ferguson Conservatives, they were no more willing to pay money for them (Oliver 1977: 216). The provincial government's continued reliance on private and municipal funding of welfare translated into a consistent refusal to accept financial responsibility for juvenile and family courts (Fiser 1966; Ontario 1968: 564; Ontario Law Reform Commission [OLRC] 1974: 7; Pukacz & Noble 1965: 28).

Consequently, the attorney general would entertain no requests for the establishment of socialized tribunals unless they were accompanied by a written agreement from the local council in question to meet specified expenses.[32] Such expenses could not exceed fixed amounts, stipulated in the Juvenile Courts Act, which were calculated on a sliding scale related to population. The written statements from the municipalities agreeing to shoulder the cost of children's courts protected the province from financial liability. Moreover, although the government was usually careful to defer to local suggestions about appointments, what emerged as the result of the attorney general's policy was an arrangement whereby the province selected juvenile-court personnel and fixed their salaries, while local councils paid the bills.

Throughout the 1920s and 1930s, then, despite pressure from J.J. Kelso within the government and sections of the social-welfare constituency on the outside (see chapter 3), attorneys general consistently refused to have the Juvenile Delinquents Act proclaimed throughout Ontario and to implement a province-wide system of juvenile courts because of the financial (and political) implications; the government would either have to provide funding itself or force municipalities to finance courts they had not asked for. In 1920, for example, Kelso attempted to impress upon Attorney General Raney the deleterious consequences of the government's past failure to fund children's courts. That policy, he said, had had 'the effect of killing the [juvenile-court] movement as the Councils were afraid to commit themselves to unknown charges.'[33]

During the Great Depression, existing financial arrangements were adhered to even more rigidly (Ontario Inspector of Legal Offices [OILO] 1932: 6; Price 1934: 17). The only new juvenile and family court established was in York County (Dingman 1948: 34).[34] When responding to local requests for financial assistance, the Ontario government routinely stressed that juvenile courts were in an experimental state and it was 'inadvisable to push their development too rapidly'; it was 'better to gain ground slowly and make sure the work [was] successful.' Moreover, since different conditions prevailed in different parts of the province, the government had to be 'careful not to dictate to people in other communities.'[35]

The onus placed on the municipalities to assume the costs of juvenile and family courts explains the complete heterogeneity that characterized the establishment of such tribunals. Without central organization and funding of these courts by the province, the presence or absence of socialized courts in different locales and the form they took 'depended on the individual community's resources, financing and encouragement' (OLRC 1974: 7). For that reason, the attorney general followed no consistent policy about how juvenile and family tribunals were to be constituted, except for the ongoing insistence that financial responsibility lay with the municipalities. Basically, anything the local governments were willing to pay for was acceptable to the province. For example, in 1929, the Oshawa council agreed to finance a juvenile court for the city but balked at extending coverage to the county. J.J. Kelso wanted to hold out for the more comprehensive option, but he was hastily advised by the attorney general's solicitor, A.N. Middleton, to immediately proclaim a children's court in the city and try later to extend the jurisdiction: 'I always like to strike when the iron is hot.'[36]

The fiscal responsibility of the municipalities for juvenile and family courts not only promoted ad hoc development but also pushed local councils towards the utilization of existing facilities and personnel in the lower courts. As late as 1945, the Guelph Board of Education defeated a resolution approving the creation of a separate juvenile court in the city on the grounds of probable cost (Dingman 1948: 92). The board felt the general citizenry was not convinced of the necessity for an entirely new court when the magistrates' court was already available: 'It was felt in some quarters that minor and much less expensive additions to existing facilities were the obvious solution: the existing Magistrate could be Judge; the Police Court Clerk could act as juvenile court clerk; and the Children's Aid Society could look after the probation duties' (ibid: 92–3).

The same mentality was at work when the early family courts were established. In Hamilton, for example, the city council continually refused to entertain the idea of creating a juvenile court outside the existing police court. This was another reason why the attorney general encouraged Magistrate Burbidge to develop a domestic-relations division in the police court; the alternative was to have no socialized courts in the city at all. Thus, 'the Family Court was simply superimposed on the Juvenile Court structure' within the magistrates' court (Burbidge 1950: 4).

Similar eclecticism had a determining influence on the creation of the family court in York County. From the early 1920s, Judge Mott had been pressing for an extension of his jurisdiction to cover at least part of the county, but the provincial government ignored his requests until a Toronto Grand Jury report in 1928 recommended the extension of juvenile court authority to include adjacent rural areas.[37] When Attorney General Price solicited Mott's comments on the report, the judge seized the opportunity to reiterate the urgent need for a method of dealing with county children, through either the extension of his jurisdiction or the establishment of a separate juvenile court in the county.[38] During a subsequent interview with A.N. Middleton, Mott convinced him of 'a real necessity' for a children's court in the county and, more important, of the advisibility of extending the jurisdiction of the Toronto Juvenile Court since it would be cheaper than developing an entirely new court.[39]

The County of York, however, had its own ideas about the matter. Both Judge Mott and the attorney general were thwarted by local politics when the county council opted to create a juvenile and domestic-relations court within the existing police court. As a result, two family courts operated side by side, one organized separately from the magistrates' court and one an integral part of the municipal police court. At the same time, the York County court utilized the clinical facilities of the Toronto Family Court. This overlap is just one more indication that the attorney general was willing to accept any type of arrangement so long as the province did not have to pay. And, in fact, the two family courts remained separate until their amalgamation following the creation of the Municipality of Metropolitan Toronto in 1954 (Stewart 1971: 34, 69).

The provincial government's refusal to assume financial responsibility for the development of a socialized-justice system in Ontario was also the determining influence on the establishment of adult probation. Compelled to assume fiscal responsibility for the payment of adult-probation officers after an abortive attempt to fob off the responsibility to

the local level, the attorney general adopted the policy of selective implementation, described previously, thereby minimizing the cost to the
province. Developing adult probation under the direction of a juvenile-
court judge meant that the probation officers, who supervised juveniles
and were paid by the city, could now be used in cases involving adults
as well. By simply adapting the existing facilities of the Toronto children's tribunal to accommodate adult probationers, the province needed
only to hire and pay a few additional probation officers.

Although the Drury administration did the minimum in launching
adult probation, a precedent had been set. However, their Conservative
successors resisted all attempts to expand the new system outside York
County. For example, when Judge Mott asked if his report on adult
probation for 1925–6 would be printed and distributed, Attorney General Price concurred with the sentiments of A.N. Middleton, who was
predictably and emphatically opposed to publication. Middleton pointed
out that it would simply become 'useful propaganda for the purpose of
extending the application of the [Probation] Act to other portions of the
Province.' Since the municipality provided only office space and the
government had to pay the salaries and other expenses of the adult-
probation officers, he continued, 'I would think that there is no necessity in any view for the printing of this report.'[40]

Yet the Conservatives did expand the adult-probation system in 1929,
and this expansion resulted in the creation of the Toronto Family Court.
A new Probation Act (S.O., 1929, c. 88), empowering magistrates to grant
probation to adult offenders without first having to register a conviction
against them, was enacted. This statute, together with various other
legislative enactments and the appointment of the Ross Commission
(Ontario 1930), was part of the Ontario government's pre-election response to growing demands for an overhaul of the province's 'vaunted'
social-welfare system (Oliver 1977: 308–9). Attorney General Price had
actually been thinking about both juvenile courts and adult probation
for some time before he began the process of extending the jurisdiction
of the Toronto Juvenile Court. He envisaged a policy that would lead
to the creation of children's courts 'in each County, or large City, and
this combined with the probation work would be a very valuable thing.'[41]
After all, if children under sixteen could be placed on probation, why
not older people? A person who commits a crime, Price asserted, is
usually 'child-like or they would not do it'; there is some 'weakness which
may be overcome.'[42]

Price elaborated on these views in a statement to the province's crown attorneys which appeared in the newspapers on 1 July 1929, shortly after the opening of the Toronto Family Court. He said he was 'particularly anxious that Juvenile Courts be established wherever possible throughout the Province' and, further, that where the 'volume of work warrants it, there should be established a Domestic-relations Court, probably in conjunction with the Juvenile Court, where all cases related to family matters can be disposed of.'[43] Turning to the topic of probation, Price predicted that eventually every county and large municipality would have at least one adult-probation officer. Anything that built up 'good citizenship,' he said, would also 'be a money-saver for the municipality' by keeping family breadwinners out of jail. A 'few thousand dollars spent on Probation,' he concluded, would 'greatly cut down on the expense of the present system and at the same time be a great factor in the improvement of social conditions.'[44]

A few months later, in November 1929, Deputy Attorney General Humphries reiterated the government's desire to expand adult probation. Responding to a query from a juvenile-court judge in British Columbia, he explained that the attorney general's department had decided to extend the probation system to include adults and to remove certain cases from the general police court. They had begun in Toronto but the policy was going to be 'implemented throughout the province.'[45] Two years later, Humphries was even more explicit about the government's motives. In a letter describing the establishment of the Ottawa Family Court, he emphasized that the extended jurisdiction accorded Judge McKinley in 1931 was 'not in connection with the Juvenile Court but as an Adult Probation Officer ... Certain Counties were grouped as a tryout so that Probation Officers might be of use to the different Magistrates in dealing with Adult Cases.'[46]

It seems clear, then, that the driving impetus for creating the first family courts in Ontario was the desire of the provincial government to expand the adult-probation system with the least amount of expenditure. The attorney general was excited at the prospect of enlarging both the juvenile-court and adult-probation systems simultaneously, primarily at the expense of local governments. He even briefly contemplated the feasibility of using his power as attorney general to create juvenile courts that would be financed by the particular county or city even when there had been no local demand for them. If he could possibly implement such a policy, the juvenile-court and adult-probation systems would become province-wide. Although apprised by his departmental solicitors of the traditional policy whereby the attorney general acted only upon formal requests from local governments for the establishment of juvenile courts and only after there was agreement by the latter 'to bear the expenses of the Court,'[47] Price apparently still entertained the idea of imposing such courts on every community in Ontario whether a request had been received or not.[48]

This notion was not translated into policy, however, probably because the attorney general came to realize that forcing local governments to implement and pay for juvenile courts as a way of expanding the adult-probation system would have extremely negative political consequences and/or generate immediate requests for provincial funding. For example, when A.N. Middleton conducted a survey of the municipalities with juvenile courts to discover how those courts were organized, he received virtually identical responses from all of them, namely, that their courts were badly underfunded and they would appreciate some financial assistance from the province.[49] Given the replies from centres that had already established children's courts, it seemed highly unlikely that areas without an existing juvenile court would willingly develop one without some money from the attorney general's department. In the end, the provincial government simply let well enough alone and continued the piecemeal, ad hoc implementation of socialized justice within the lower courts.

Sloughing Off the Poor

Family courts were not created only because it was most convenient for the provincial government to develop an adult-probation service by extending the jurisdiction of selected juvenile courts. The establishment of domestic-relations courts within the magisterial system was also facilitated by the growing reluctance of legal personnel to process domestic cases, especially those related to the Deserted Wives' and Children's Maintenance Act. Police, prosecutors, and county judges were not at all happy about having to cope with family-welfare law. For example, the Toronto Police Department, which had expended considerable resources on domestic cases over the years, grew increasingly restive about assuming this responsibility in the postwar period. By 1902, the Staff Department had been adjudicating family matters 'without the aid of the Courts' for some time (Toronto Police Dept [TPD] 1902: 38). A decade later, it was collecting support money for wives 'who were in a destitute condition' (TPD 1912: 30).

During the 1920s, however, the annual reports of the police department began to lament the time spent by police officers on the collection of support money, which could 'scarcely be classed as police work' (TPD 1925: 7). At the same time, the police felt compelled to continue the work 'in the interests of society' (ibid) since the women and children involved would otherwise be 'a charge on the City or Municipality' (TPD 1926: 9). Seemingly, the police were prepared to transfer their collection responsibilities to any other agency willing to accept them, including the probation department of a juvenile court, which used non-legal personnel and methods.

Similarly, many crown attorneys resented having to act as counsel in welfare cases. The issue was money. Although in the early 1920s a few reform-oriented lawyers urged the Drury government to compel prosecutors to assist deserted wives and children as a duty, many practising crown attorneys desired payment for services rendered.[50] In typical fashion, the government attempted to satisfy everyone. The Toronto and York Crown Attorneys Act (S.O., 1921, c. 40) did make it compulsory for the county prosecutors to represent complainants in cases arising under the Deserted Wives' Maintenance Act and the Children of Unmarried Parents Act without additional compensation.

Outside Toronto, however, crown attorneys were to be paid 'a reasonable remuneration' to act in CUPA cases (Ontario 1924: 16). So far as the DWMA was concerned, the attorney general's department adopted the position that the crown attorney was required to attend and prosecute only in cases where the complainant was anyone other than the deserted wife, child, or person with the care and custody of a deserted child. If he acted as counsel when such attendance was not part of his duty, 'it would be private practice and he would be entitled to charge a fee to the party for his services and such collected are not fees of his office as crown attorney' (Ontario 1926: 109).

Despite the official government policy, however, crown attorneys frequently failed to receive payment for legal services rendered because the complainants were unable to pay them. Protests from prosecutors were met with a reiteration of the attorney general's position on the issue but little changed. Gordon D. Conant, Oshawa crown attorney and future attorney general, complained to the government in 1934 and again two years later about having to do considerable work under 'your [welfare] Acts without remuneration.'[51] The inspector of legal offices acknowledged the dilemma posed by the fact that neither the counties nor the province had funds available to pay prosecutors: 'It seems to me that the [DWCMA] could not properly be enforced the way it is at present, unless the Government wants to spend some money.'[52] The government did not. As a result, there was a tendency for crown attorneys to favour informal settlement of social cases, which thus eliminated the need for counsel. And it was the juvenile and domestic-relations courts that relied heavily on out-of-court settlements, mediated by probation officers and other non-legal personnel.

During the 1920s, some county and district judges, and even a few police magistrates, also began to balk at performing duties related to family-welfare law. The attorney general first confronted this problem in 1924 when the county-court judge in Parry Sound steadfastly refused to handle any cases under the Children of Unmarried Parents Act involving travel on his part (see chapter 3). Since county- and district-court judges were federal appointees, the provincial government was virtually powerless to force them to do anything. Thus, although the attorney general's solicitors felt strongly that the Parry Sound judge ought to process all CUPA cases, A.N. Middleton finally conceded that 'it might be a great convenience to the parties' if two of the local police magistrates were appointed under the statute, especially the one who also acted as a juvenile-court judge. 'Matters of this kind,' he said, 'would seem to be essentially matters which should be dealt with by a Judge of the Juvenile Court.'[53]

As with crown attorneys, the reluctance of federal judicial appointees to process domestic cases was money-related. The Ontario government discovered this fact with a vengeance when it attempted to restrict jurisdiction over the child-welfare statutes to the county and district courts following the 1927 Law Revision, a move that would also have saved the province money because Ottawa paid the salaries of the judges in those courts (see chapter 3). However, county-court judges reacted swiftly and negatively to the imposition of more responsibility for the administration of welfare law than they already had. In a strong letter to the attorney general, requesting that the police-magistrate and juvenile-court judge in his county be designated under the Children's Protection Act, Judge Hopkins of Cayuga, Ontario, stated the case bluntly: 'It is really Police Court work and a County Judge should not be required to do this work without any compensation and I decidedly object to doing this work.'[54] Judge Hopkins was not the only disgruntled member of the judiciary. As A.N. Middleton discovered, there was general dissatisfaction among county judges and a few police magistrates who, since there was 'no fee' accorded them, were not 'anxious to do the work' entailed by social legislation.[55] At the same time, the attorney general received many requests from magistrates to be redesignated under the Children's Protection Act.[56]

Protests to the attorney general from county judges and the requests from police magistrates to have their authority under the CPA restored were matched by the flood of letters to the provincial secretary's department from local Children's Aid Society agents who found their work under the act completely untenable without access to the police and juvenile courts. A communication from the Hamilton CAS was typical. It asked for the redesignation under the CPA of the police-magistrate and juvenile-court judge 'who has been acting in these capacities in such cases for a long period of time' so that the CAS could deal promptly with cases which otherwise would have to go to county court.[57]

Continuing pressure from social workers, J.J. Kelso, and justice-system personnel forced the government to reconsider its decision to shift the adjudication of most domestic and child-welfare law to the higher courts. In a move with momentous implications for the future development of family courts in Ontario, the deputy provincial secretary, F.V. Johns, met with the inspector of legal offices, I.A. Humphries, to select forty-nine or fifty police magistrates with jurisdiction over large districts for reappointment under the Children's Protection Act.[58] Within a few weeks, the attorney general had prepared the requisite order-in-council and, by 1930, eighty-three magistrates had been redesignated under the CPA and two empowered under the CUPA.[59]

It seems evident, then, that political pragmatism – money and votes – was the impetus for the creation of Ontario's early family courts. Reform demands were filtered through and reshaped by the provincial government's own priorities. Thus, the attorney general was not responding directly to the reform demands of any individual or group but the policy of creating family courts on a selective basis within the magisterial system allowed him to achieve his objective of extending adult probation at minimal cost while simultaneously appearing to meet the demands of as many different constituencies as possible. Consequently, no individual or group with opinions and proposals on socialized tribunals received everything demanded of the government, yet none was left entirely unhappy.

On the one hand, the fact that police magistrates and juvenile-court judges could be empowered to process cases under provincial welfare legislation meant that most of the work under those statutes could be relegated to the lower courts. This situation was pleasing and convenient for many county- and district-court judges and other legal personnel because they were able to hand over responsibility to those who seemed more than willing to accept it, namely, the probation departments of the socialized courts. On the other hand, the government was able to mollify both the supporters of a province-wide system of juvenile and family courts and those who were leery of creating such a comprehensive system. The establishment of family courts in Toronto and Ottawa placated the juvenile-court personnel and their allies, who had been among the most vociferous advocates of expanding the boundaries of socialized justice. At the same time, the government's piecemeal approach appeased lawyers such as Allen Dymond and social workers such as Charlotte Whitton, who supported social legislation and socialized courts but opposed the wholesale expansion of the existing juvenile-court system.

The Toronto and Ottawa Family Courts

The family courts established in Ontario during the interwar years were truly a product of the marriage between 'conscience and convenience,' albeit not in any instrumentalist sense (Rothman 1980). But why did the attorney general choose to create the province's first domestic-relations courts by extending the jurisdiction of the Toronto and Ottawa juvenile courts? In Toronto, for example, the attorney general had to dismantle a thriving domestic-relations division within the city's police court to turn into reality what had been talked about 'for the past ten or fifteen years.'[60] An analysis of developments leading to the selection of Toronto and Ottawa as family-court sites reveals the familiar interplay of idealism and pragmatism at work. Seemingly, the most important factors governing the political decision makers were: the consolidation of jurisdiction, personnel, and facilities by the juvenile courts of those cities during the 1920s; the political connectedness of the Ottawa Juvenile Court judge; and the desire of the attorney general to remove the presiding magistrate in the Toronto Women's Court.

By the time family courts were officially proclaimed in Toronto and Ottawa, Judges Mott and McKinley had both managed to expand their powers far beyond the administration of the Juvenile Delinquents Act. Mott's tenacious badgering of the attorney general and the provincial secretary for jurisdiction over the various pieces of family-welfare legislation enacted in the postwar period had frequently generated resistance but, none the less, he increased his authority at a fairly steady pace throughout the 1920s. Initially, he was the only juvenile-court judge in the province to be designated under the Children of Unmarried Parents Act and the Adoption Act after they were enacted in 1921. Then, after 'nearly a year's experience' in dealing with the CUPA, Mott asked for an amendment that would have made *all* agreements under the statute subject to court approval (see chapter 3).[61]

While this suggestion was not incorporated into the statute, the number of judge-approved agreements under the CUPA did increase over the years. More important, Mott seemed to appropriate jurisdiction under the law where none existed. Like that of the regular police magistrates, his jurisdiction as a judge was limited to the area in which he worked, yet Mott apparently acted as if it were province-wide. Thus, even J.J. Kelso was taken aback to learn that Mott believed he could exercise 'general jurisdiction' under the CUPA and 'have men brought before him from other parts of the Province notwithstanding the fact that they do not reside here.'[62]

Although it took him an additional year to do so, Mott also acquired jurisdiction under the Deserted Wives' Maintenance Act after it was amended to include children abandoned by their providers. Initially, when the statute was changed in 1922, only police magistrates were accorded authority over the sections pertaining to child desertion but, the following year, juvenile-court judges were empowered as well (S.O., 1922, c. 57, s. 3, ss. 1; S.O., 1923, c. 32, s. 3, ss. L). Then, after the 1927 Law Revision fiasco, Mott was one of the juvenile-court judges who was redesignated under the legislation pertaining to adoption, child protection, and illegitimacy.[63] Thus, despite frequent rebuffs from the attorney general's law clerks and solicitors, Mott, through a combination of sheer persistence and luck, found himself at the head of a small empire in the late 1920s. By 1928, he had acquired authority under all the major pieces of family-welfare law except the sections of the Deserted Wives' and Children's Maintenance Act pertaining to wife abandonment and several sections of the Criminal Code governing non-support and spousal assault.

Following his appointment in 1922, Ottawa Juvenile Court Judge John McKinley pursued a comparable expansionist strategy. The next year, he was granted jurisdiction over the Adoption and Children of Unmarried Parents acts. In recommending McKinley's designation, F.V. Johns told the provincial secretary, Lincoln Goldie, he felt it 'quite proper that the judicial duties of these [District, County, Magistrates' and Juvenile] Courts should be linked up,' and the Ottawa judge's appointment was desirable because he was 'eminently qualified for the work.'[64]

Like Mott in Toronto, McKinley also 'appropriated' jurisdiction. On 1 February 1928, for example, he reached an agreement with the Ottawa police that matters 'involving members of the same family' would be tried in the juvenile as opposed to the police court (McKnight 1963). The police magistrate had been conducting a 'so-called Court of Domestic-relations' since the early 1920s, but it was 'merely a separate sitting of the Police Court held at another part of the day from the regular sittings, and from which public and reporters were excluded' (Harkness 1924: 13). In contrast, when the Ottawa Juvenile Court began to process family cases and operate as an unofficial domestic-relations court, the primary concern was to 'do good': 'The thinking behind this was that if charges laid between husband and wife were tried privately and in the same court as the Juveniles, help might be given to these families, and some children prevented from becoming delinquents or neglected children' (McKnight 1963; Ottawa Family Court 1950: 6).[65]

By 1931, McKinley not only exercised jurisdiction over the same legislation as Judge Mott did prior to the establishment of the Toronto Family Court, but was also authorized as a deputy magistrate to process adult cases under the Criminal Code sections governing non-support and the Deserted Wives' and Children's Maintenance Act (ibid). Thus, the Ottawa Juvenile Court was really operating as a comprehensive family court three years before receiving official sanction by the provincial government. In addition, Judge McKinley exerted influence beyond the confines of his court following his appointment to the Ontario Parole Board in 1927, influence that increased when he became the chair five years later.[66]

The acquisition of extended jurisdiction over family-welfare law by the juvenile-court judges in Toronto and Ottawa would not, in itself, have resulted in the official proclamation of family courts. However, when the attorney general decided to expand the adult-probation system using the juvenile courts, it was logical to begin in the two cities that had the oldest and, arguably, the best-administered courts in Ontario. The Toronto Juvenile Court, in particular, had intensively developed the adult-probation and clinical services established under its aegis during the early 1920s. Over the first five years of operation, between 1922 and 1927, for example, the Adult Probation Department for York County had processed 2,319 probationers (County of York Adult Probation Dept 1927). In determining whether a convicted person was probation material or not, the investigating department of the juvenile court generally conducted a study of the individual's mental background and social circumstances, after which the court psychiatrist submitted a report to the judge or magistrate presiding in the case. If the diagnosis favoured probation as a disposition, the judge or magistrate usually turned the offender over to the adult-probation officer attached to that particular criminal court, who worked under the overall supervision of Judge Mott (County of York APD 1923: 7).

This system was entrenched in the Toronto Juvenile Court during the

1920s not only because court workers desired it but also because of enthusiastic support from justice-system personnel in York County. Judge Mott's administration of the Adult Probation Department was the subject of glowing testimonials by the crown attorney, police magistrates, and county judges, all of whom stressed how efficient, economical, and humanitarian probation was compared to the old procedures employed with adult offenders (ibid: 12–13). Senior police magistrate Emerson Coatsworth, one of the architects of the new system, was also pleased to have a means of 'dealing ... with first offending prisoners and keeping a control over them that we did not have before' (ibid: 12).

Judge Mott certainly lost no time in extending that control over adult offenders. In his fifth annual report, he discussed the additional work performed by the probation officers, which, although 'without legal sanction or authority,' was commendable from 'the humanitarian and social standpoint' (County of York APD 1927). Two classes of cases were involved: those where informal and unofficial probation was used and those where 'preventive probation' was employed. With the former, adults were placed on probation 'without formal conviction ... to avoid the stigma of a court record.' Such was generally 'the practice in cases of non-support of family, and assault, where a conviction of the husband might act as a hindrance rather than a help to his improvement.' With the latter, potential delinquents were brought to the attention of the court, usually by their parents, and the probation department was able to prevent future criminality 'through early unofficial treatment' (ibid).

As was the case for adult probation, clinical facilities developed in the Toronto Juvenile Court for a number of reasons. As the first Canadian court clinic providing psychiatric, psychological, and medical services, it attracted the attention of well-known professionals, many of whom offered their 'expertise' on a volunteer basis. In 1921, three psychiatrists – C.K. Clarke, C.M. Hincks, and E.K. Clarke – and three psychologists were appointed as consultant staff. They were joined soon after by Dr Edna M. Guest of Women's College Hospital, who became the gynaecological adviser to the court (Stewart 1971). At mid-decade, Dr William Blatz, the acknowledged leader of the child-psychology movement in English-speaking Canada during the interwar years (Strong-Boag 1982, 1988), joined the court as a consultant, an affiliation he was to retain for at least twenty-seven years. Thus, each delinquent child, and, increasingly, each adult before the court, was subjected to an exhaustive mental, physical, and social analysis by the experts. A statistical survey of all cases handled by the clinic every year appeared in the annual court report (Toronto Family Court 1925, 1952).

What the mental-health professionals received in return for their volunteer work was a unique chance to research the differences between delinquents and non-delinquents and, for some, to pursue their theories on the links between mental defectiveness and crime. Court personnel and workers in outside organizations conducted various cooperative experiments over the years. In 1925, for example, the Clinic launched an intensive three-year study in conjunction with the Canadian National Committee for Mental Hygiene. Difficult cases were deliberately selected for investigation in an attempt to prove that 'some seemingly impossible cases can be cured or reformed when all the factors are known and understanding treatment is applied' (TFC 1924: 22). Another experiment in the use of psychiatry for 'preventing delinquency' involved the court clinic, the Big Brother Movement, and the Big Sisters Association of Toronto. Doctors Anderson and Blatz set up a system of examination, recommendation, and follow-up for use by the three participating groups in the project: 'By a system of reporting back to the examining Psychiatrist the result of treatment recommended by him, and recording the success or failure of such, very practical results [were] ... noted' (Anon. 1927: 29).

As well as providing research data for mental-health practitioners and academics, the Toronto Juvenile Court clinic was the only facility in the province for the assessment of delinquents, and its increasing utilization by community social agencies guaranteed its survival and expansion. For example, the clinic was used extensively by the Big Brother Movement of Toronto to obtain a 'mental study' of boys who presented special difficulties and who had not necessarily appeared in court (Brett 1953: 71–2). Indeed, Dr Kenneth H. Rogers, appointed director of the BBM in February 1936, had formerly been a consultant psychologist for the juvenile court and conducted collaborative research with the BBM court secretary (ibid: 139). The extension of clinical services to adult offenders following the introduction of adult probation in 1922 further entrenched the court clinic.

Probably the most important reason for the continuation and expansion of the court clinic, however, was the initial and ongoing funding provided by the Rockefeller Foundation. In 1926, the foundation awarded Dr Anderson a six-month travelling scholarship to pursue studies in London, under Dr Cyril Burt, and in several other European countries, and also agreed to pay for a temporary replacement psychiatrist, Dr McGhie, who was hired on the joint recommendation of the National Council of Mental Hygiene and the University of Toronto.[67] Moreover, when Anderson's scholarship period was extended another six months, the foundation and the National Hygiene Council continued to meet all his expenses and supply the court with a capable psychiatrist to carry on the clinical work 'without any added cost to the City.'[68] Given this outside financial support for the clinic, neither the city nor the province was likely to object to its location in the juvenile court.

The enlarged jurisdiction acquired by Judge Mott and the consolidation of probation and clinical services for both adult and juvenile offenders under the administration of the Toronto Juvenile Court during the 1920s were obvious advantages in the quest for family-court status. The Ottawa situation was not so clear-cut. On the one hand, Judge McKinley had amassed very wide powers, either officially or unofficially, long before the family court was officially proclaimed in 1931. On the other hand, the Ottawa children's court did not establish the extensive probation and clinical services of its Toronto counterpart. Thus, one of the key factors in the selection of Ottawa for family-court status seems to have been the political connectedness of Judge McKinley. Following the 1925 Conservative electoral victory, he enjoyed 'a fairly intimate and confidential approach to some of the members of the Cabinet.'[69] He also seems to have been on very friendly terms with the deputy ministers in both the attorney general's and provincial secretary's departments.

In 1930, at a meeting with Deputy Attorney General Humphries about the organization of probation, McKinley raised the question of officially extending the Ottawa Juvenile Court jurisdiction. After some discussion about cutting expenses by grouping counties, McKinley was quick to suggest a trial using himself, his assistant, 'plus a third whom the premier knows and wants appointed.'[70] Attorney General Price did not immediately jump at the proposal to extend McKinley's jurisdiction, however. On the contrary, he felt the proposal required more thought because it meant granting the Ottawa Juvenile Court judge and his assistants authority over several counties 'and practically [entailed] the setting up of a district for dealing with Juvenile Courts and Domestic Relations.' Under such a reorganization, McKinley would exercise far wider powers than Judge Mott in Toronto, and Mr Price feared that he might then be inundated with requests from that city, the County of York, and London for similar arrangements.[71] Yet the advantages of using the Ottawa Juvenile Court personnel and a few new government-paid adult probation officers to cover seven counties became increasingly obvious and appealing – the more so since Judge McKinley, being independently wealthy, took on the juvenile-court work outside the city of Ottawa as 'a voluntary duty.'[72]

Ultimately, McKinley prevailed. Indeed, his political connections even seemed to help speed up the implementation of the new system. At the beginning of January 1931, in pressing Deputy Attorney General Humphries to appoint a particular man as a probation officer, he said: 'I sincerely hope you will be able to hustle the thing through, as the Parole work is getting very heavy here, and for reasons best known to yourself, I don't want the new venture to fail.'[73] By the end of the month, the new system was operational.[74] The domestic-relations court, which had been operating for three years with the complete cooperation and approval of both the city police and the magistrate, had received official sanction. Moreover, Judge McKinley had been granted permission to handle family matters in six additional counties, using the non-legal methods and personnel he had developed in the Ottawa Juvenile Court.

In Ottawa, then, the acquisition of extended jurisdiction by Judge McKinley during the 1920s and his political connections were apparently the major reasons for the conversion of the children's court into a family court. In Toronto, the expanded authority secured by Judge Mott prior to 1929 and the simultaneous consolidation of probation and clinical services in the juvenile court were two primary factors behind its transformation into a family court. However, it is important to note that the latter decision could not be implemented without dismantling a well-established domestic-relations division of the women's court, presided over by Magistrate Margaret Patterson. Adult members of problem families, particularly women, had not been exposed to the horrors of the ordinary police court in Toronto since her appointment to the Bench in 1922.

On the contrary, Dr Patterson had reorganized the domestic-relations section of the women's court into 'a sort of social adjustment bureau' whose purpose was to 'prevent and correct wrong, and the conditions that led to wrong, rather than to distribute punishment.'[75] To that end, she employed socialized procedures such as informal settlement of most domestic disputes (Gordon 1980: 26), 'follow-up work,' and private hearings 'as any publicity is detrimental to re-establishing the home.'[76] Magistrate Patterson also made extensive use of probation and frequently placed problem homes under supervision for varying lengths of time before final disposition was made.[77]

What is more significant is the fact that Dr Patterson never asked to be relieved of her domestic case-load. Indeed, when she learned of the attorney general's plans to establish a family court under the aegis of Judge Mott, she went straight to the women's organizations for help in preserving her own domestic-relations court. Why, then, did Mr Price press ahead with his plans? It would appear that the creation of a family court in Toronto through the extension of juvenile-court jurisdiction was not only a means of expanding the adult-probation system at minimal expense to the province, but also a way of removing Magistrate Patterson from the women's court. Although always well supported by the Toronto Children's Aid Society, the Child Welfare Council of Toronto, and other social-work agencies, she had problematic relations with other individuals and groups.

First of all, her insistence on private hearings of the cases that did come to court roused the ire of the local media (Gordon 1980: 15). There were also minor complaints from recidivists about her trial procedures. But, perhaps most important, she was a thorn in the side of successive provincial governments, especially the Conservatives, who in all likelihood would never have appointed her to the Bench (Chunn 1988a). At one point, for example, Patterson was publicly censured by Attorney General Price after jailing a man for the non-payment of one dollar and fifty cents (Gordon 1980: 26).

It seems likely, therefore, that Mr Price saw an opportunity to remove a constant irritant by transferring Patterson's authority over domestic-relations cases to the Toronto Juvenile Court. However, Mrs Patterson was not going to be displaced without a fight. The women's organizations to whom she appealed for assistance were largely responsible for securing her appointment in the first place and they presented the only strong, vocal opposition to the proposed elimination of her court. In November 1928, the Local Council of Women launched a letter campaign to try and block the creation of a family court under Judge Mott.[78] Each of the sixty-three women's groups associated with the local council were urged to write Senior Police Magistrate Emerson Coatsworth, Patterson's superior, to 'strongly protest against any curtailment' of her court.[79]

In addition to the letter campaign, the Local Council of Women arranged a meeting with Judge Mott to discuss the attorney general's decision. Understandably, Mott tried to be a peace-maker. He said it was his hope that, in light of the 'peculiar situation' that had developed, whatever change was implemented would be 'beneficial to the Community.' Despite their conference with the judge, council members were obviously not appeased. They remained adamant that the jurisdiction of the women's court should not be 'interfered with' and proceeded to mobilize a 'large deputation' to approach the attorney general about the matter.[80]

Women's church groups concerned about the fate of Patterson's court also directed protest letters to both the Toronto City Council and the

Board of Control. Then, in March 1929, a 'large deputation' of the Toronto Ministerial Association visited Mayor McBride to impress upon him the need for retaining a women magistrate on the Bench in the women's court. If Patterson were transferred to Judge Mott's court, as the government seemed to be contemplating, she would be under his authority, and the women's court would be left to the ministrations of another man, 'a retrograde step' in the opinion of the association. The mayor prudently expressed agreement with the position presented by the delegation[81] and, subsequently, the Board of Control agreed to forward all communications about the matter to the attorney general.[82]

The attorney general's plan to transfer Dr Patterson to Judge Mott's court and replace her with a man in the women's court was only a partial success. Protests from the women's groups helped stave off that eventuality. For example, a delegation from the Women's Liberal Association in March 1929 emphasized to the acting premier, George Henry, that, having worked twenty years for the women's court, both Conservative and Liberal women in the city were 'united in their desire that it should be maintained.' With a provincial election pending, Mr. Henry said he thought he could 'assure the ladies [sic]' that the women's court would not be dismantled.[83] At the same time, the attorney general remained adamant about establishing a family court under Judge Mott. When the president of the Local Council of Women asked Price in mid-March 1929 for a definite answer about whether the women's court under Dr Patterson would be maintained, he replied 'that *nothing* would be allowed to stand in the way of establishing a Court of Domestic Relations' [my emphasis].'[84]

Part of Patterson's problem was a lack of support from her immediate superior, Emerson Coatsworth. He was briefed by Israel Humphries about what the attorney general proposed doing since it meant 'taking work from the present Police Magistrate in the City Hall [Patterson] and giving it to the Juvenile Court Judge and the Deputy Juvenile Court Judge.' He also solicited Coatsworth's 'considered views' about the proposed organization of the new domestic-relations tribunal, particularly the matter of giving the judges jurisdiction over specified Criminal Code sections.[85] Although Coatsworth consulted Margaret Patterson about the situation and received a report on the operations of her domestic-relations court, the senior magistrate ultimately expressed general agreement with the proposed organizational changes within the Toronto Juvenile Court.[86] His sole reservation, he told Humphries, concerned the provision allowing non-lawyers to administer the Criminal Code sections pertaining to family matters.

However, the deputy attorney general was strongly in favour of granting such authority to the two juvenile-court judges since it would mean that 'this Court will practically be dealing with all matters of a Domestic nature.'[87] Coatsworth's doubts were obviously dispelled (or repressed) by the time the Toronto Family Court was officially launched. In his press statement at the opening, Attorney General Price made a point of mentioning that the chief magistrate was 'entirely satisfied with the arrangements.'[88] Ultimately, then, Patterson's jurisdiction over domestic-relations cases was transferred to the Toronto Juvenile Court. Thus, the new family court was established at virtually no additional expense to the province simply by adding several government-paid adult-probation officers to the existing juvenile court personnel who did probation and investigative work and by reassigning the staff of three who had been handling non-support and maintenance matters at the Toronto City Hall. The salaries of the latter therefore continued to be the city's responsibility.[89]

None the less, because of the vociferous opposition by women's organizations to the dismantling of Patterson's court, Attorney General Price did feel compelled to offer an explanation of events. At the opening of the family court, from which Dr Patterson was notably absent, Mr Price announced that he wished to clear up 'a little misapprehension.' He was at pains to emphasize that Magistrate Patterson 'had a chance to come' to the new court but had preferred to remain in the women's court, where she felt there was work for her to do.[90] This was a euphemistic way of admitting that the government had intended to remove Patterson from the Bench altogether but was forced to bow to the pressure from her numerous supporters. However, by successfully stripping away her domestic-relations jurisdiction in 1929 and restricting her to the adjudication of what he deemed to be 'minor cases' involving female offenders, the attorney general set the stage for Patterson's eventual eclipse in 1934.[91]

In retrospect, then, the attorney general created family courts in Toronto and Ottawa because those sites best enabled him to meet his objective of expanding the province's adult-probation system at minimal cost and without any fatal political fallout. He also discovered, and was quick to take advantage of, the untold propaganda advantages that could be reaped from the ventures in those cities. During the early 1930s, with the Great Depression providing a legitimate excuse for not expanding the adult-probation system to other jurisdictions in the province, Price made numerous speeches to community service clubs, social-work agencies, and young Conservatives; gave radio broadcasts; and addressed

CHAPTER FIVE

The Legal Challenge to Socialized Justice: Family Courts in Jeopardy

> For my part I think that whatever its faults may be, the Confederation scheme for the administration of law in Canada is the finest that human ingenuity has yet devised for the legal ordering of the relations between man and man and man and the state.
>
> McGillivray, JA (*Kazakewich* v *Kazakewich* [1937] 67 CCC 379)

The question of how family-welfare law ought to be administered was not laid to rest with the official proclamation of the Toronto Family Court in 1929. The attorney general's decision to establish family courts on a selective basis within the magisterial system and through the extension of juvenile-court jurisdiction did not persuade those who had consistently 'disowned' the issue to reverse their stance. Indeed, the ongoing resistance to both socialized justice and a welfare state that characterized the interwar period was reflected in strong opposition to any tampering with the legal structures, entrenched under the British North America Act, which were premised on a strict division of civil–criminal and judicial–administrative powers between the federal and provincial governments. None the less, from the late nineteenth century onward, the social-welfare systems of the various provinces had been subject to increasing infiltration by non-legal personnel, discourses, and methods. As a result, it was very obvious by the 1930s, especially in Ontario, that the domestic problems of the working and dependent poor were being processed almost exclusively by magistrates' courts, many of which had been extensively socialized.

Growing dissension about whether the provinces had the authority to do what they had done to their respective social-welfare systems was evident in a number of court appeals against maintenance orders issued by lower-court 'judges' under provincial desertion statutes. The decisions in these cases revealed that the judiciary were just as divided on the issue of the provincial governments' constitutional power to alter traditional legal structures as anyone else. In 1937, however, the debate seemed to be over when the Ontario Supreme Court decreed that provinces did not possess such authority. Suddenly, the socialized-justice system that had evolved in an ad hoc manner over a forty-year period in Ontario's lower courts was threatened with extinction. Yet, initially, social-work leaders and government lawyers and bureaucrats appeared oblivious to the danger.

Creating a 'Poor Law System' on the Instalment Plan

The transformation of the nineteenth-century legal structures governing marginal populations from the 1880s to the 1940s reflected, but was not wholly the product of, the emergent welfare state in Ontario/Canada. Two historical antecedents were arguably the determining influences on the way in which socialized justice, including family courts, and the welfare state took shape. The first was the province's explicit rejection of the English Poor Law in 1791. Enacted during the sixteenth century, the Elizabethan poor laws 'guaranteed the indigent outdoor relief in the parish of their birth,' thereby establishing a modicum of public responsibility for maintaining the poor in the community (Struthers 1983: 6). Thus, while Ontario invariably emulated English welfare statutes, both before and after Confederation (Komar 1975), the rejection of the Poor Law statute meant that the province had no accepted tradition of state responsibility for the working and dependent poor.

The second major historical influence on the development of socialized justice and the welfare state in Canada was the ambiguity generated by the division of legislative powers between the federal and provincial states set out in the British North America Act (Varcoe 1954: 230–6). Although sections 91 and 92 ostensibly accorded Ottawa and the provinces exclusive jurisdiction over criminal law and property and civil rights, respectively, this compartmentalization of powers was not at all clear-cut in practice. Thus, each level of government exercised jurisdiction over different issues pertaining to marriage and marital breakdown, leaving neither with 'the constitutional leverage to regulate all aspects of family-related disputes' (Russell 1987: 226). In addition, because both Ottawa and the provinces could enact legislation governing domestic issues, establish courts to administer it, and appoint the presiding officials in those courts, overlap and jurisdictional disputes between the two levels of state were inevitable.

Over time, then, Ontario enacted numerous welfare statutes, which collectively produced the rough equivalent of a 'poor-law system.' Consequently, when the erosion of legal formalism in the lower courts accelerated during the late nineteenth century, the existence of such a system, created more or less on the instalment plan, became a contentious issue. The proliferation of social legislation in many provinces and the establishment of socialized tribunals to administer it were not universally acclaimed.

Active opposition to the socialization of family-welfare law culminated during the 1930s with a spate of court cases challenging the constitutionality of deserted wives' legislation and its enforcement in several provinces, including Ontario. The court judgments in these appeals reflected obvious confusion among the judiciary about the status of the socialized justice that was becoming characteristic of provincial magisterial systems and, more generally, of the new form of social and legal organization that was taking shape in Canada. Thus, while the various appeal courts examined the same questions in relation to the deserted wives' legislation of their respective locales, they handed down very divergent answers.

The immediate issue in all these cases was ostensibly a very simple one. Did provinces have the right to appoint magistrates and juvenile-court judges, who were frequently non-lawyers, and to grant them judicial powers they had not been accorded prior to Confederation? However, the larger question being addressed by the courts was whether the provinces, who were given responsibility for social-welfare under the terms of the British North America Act, had the constitutional power to alter existing legal structures in order to accommodate their increasing obligations in this area. The case of most immediate interest to the Ontario attorney general in relation to these queries was *Kazakewich* v. *Kazakewich* ([1937] 67 CCC 346). Mr Kazakewich challenged the legality of a maintenance order issued by a magistrate under the Alberta Domestic Relations Act, first, to a district court judge, who upheld the original order, and, then, to the Supreme Court of the province, which overturned it.

Significantly, the Supreme Court Judgment was not unanimous, and the opinions expressed are illustrative of the unique difficulties generated by the split-level nature of the Canadian state. The majority determined that Alberta had clearly violated the constitutional division of powers set out in the British North America Act by granting inferior courts the authority to award alimony. This power was not possessed by magistrates and justices of the peace prior to Confederation, but was clearly exercised by the superior courts in Canada long before 1867 (ibid). Moreover, they believed that the province had erred in conferring judicial powers on its own tribunals. Speaking for the majority, McGillivray, JA, said they were not unaware of, or even opposed to, 'the widespread modern legislative tendency' to create administrative tribunals for determining 'specific matters of controversy.' On the contrary, they conceded that it seemed 'to be of great public advantage to set up regulatory tribunals such as railway commissions and public utility boards' (ibid: 377–8).

That said, however, the majority saw absolutely no 'legal justification' for any attempt by the courts 'to mould and fashion the Canadian Constitution by judicial legislation so as to make it conform according to their views to the requirements of present day social and economic conditions' (ibid: 367). It was not up to courts of justice to make the law but, rather, to apply it. Thus, with regard to tribunals such as magistrates' courts, 'which are administrative in name but ... whose functions are not incidentally but primarily judicial' and where the presiding appointees exercised jurisdiction as extensive as that of judges appointed under section 96 of the British North America Act (see appendix D), the majority concluded that 'the power of appointment to such bodies is beyond the competence of the Province' (ibid: 378). Indeed, the very fact that superior courts were assigned responsibility for deciding the limits of federal and provincial powers demonstrated the 'wisdom of the Imperial Parliament' in committing such legal questions to 'the decision of Judges who are trained lawyers rather than to say, butchers, who may be excellent Justices of the Peace' (ibid: 375).

By contrast, the dissenting justices in the *Kazakewich* case expressed the view that Alberta did indeed have the constitutional authority to enact the deserted wives' legislation. Noting that 'similar acts' were and had been on the statute books of different Canadian provinces 'for many years,' they hesitated to say 'that the jurisdiction conferred in the present case is beyond the powers of the Province' (ibid: 349). Furthermore, since there was provision in the legislation for appeals to both the district and supreme courts of the province, 'certainly no injustice can arise by reason of its exercise by an inferior Court' (ibid). In conclusion, the dissenting judges pointed out that since Confederation the federal Parliament had 'from time to time increased the jurisdiction of justices of the peace in criminal matters under its powers to regulate criminal procedure,' thereby establishing the precedent that provinces might 'appoint the judges of a court of a considerable jurisdiction,' and section 96 of the British North America Act did not distinguish 'between courts of civil and courts of criminal jurisdiction' (ibid: 354).

Similar questions were addressed by the Ontario Supreme Court in *Clubine* v. *Clubine* ([1937] 68 CCC 327). This time, however, the court was unanimous in upholding the appeal of Ivan Clubine against a maintenance order issued by a Toronto Family Court judge in March 1937. Although the Ontario Supreme Court followed the Alberta precedent reluctantly, the consensus among the justices must be underscored. The Judgment was delivered by Justice W.G. Middleton, who had been the chair of the province's Law Revision Commission in the 1920s. At the time, although sympathetic to the principles underlying the family-welfare legislation, Middleton had objected to its administration by inferior courts on two grounds: it denied due process to the men who were subject to maintenance orders and it violated the '1867 rule' whereby superior courts had sole responsibility for determining cases related to alimony and custody (see chapter 3).

Ten years later, although he agonized hard and long about the *Clubine* decision, Justice Middleton ultimately adopted a position entirely consistent with his earlier one. On the one hand, having had 'intimate contact with Judge Mott and the most excellent work he is carrying on with his band of associates,' Justice Middleton admitted he did not want to disrupt this 'valuable work' of the Toronto Family Court or make a decision which would be against 'a personal friend.'[1] On the other hand, he and his judicial colleagues felt that, for several reasons, they had no choice but to support Ivan Clubine. First of all, the Ontario Deserted Wives' and Children's Maintenance Act (DWCMA) was even more sweeping than its Alberta counterpart as the result of a 1934 amendment that eliminated the upward limit on the amount men could be ordered to pay for maintenance of their wives and children (S.O., 1934, c. 10, s. 2, ss. 1). The justices concluded that, since magistrates' courts could now award 'unlimited amount' and had the power to imprison in case of default, a power not possessed by the Court of Chancery or the Supreme Court, in effect what had happened was 'the practical transfer of the entire alimony jurisdiction from the Supreme Court to the Magistrates' Court.'

Moreover, the Ontario Supreme Court judges agreed with their Alberta brethren that a province could not constitute a tribunal and transfer to it jurisdiction previously vested in a higher court without contravening the British North America Act. Although the family courts, in particular, were highly commendable tribunals, the fact remained that they had been built up through dubious means:

> The action of the Province in creating Magistrates, many of whom are laymen, and giving to the tribunals constituted the name of a Court, and to the officers presiding, the title of Judge and Deputy Judge, and conferring upon this tribunal part of the jurisdiction of the Supreme Court is manifestly a violent and indefensible departure from this principle, and cannot be defended merely by the appointment of Magistrates who already had some jurisdiction under the *Criminal Code* and provincial statutes. (ibid: 331–2)

Notwithstanding the above, the Ontario justices recognized that the *Clubine* case raised questions 'of great public interest and importance' and that they 'should be settled by the Court of final resort' (ibid: 327). They regretted the unfortunate circumstance that, because of the form in which *Clubine* had been presented to them, there could be no appeal from their Judgment and expressed the hope that through cooperation between the federal and the Ontario governments it would be possible to continue 'the existing state of affairs subject to such limitations and modification as may be deemed expedient' (ibid). Although alimony was a 'difficult and delicate ... subject,' they agreed that it would be best dealt with 'by the exercise of the kindly and familiar jurisdiction of a Court of Domestic Relations' (ibid: 333).

While the Ontario Supreme Court felt compelled to follow the majority decision in the *Kazakewich* case, their New Brunswick counterparts felt no such compunction to do so. Six months after the *Clubine* decision, the New Brunswick Supreme Court handed down a Judgment in the case of *Rex* v. *Vesey* ([1938] 69 CCC 371), which involved an appeal under the deserted wives' legislation of that province. This time, the maintenance order issued by the lower court against the appellant was unanimously upheld. In disregarding the precedents set by the Alberta and Ontario cases, the New Brunswick justices adopted the position that desertion was essentially the 'poor man's [*sic*] divorce' and the deserted wives' statute was intended to be the equivalent of a poor law provision. Therefore, concluded the chief justice, even if the payment ordered were 'alimony in the sense in which that term is used in the Divorce Court, which I think it is not, ... a provincial Legislature may quite competently in the class of cases intended to be dealt with by [the DWCMA] enact such provisions and such legislation would be in force until disallowed by the Federal authority' (ibid: 382).

What the New Brunswick statute did was enable a wife 'who may practically be starving' to go before a magistrate 'in the locality in which she lives and speedily and effectively obtain relief when her husband is able to maintain her. If the Province cannot confer this jurisdiction, the Dominion cannot do so except through the medium of the criminal law' (ibid: 383). Furthermore, continued the justices, if only higher court judges were empowered to make orders under desertion legislation, it would make court proceedings more expensive and often create the problem of a wife having to travel to the court (ibid).

None the less, although the New Brunswick decision came after *Clubine*, the latter Judgment ultimately had the gravest implications for the future development of socialized justice in Canada. By unanimously reaffirming the conclusions of the majority in *Kazakewich*, the Ontario Supreme Court justices essentially declared that the existing family courts were illegally constituted tribunals. This decision threatened all the sociolegal structures that had been created for regulating the poor since the late nineteenth century. However, neither the Ontario attorney general's department nor the Canadian Welfare Council (CWC) under Charlotte Whitton initially had any intention of going before the Canadian Supreme Court to defend the status quo.

The Canadian Welfare Council and the Non-issue of Family Courts, 1920–1937

Indeed, the fact that the CWC did eventually participate in a Reference before the Supreme Court of Canada on the issues raised in the *Clubine* case (see chapter 6) was a complete surprise, given the lack of active interest in the establishment of family courts that had always characterized the organization. Although it had issued pamphlets on this topic (Harkness 1924; Hosking 1930), the council articulated no official policy on family, as opposed to juvenile, courts before 1937. Thus, until the CWC began to grapple with the ramifications of the *Clubine* Judgment in December of that year, Charlotte Whitton had the mistaken impression that Ottawa and Toronto were the sites of the only family courts in Ontario.[2] Even more revealing of her attitude is the fact that Whitton did not remember the number of publications about domestic-relations courts that she had commissioned and released under the auspices of her own organization. Responding to a query from the Canadian high commissioner in London, she mentioned only one, whereas, in fact, there were two.[3]

This dearth of council attention to the family-court issue stemmed partly from Whitton's primary focus on child protection and the Children's Aid societies rather than spousal problems. She was always far more interested in the administration of the Children's Protection Act than any of the other social statutes governing intrafamilial relations (Rooke & Schnell 1987). A second reason for the absence of an official council policy on family courts was related to the ongoing dilemma, never resolved, about how these tribunals ought to be constituted (see chapter 3). Certainly, the Canadian Welfare Council exhibited an active concern with the problem of desertion during the interwar years and made sustained, somewhat successful, efforts to achieve the enactment of legislation for the reciprocal enforcement of maintenance orders (see chapter 2). At the same time, Whitton remained unalterably opposed to the creation of juvenile or family courts as administrative, rather than legal, tribunals exercising jurisdiction and incorporating services she felt belonged with social-work agencies in the community, particularly the Children's Aid societies.

Such had been Whitton's position since at least the mid-1920s. During the Ontario Statute Law Revision between 1925 and 1927, for example, she agreed with the Law Reform commissioners that legal professionals ought to preside over the courts administering social statutes. From her perspective, the tendency for 'certain courts to become really administrative social agencies' and the further tendency 'to have a lay presiding officer exercise judicial functions' were deplorable.[4] At the same time, she wanted social workers in community agencies, particularly the CASs, to have the primary decision-making power with respect to the treatment and supervision of deviant families. Thus, Whitton frequently expressed the opinion that the emphasis of the commission on the 'legal rather than the social aspects of the legislation' relating to child and family welfare was regrettable since it granted judges more power at the expense of the Children's Aid societies and the provincial secretary's department (Whitton 1927: 14–19).

Of course, for his own pragmatic reasons, Attorney General Price ultimately opted for selective implementation, continuing the established policy of proclaiming juvenile and family courts only in municipalities willing to shoulder the associated costs. However, although this piecemeal approach coincided with Whitton's own strategy of not supporting the creation of socialized courts on a province-wide basis unless the requisite professional personnel and essential community social services were made available, she had always regretted the passage of the

Magistrates' Jurisdiction Act, 1929, which enabled the Ontario attorney general to establish family courts through the extension of juvenile-court jurisdiction. She was also well aware that her attitude had generated some negative repercussions within the social-welfare constituency, especially among those working in the existing family courts and the social agencies closely linked to them: 'Part of my unpopularity in certain quarters in Toronto and my clash with McKinley here [in Ottawa] were because I was absolutely satisfied from my contacts with the Department of Justice that this whole trend under the amended *Jurisdiction Act*, creating the Family Court in 1929, was very questionable and might start hounds that we could not stop.'[5]

Unable to control the legal form of socialized tribunals, Whitton concentrated on bringing the existing juvenile and family courts into her sphere of influence. She appears to have been extremely successful in forging close links with the Toronto Family Court. Although not keen that Judges Mott and Hosking were both laymen, Whitton applauded the fact that much of the social work of the court was performed by established community agencies, such as the Toronto Children's Aid Society, the Big Brother Movement, and the Neighbourhood Workers' Association, which were supervised by professionally oriented personnel. She also managed to imbue the Toronto court workers with her vision of professional social work and to tie them to the council committees where those ideas were reinforced. Thus, Judge Mott served as a vice-chairman of the council's Delinquency Services Division for at least a year,[6] and Deputy Judge Hosking was involved with the division's work as well.

Having thus attained a certain sway over the Toronto court, Whitton frequently mentioned it as a model to be emulated by others. When Prince Edward Island was thinking of legislation to establish family courts in 1933, for example, Whitton immediately suggested that the Canadian Welfare Council 'arrange to have one or even two of the Toronto workers go down to the Island and help you in setting up your services on the job.' She had nothing but praise for Judges Mott and Hosking, who so wholeheartedly embraced her views: 'there are no two men in this field in Canada, who are more insistent on the importance of the prior creation of the child protection and family services on which the Family Court may rest.'[7]

Although successful with the Toronto court, Whitton was unable to attain the same influence over Judge McKinley in Ottawa. Notwithstanding his membership in the Canadian Welfare Council, he was too keen to expand his judicial powers, too unwilling to espouse Whitton's brand of social-work professionalism, and too intimately linked to the provincial government to suit Whitton. Indeed, it is most likely that her 'clash' with John McKinley predated the official proclamation of the Ottawa Family Court in 1931. Whitton had been voicing misgivings about him since at least the mid-1920s when the Ontario Statute Law Revision was carried out.

For example, in January 1927, she was extremely perturbed by a proposed amendment to the Children's Protection Act, suggested by McKinley, 'whereby no child could be committed to the care of any institution, agency, etc., even for a temporary period without an order from the court.'[8] Two months later, she commented that many of the changes to the CPA were 'deplorable' from the viewpoint of the Children's Aid Society, yet '[our] Judge here has no doubt that they transfer the power of designating as to the foster home in the hands of the judge.'[9] And, when Whitton spoke of 'the present attitude to lay judges, and the justification of that attitude in certain quarters in respect to certain judges,' there seems little doubt that she was thinking of John McKinley.[10]

Despite the fact that the Canadian Welfare Council had adopted no official policy on family courts, then, Whitton's perspective on juvenile and family courts tended to prevail, both inside and outside the organization. For example, the 1935 report on the Ontario reformatory system incorporated her views for the most part, but that is hardly surprising, given the presence of Judge Mott, W.L. Scott, Frank Sharpe, and Whitton herself on the committee (Ontario 1935: 1). The report recommended that juvenile and family courts be established throughout Ontario on a district basis and that the Juvenile Delinquents Act be proclaimed in each district (ibid: 17, 52). However, such was to occur only when 'the proper officials have been appointed, and the necessary machinery provided in order that the Court may function efficiently' (ibid: 17). Moreover, while the courts were to incorporate basic probation services, the committee recommended 'close correlation of their services with all existing community services, public and private, especially those of the Children's Aid Societies' (ibid: 52).

However, in retrospect, it is also evident that the Canadian Welfare Council could be remarkably pragmatic about the establishment of juvenile and family courts, depending on the circumstances. In a 1929 conference paper, Elizabeth King raised the question of whether the juvenile courts ought to do social work. King, who was involved in much of the survey research conducted by the council, emphasized how essential it was that children's courts be allowed to do casework.[11] This position seems to contradict Whitton's.

Furthermore, in situations where it was clear that a community would not agree to establish a juvenile or domestic-relations court independent of the police court and/or where the community did not have extensive social-work services available outside a socialized court, the council adapted to the prevailing conditions. Thus, in its *Report on Child Protection and Family Welfare Services for the City of Kingston* (1931: 21), the CCCFW accepted the reality that the local government would not create separate juvenile and family courts in the city and recommended, perhaps reluctantly, that to achieve 'the greatest possible flexibility' in dealing with cases involving both adults and juveniles, 'an effort be made to have the *J.D.A* (1929) proclaimed and the services of a Juvenile Court and a Domestic Relations Court established' within the existing magistrates' court.

Ultimately, Ottawa's appointment of the Royal Commission to Investigate the Penal System in February 1936, under the Hon. Mr Justice Archambault, provided the catalyst for the Canadian Welfare Council to develop an official policy on the relationship between juvenile and family courts. The Division on Delinquency and Related Services was charged with preparing a memorandum on the youthful offender for submission to the commission. Significantly, although the committee struck included W.L. Scott, it was dominated by people who worked in the juvenile-justice system, including Harry Atkinson, superintendent of a Manitoba training school; Richard S. Hosking, deputy judge of the Toronto Family Court; and Kenneth Rogers, director of the Big Brother Movement of Toronto. Atkinson, the committee chair, circulated a questionnaire to his fellow members, soliciting their opinions on specific issues related to socialized courts: Should the juvenile court be a court of justice or a social agency? What was the place and function of the family court? Should it be linked up with the juvenile court?[12]

Only Scott's response survives. Almost predictably, he reiterated his long-time position, which was also that of Whitton: the juvenile court 'should ... be primarily a Court of Justice. Although a different principle has been followed in the United States and other countries, it seems to me that any other view would not be acceptable to the people of Canada.' On the question of the family court, Scott retained his personal preference, first articulated in the 1920s, that it ought to be separate from the children's court. However, acknowledging 'it would be difficult, if not impossible to have two sets of courts ..., [he concluded] that apart from its desirability on other grounds, the Juvenile Court must of necessity be linked up with the Family Court.'[13]

But how were they to be linked? Seemingly, the council's Archambault submission was virtually complete when Scott suggested to Charlotte Whitton that they should address the implications of the *Clubine* case in their presentation to the commission. Scott proposed that the CWC adopt the proposal outlined in the Ontario Supreme Court Judgment on *Clubine*, namely, to seek cooperation between Ottawa and the provinces, which would result in legislation allowing a family court to function. He envisaged domestic-relations courts or 'courts in social causes,' the name preferred by Whitton, that would be constituted through a federal legislative enactment. They would be 'considered as socialized tribunals absorbing and continuing the functions of the Juvenile Court System and adapted to conditions pertaining locally in the respective provinces.' Supervision of standards and services, however, 'might rest with the appropriate provincial authority.'[14]

Scott's suggestions were incorporated into the council's proposed Archambault submission, but there was to be a further change.[15] On 18 December 1937, Whitton sent him yet another revision for comment. Because the *Clubine* decision 'raised in sharp form the whole question of the organization and status of Family Courts in Canada,' she had felt compelled to re-examine the whole question once again.[16] Consequently, the council's final presentation to the commission, titled *The Problem of the Juvenile and Youthful Offender* (1938c), proposed the development of inclusive courts in social causes, which would not be new tribunals but, rather, specialized adaptations in the existing court systems (1938c: 53). They would exercise jurisdiction over children's, family, and social-problem cases, not only absorbing and continuing the functions of the juvenile-court system, but also assuming responsibility for domestic proceedings under various social statutes (ibid).

The Canadian Welfare Council offered no specific suggestions on how the necessary adaptations in practice and procedure would be achieved, however. Seemingly, the first objective was to obtain the 'appropriate legislation' through federal-provincial cooperation, which would overcome the difficulties arising in the *Clubine* case and enable a court in social causes to function (ibid). Once the council's Archambault submission was finalized (1938c), Whitton mailed copies to a diverse group of individuals for comments and suggestions, particularly in relation to 'possible federal and provincial enactments which might make the constitution of such Courts possible.'[17] After seventeen years, the CWC had produced an official policy on the family-court issue.

The Ontario Attorney General, Provincial Rights, and Socialized Courts, 1920–1937

Like the Canadian Welfare Council, the Ontario Department of the Attorney General had never considered the establishment of family courts to be a high priority during the interwar years. The existing courts were simply by-products of the Ferguson government's decision to expand adult probation as cheaply as possible (see chapter 4). Moreover, when the Liberals assumed power in 1934, they exhibited no interest in creating any new domestic-relations tribunals. Indeed, extending the jurisdiction of the Hamilton Family Court to cover Wentworth County was their only contribution to the development of such courts in the province. Consequently, when the Ontario Appeal Court handed down the *Clubine* Judgment in June 1937, the acting attorney general, Paul Leduc, expressed no intention of trying to overturn the decision.

It is important to underscore the complete lack of interest in juvenile and family courts per se that characterized all provincial governments in Ontario throughout the interwar years. The question of whether the appointments of juvenile-court judges made by the province were constitutional without ratification by the federal justice department was clearly of no special concern to the attorney general's department prior to *Clubine*. For example, the government's response in the mid-1920s to queries from Hawley S. Mott about his status was a typical one during this period. He first became anxious about the constitutionality of provincially appointed juvenile-court judges after the BC Supreme Court set aside the appointment of Helen Gregory MacGill, a Vancouver juvenile-court judge (MacGill 1955). In the wake of that decision, Mott initially consulted W.L. Scott, honorary counsel to the Canadian Welfare Council, who replied that he was 'inclined to think the decision of the [BC] Court' was correct because it had always been the position of the federal justice department that appointments of juvenile-court judges had to be made by them to be effective. However, Scott said, Ottawa had always been willing to confirm the appointment of 'anyone who has been appointed by the Provincial authorities' and he advised Mott to apply directly to Justice for confirmation of his position.[18]

For whatever reason, however, Mott ignored Scott's advice and approached the Ontario attorney general, W.F. Nickle, about the 'doubt in my own mind' concerning his status.[19] Nickle's departmental solicitors had no such doubt. The appointment of a juvenile-court judge was 'clearly within the powers of a Provincial Government,' they assured Mott, and there was absolutely 'no reason' to ask for a federal commission since the British North America Act gave provinces jurisdiction over both the administration of justice and the constitution of courts not included in section 96 (see appendix D).[20] Mott's appointment thus remained a provincial one, without the federal stamp of approval. Moreover, a decade later, the province had accorded him even more powers as a family-court judge, including jurisdiction under the desertion statute, which, as was noted earlier, had been amended to eliminate the upward ceiling on the amount of weekly maintenance a man could be ordered to pay.

Understandably, Mott became apprehensive about his legal status once again following the Alberta Supreme Court decision in *Kazakewich* v. *Kazakewich*. Finding Mr Magone, a departmental solicitor, 'quite non commital [*sic*] on the matter,' the judge approached Attorney General Arthur Roebuck directly: 'I have known for some time that there has been a feeling that we [family-court judges] had no jurisdiction' under the Deserted Wives' and Children's Maintenance Act, he said, because 'our appointments were made by the Province of Ontario.' And, although there had been no appeals to that point against orders issued by Ontario courts, Mott wondered 'if we wouldn't be well advised in this matter to have the appointment of the Judges of the Family Courts approved by Ottawa, which would overcome this objection.' Evidently afraid of antagonizing the attorney general, he hastened to add that he was only 'thinking out loud' and not 'making a suggestion.'[21]

Once Mott had raised the issue, it became clear that now the attorney general's department also entertained doubts about the legality of their prior decision to accord a family-court judge jurisdiction over matters related to maintenance. Mr Roebuck admitted to his deputy, I.A. Humphries, that he was 'not sure of the answer to this problem' because he had felt 'for some time' that support orders were a matter for a federally appointed lawyer-judge to adjudicate and 'had questioned the constitutionality' of the DWCMA. None the less, the attorney general conveyed a somewhat contradictory message to Humphries. On the one hand, he said, the question did 'not seem to be pressing for the worst that can happen is that some of us do not go to jail.' On the other hand, he admitted, if an Ontario court were to follow the Alberta decision, 'it might upset our present system quite a bit' and, therefore, Humphries ought to 'give a little time to the matter.'[22]

The deputy attorney general did not have much time to think. Less than two weeks later, Ivan Clubine posted Notice of Appeal against a maintenance order issued by Judge Hosking of the Toronto Family Court. When informed of this development, Humphries, who had been actively involved in helping Attorney General Price launch the court in 1929 (see chapter 4), revealed his own reservations on the question. He had been 'apprehensive for some time' that this issue would arise: 'It [maintenance] is more in the nature of granting of alimony and possibly would be argued along that line.'[23]

Seemingly, then, officials in the attorney general's department had been privately pondering the legality of their actions in the area of family-welfare law for a while but had gone ahead anyway. Now their bluff had been called, what would they do to resolve the situation? In retrospect, the strategies adopted by the Ontario attorney general in relation to the *Clubine* case over the next year appear to have been heavily influenced by two internecine political conflicts. The first was a dispute within the provincial cabinet, which strongly influenced the government response to *Clubine* for much of 1937. Premier Hepburn split with both his attorney general, Arthur Roebuck, and minister of welfare, David Croll, over the extent of the government's commitment to genuine reform.

This cabinet dissension was specifically centred on the resolution of labour issues and culminated during the 1937 strike of auto workers in Oshawa. Following his 1934 electoral victory, Premier Hepburn showed no inclination to translate his radical, populist campaign rhetoric into concrete reform policies. However, the attorney general and minister of welfare were both staunch proponents of certain reforms, including the implementation of legislation governing conditions in Ontario's industrial plants. Thus, although Hepburn had enacted the Industrial Standards Act, 1935, he had no compunction about subverting it by adopting a policy of strike-breaking as the province began to experience a revival of industrial trade unionism in the mid-1930s (McKenty 1967: 101–2). After the CIO sent representatives to Canada to organize Oshawa auto workers, the premier openly assisted General Motors in attempts to prevent unionization. When Roebuck and Croll opposed Hepburn's action, the premier immediately demanded, and received, their resignations on 14 April 1937 (ibid: 110–11). As a consequence of this political infighting, Ontario had three different attorneys general that year. Arthur Roebuck was still in charge during the initial appeal of the *Clubine* Judgment to the county court; Paul Leduc became the acting attorney general on 14 April; and, Gordon D. Conant assumed the cabinet position on 11 October 1937 (ibid: 137–8).

The second internal party conflict that shaped the province's response to the *Clubine* case was the growing animosity between the federal Liberal party under Mackenzie King and the Ontario Liberal party under the leadership of Mitch Hepburn (Schull 1978: 296–301). The acrimony revolved primarily around the issue of fiscal responsibility for social-welfare, specifically unemployment relief, which had become a crushing burden for the municipalities during the 1930s depression. Working in tandem, Premier Hepburn and Maurice Duplessis of Quebec consistently rejected any proposals that would have entailed the surrender of provincial rights to the national government. Hepburn feared that, if Ontario agreed to transfer some of its welfare powers to Ottawa so the latter could implement unemployment-insurance legislation, the province would end up subsidizing poorer provinces.

Ultimately, this internecine struggle between the Ontario premier and Prime Minister Mackenzie King erupted into the open. Hepburn broke publicly with the federal Liberals on 3 June 1937, only a few weeks before the provincial Supreme Court handed down its Judgment in the *Clubine* case (McKenty 1967: 125; see also Struthers 1983). His tenacious defence of provincial rights not only carried Hepburn to a second sweeping electoral victory in October 1937 (McKenty 1967: 135), but also set the stage for the eventual showdown before the Canadian Supreme Court on *Clubine*.

That eventuality could not have been predicted, however. During the months before the Ontario Supreme Court decision on *Clubine*, the attorney general essentially adopted a holding policy in relation to the case. Two lines of action were pursued. First, the government acceded to requests from the Toronto crown attorney, Judge Mott of the family court, and others to have a departmental lawyer present at the *Clubine* appeal hearings, both at the county-court level in April 1937 and before the Supreme Court of the province in early June. The attorney general and his aides slowly began to realize that potentially disastrous consequences might stem from a successful appeal by Ivan Clubine because almost every Ontario magistrate exercised power in proceedings under the Deserted Wives' and Children's Maintenance Act.[24]

The other tack followed by the attorney general in the early stages of *Clubine* was to determine what, if anything, the Alberta government planned to do about the *Kazakewich* Judgment. Was further action being contemplated and could they provide any information that would be 'useful' in the argument that 'no doubt will come forward in Ontario'?[25] The Alberta attorney general's department replied that their attempt to appeal *Kazakewich* at the provincial level had been quashed, but they were considering a Reference to the provincial Supreme Court, followed by an appeal to the Supreme Court of Canada in which they hoped that 'some of the other provinces might intervene and assist us.'[26] In his response, Deputy Attorney General Humphries stated that Ontario might well 'intervene in the matter' because the question was 'one of very great importance.'[27] Thus, in the early months of the *Clubine* case, the attorney general basically adopted a wait-and-see attitude, formulating no changes in the administration of family-welfare law before the appeals were over and, presumably, until it was determined whether Alberta was going to fight the constitutional battle for them.

Once the Ontario Supreme Court handed down its Judgment on 29 June 1937, however, Acting Attorney General Paul Leduc was forced to consider the implementation of a new policy on the administration of social legislation in the province. There were several options to be weighed, one of which was to request a Reference before the Supreme Court of Canada. That course of action certainly generated some interest and support. Various crown attorneys wanted to know the government's intention because they had cases pending that were similar to *Clubine*.[28] The Alberta attorney general's department was also anxious to know if Ontario planned to go before the federal Supreme Court because they were still considering a provincial Reference on *Kazakewich*.[29]

Notwithstanding these sentiments, officials in the Ontario attorney general's department discussed and then decided against the Reference option as a response to the *Clubine* Judgment. By the end of July, it was 'rather doubtful' that the province would go to the high court.[30] At the beginning of August, Deputy Attorney General Humphries could definitely state that it was not 'the intention of the Province to appeal the decision in connection with the *DWCMA*.'[31] Consequently, several months later when an appeal was launched against a maintenance order issued by a Windsor magistrate, the attorney general's department said it was not 'necessary' for the provincial government to be represented at the hearing since the county judge would be bound by the *Clubine* decision and, more important, because the constitutional issue had been settled by the Ontario Supreme Court justices.[32]

Extant archival materials do not reveal why the Ontario government declined to request a Reference to the Canadian Supreme Court in the immediate aftermath of the *Clubine* decision in late June 1937. Surviving documents do contain scattered comments, however, that indicate that, in addition to the political conflicts described previously and other issues with higher priority, the attorney general's department did not think they had a case. When Judge Mott queried the constitutionality of his appointment in March 1937, for example, both the attorney general and his deputy had expressed apparently long-felt reservations about the legality of the system they had established in the lower courts of the province to administer family-welfare law. Moreover, even when the Ontario government finally did request a Reference before the Canadian Supreme Court, it was done with the expectation that they would lose (see chapter 6). Their own solicitor clearly thought there was little chance the high court would uphold the jurisdiction of magistrates under the Deserted Wives' and Children's Maintenance Act.[33] Thus, the attorney general fully expected that he would have to amend the existing welfare statutes, making provision for their enforcement outside the lower courts.[34]

A second course of action considered by the attorney general's department in the immediate wake of the *Clubine* Judgment was to seek federal support in maintaining the status quo. The Ottawa Family Court judge, John McKinley, wondered whether it would be 'possible and practical, as well as legal,' for the provincial government to ask its federal counterpart to enact the Ontario Deserted Wives' and Children's Maintenance Act, as it stood, 'making it effective in the Provinces that see fit to proclaim it.' Then, if Ottawa agreed, a clause could be added to the statute, giving magistrates and family-court judges jurisdiction under the act.[35] The Toronto and Ottawa family-court judges, as well as some municipalities, also pressed for federal confirmation of all presiding juvenile- and domestic-relations-court judges who held only provincial appointments.

The basic concern of the municipalities was a monetary one. They feared that relief costs for maintaining deserted families would soar if the DWCMA were no longer within the jurisdiction of the family and magistrates' courts, since all the orders previously made by these tribunals under the statute would be invalid. Immediately following the county-court decision on *Clubine* in April 1937, which overturned the maintenance order issued by Judge Hosking, the York County Council discussed the ramifications of the Judgment and agreed that they must seek federal confirmation of the appointments of their own family-court judges before the municipality was confronted with more husbands having support orders quashed.[36] Subsequently, after the Ontario Supreme Court ruling on *Clubine* in June, the warden of York County, W.E. MacDonald, wrote to Premier Hepburn, expressing alarm and concern that 'scores of women' were going to be left without support because orders issued by the county family court had been 'nullified.'

Furthermore, he pointed out, deserted women could now 'only secure help if they [had] sufficient money to issue a writ in one of the Higher Courts' and the result was 'bound to be that these women will have to forego [*sic*] court proceedings and ask for help or relief from the municipalities.' To cope with the situation, the county council was 'considering sending a delegation to Ottawa' to request that 'pending the necessary Dominion legislation ... the County men be given the authority of County Judges in so far as domestic relations matters are concerned.' MacDonald wanted to know the 'attitude' of the provincial government and wondered if Premier Hepburn would 'personally discuss the Matter' with his attorney general because the county would 'get further [in Ottawa] if we had the support of your Government.'[37]

The idea of seeking a means through which administration of the DWCMA could be left to the magistrates' and family courts also received support from some crown attorneys. Gordon Conant, the Oshawa crown and soon-to-be attorney general, wrote the government in July to say he had been dissatisfied with the desertion statute over the years (see chapter 4) and still felt the 'whole business' about the DWCMA remained 'in an unsatisfactory condition.' Conant proposed that the Children's Aid Society superintendents in the various counties be put in charge of DWCMA matters since such matters 'invariably involve children and in any event they are a social problem.' And where there was a juvenile-court judge 'as we have here [in Oshawa],' these cases should be handled by him as opposed to the 'ordinary Magistrates' Court.'[38]

These proposals for maintaining the status quo in the administration of family-welfare law, especially the suggestion that the province seek confirmation from Ottawa of the juvenile- and family-court judges it had appointed over the years, were rejected by the attorney general's department. Government solicitors, particularly Mr Magone, were entirely opposed to such a course of action. In a July memorandum to Acting Attorney General Paul Leduc on the implications of the *Clubine* Judgment, Magone pointed out that asking the federal minister of justice to designate family-court judges and magistrates as judges, with the powers of a superior-court judge in alimony cases, was simply not feasible strictly on legal grounds. Many of the former were 'laymen,' and section 97 of the British North America Act expressly stated that judges had to be selected 'from the respective Bars of the Provinces' (see appendix D).[39]

Even if it had been possible to circumvent section 97, however, Magone would not have approved of granting non-lawyers extended judicial powers. The legal professionalism, which had been so evident in the 1920s (see chapter 3), still shaped the thinking of at least some departmental solicitors, as Magone's reply to Warden MacDonald reveals: it was 'quite futile' for the county council to send a delegation to Ottawa, he said, since the federal Parliament 'had absolutely no power to clear up the situation'; neither of the family-court judges in York County was a lawyer and non-lawyers could not be appointed county-court judges.[40] Magone also expressed his disapproval of lay judges to G.D. Conant: 'There has been an agitation, of course, to have the Department approach Ottawa,' he said, but there was the section 97 problem and, more important it seems, Magone's resistance to the ideology of socialized justice.[41]

What Mr Magone advocated, and what the Ontario attorney general adopted over the course of the summer as the projected long-term solution to the *Clubine* dilemma, was the transfer of the DWCMA jurisdiction pertaining to the maintenance of deserted wives from the magistrates' to the county courts. However, since the statute could not be amended until the next legislative session in the spring of 1938, Magone also formulated a stopgap policy. In the interim, he suggested that the family and magistrates' courts continue to administer the DWCMA as it pertained to the maintenance of children, since alimony did not apply to children, and use the relevant Criminal Code sections in cases related to the support of deserted wives (see appendix C). The Toronto Family Court judges had already been 'told to carry on under this provision'[42] and similar instructions conveyed to John McKinley in Ottawa.[43]

After consultation, both Acting Attorney General Leduc and Deputy Humphries concurred with Magone's suggestions and told him to prepare instructions for the various court officials across the province who were directly affected by the *Clubine* decision. When he sent copies to family-court judges Mott and McKinley, Magone, who perhaps anticipated resistance, was extremely vague about the long-term solution, worked out and adopted unofficially by the government, which would considerably reduce their powers by moving the administration of the Deserted Wives' and Children's Maintenance Act to the county courts. He said only that at the 1938 legislative session 'some method will be worked out whereby the machinery at present used under the DWCMA so effectively, may continue to be used.'[44] Magone was more specific in his communications with others, however. He informed both Warden MacDonald of York County and Gordon Conant, the Oshawa crown attorney, he thought it 'likely' the government would appoint county judges 'possibly as *persona designata* to take these cases' under the desertion statute.[45] In his view, this was 'the only solution.'[46]

The interim and long-term policies adopted by the attorney general's department in response to *Clubine* clearly reveal no allegiance to the principles of socialized justice in that quarter. Ultimately, the province was prepared to hand over jurisdiction under the DWCMA to the incumbent county-court judges, with no specialized adaptation of their courts. In the meantime, the attorney general had instructed magistrates and family-court judges to apply the criminal law to male deserters who appeared before them. However, although such policies seemingly reflect strong adherence to the principles of legal formalism and professionalism, there was probably a more pragmatic rationale underlying the province's decision to use the county courts for the administration of the DWCMA. The federal justice department was responsible not only for appointing, but also for paying the judges of these tribunals. Thus, if more judges were required when the transfer of jurisdiction planned by the Ontario attorney general took effect, Ottawa would have to foot the bill.

As it turned out, however, the plan for the future administration of Ontario's family-welfare law, hammered out over the summer of 1937, was not the final solution to the *Clubine* problem. Six months later, Attorney General Gordon Conant did request a Reference hearing before the Canadian Supreme Court on the issues raised by the case. This move represented a complete reversal of the government's earlier position inasmuch as it constituted an attempt to legitimize the continued administration of social legislation by socialized courts within the magisterial system. Moreover, Conant was joined in his endeavour by the Canadian Welfare Council, which also abandoned the policy on family courts incorporated in its Archambault submission and pressed for continued lower-court jurisdiction over family-welfare law.

The Legitimation of Socialized Justice: The Supreme Court Reference and Family Courts

> I am unable to accept the view that the jurisdiction of inferior Courts, whether within or without the ambit of s.96, was by the *B.N.A. Act* fixed forever as it stood at the date of Confederation.
>
> Sir Lyman P. Duff, CJC (Reference [1939] 71 CCC 128)

The 1938 Reference to the Canadian Supreme Court was framed in terms of the constitutional questions raised by the *Clubine* case.[1] Did the provinces have the right to create tribunals; appoint 'judges,' some of whom were non-lawyers; and assign them what were essentially judicial powers traditionally exercised by federal appointees in the higher courts? However, while the immediate focus of the Reference was a decision made by a Toronto Family Court 'judge,' the Supreme Court was being asked for a ruling on a much larger issue, with grave implications for the future development of both socialized justice and the welfare state in Canada. Was it legitimate for the provinces to restructure the lower courts, in the way that they had, in order to accommodate their growing welfare responsibilities?

A negative response meant that the existing system for the administration of family-welfare law would be overthrown. Thus, social-work leaders, government lawyers, and politicians, who initially had no intention of doing so, ultimately had very pragmatic reasons to seek Supreme Court sanction for maintaining the status quo. Ironically, then, the individuals and groups who so consistently 'disowned' the family-court issue during the interwar years helped bring about the historic decision by the nation's highest court that legitimated and set the future course of development for socialized justice in Canada.

The Canadian Welfare Council and the Supreme Court Reference

Anything but the Status Quo

Why did Charlotte Whitton and W.L. Scott suddenly become so interested in the *Clubine* Judgment in December 1937? After all, the Canadian Welfare Council (CWC) had shown only a perfunctory concern when the case erupted during the spring of that year. For example, after Ivan Clubine successfully appealed the maintenance order issued by Richard Hosking in March, the deputy judge of the Toronto Family Court wrote immediately to the council for assistance: 'We have a situation on our hands as the result of an appeal to a County Court Judge ... ; [although the Deserted Wives' and Children's Maintenance Act] has been in operation since 1901 [*sic*] ... now in the year 1937 we are told it is a matter which properly comes before the Supreme Court and no one with a Provincial appointment has authority to deal with it.'[2] Both Scott and Whitton were apprised of the 'situation,' but although the former discussed the issues with Marjory Bradford, Whitton's assistant, and the latter inquired at the end of August about the outcome of the Toronto appeal case, there was absolutely no notion that the Canadian Welfare Council should become involved as an organization until almost six months after the *Clubine* Judgment was handed down by the Ontario Supreme Court.[3]

Whitton was spurred to act only after doubts were raised about the legality of magistrate- and family-court jurisdiction over other social statutes. When a child-welfare case processed in the Hamilton Family Court prompted 'similar questions' by the higher courts to those raised by *Clubine*, all of a sudden it was not just a matter of whether the lower courts had the authority to administer the Deserted Wives' and Children's Maintenance Act; their powers under the Adoption, Children of Unmarried Parents, and Children's Protection acts were being challenged as well.[4] Consequently, in December 1937, when Attorney General Gordon Conant instructed the Ottawa and Toronto family-court judges and the magistrates of the province to stop handling cases under these three statutes, Whitton sensed danger. From her perspective, transferring jurisdiction over social legislation to the county courts, with no adaptation of these tribunals, meant that forty years of work and agencies in the children's field that had been built up would be 'inexpressibly impaired in the Counties': costs, distances, and the pressure of business involved in regular county-court hearings, as well as the considerations implied in the Ontario Supreme Court Judgment on *Clubine* about the very nature of the cases being processed under social laws, would all contribute to that eventuality.[5]

By December 1937, the Canadian Welfare Council was also under mounting pressure from social-work agencies and family-court personnel to help them find a quick resolution to the *Clubine* dilemma. Significantly, even Robert E. Mills, one of Whitton's staunchest allies, sent her an urgent appeal: 'Our people are in an uproar over the developments, present and threatening, in connection with interpretation of our social legislation ... Everyone thinks that the Council is our "white hope." '[6] Two days later, the director of the Children's Aid Society of Toronto (CASOT) wrote again to emphasize how awkward it was for the CASOT that cases under the social statutes now had to be taken to the county courts because of the procedures involved, increased costs, and judicial reluctance to administer welfare law.[7] Clearly, county judges were no more willing to deal with social cases in 1937 than they had been a decade earlier when the Ontario government unsuccessfully attempted to transfer such jurisdiction to them following the revision of provincial welfare statutes (see chapter 4).

Mills's entreaties coincided with Whitton's growing fears about the implications of *Clubine*. Even as she was mailing out copies of the Archambault submission for comments, Whitton had already begun to think of taking action. In a letter to C.V. McArthur, an honorary counsel to the CWC, she said: 'I am strongly disposed to have the Council go right ahead now in an endeavour to get the whole situation realigned from the point of view of these Courts in Social Causes.'[8] Almost immediately, she began to try to determine what, if anything, the Ontario attorney general intended to do about the worsening situation. She pressed her old friend, Bert Heise, to discuss the problem 'informally with the law officers of the Crown in Ontario,' not in his official capacity as head of the provincial Children's Aid Branch but, rather, as a member of the Canadian Welfare Council.[9] At the same time, Whitton suggested to Robert Mills that one line that 'might be of use' was to contact McIntyre Hood, the attorney general's private secretary, who was also an old friend of hers.[10]

When events seemed to indicate that Gordon Conant was simply 'retreating one step at a time'[11] and would probably not try to reverse the Ontario Supreme Court's Judgment on *Clubine*, Whitton began to contemplate launching an appeal that would be coordinated by the Canadian Welfare Council and include the City of Toronto and the Children's Aid societies in Toronto, Hamilton, and Ottawa.[12] She also started to think about organizing a closed conference, similar to the one held in 1929 to discuss revisions to the Juvenile Delinquents Act (see chapter 3) that would bring together federal and provincial law officers and representatives of various social agencies in the delinquency, child-protection, and family-welfare fields to try to find a solution to the *Clubine* problem.[13] Then, in the midst of Whitton's mobilization efforts, the Ontario attorney general inexplicably requested a Reference to the Supreme Court of Canada to clarify the constitutional issues raised by *Clubine*.[14] This news galvanized Whitton to focus on articulating an explicit course of action for the Canadian Welfare Council.

It is evident that Whitton continued to view the council's policy on family courts, which was outlined in the Archambault submission (1938c; see chapter 5), as the solution to the *Clubine* dilemma. Although the document did not specify exactly what form domestic-relations courts should take, Whitton's covering letters, which accompanied the copies sent to various individuals for comment, reveal her position that courts in social causes should be constituted through federal legislation, have the status of the county courts, and be presided over by lawyer-judges. The new courts would thus be primarily judicial as opposed to administrative tribunals. In her letter to Justice Middleton, author of the *Clubine* decision, Whitton very deliberately presented the Archambault submission as the council's tentative proposal for remedying the problematic situation created by the Ontario Supreme Court Judgment. The establishment of courts in social causes on a county or territorial basis would, 'in my judgment,' she said, restrict the choice of judges to bar members and 'make these Courts judicial services, with close collaboration with the social services.'[15] She expressed the hope that Middleton would agree with her.

Whitton reiterated the same sentiments in her letter to C.V. McArthur. Significantly, however, she added a pragmatic note, admitting that, if laymen were 'still to be desired' for these courts in social causes, she could accept such an alternative, provided 'the designation of such officers as Judges' was abandoned.[16] None the less, Whitton's relentless professionalism predisposed her towards the idea of having lawyers preside over courts 'charged with such responsibility' in social causes. Moreover, she believed there would be no 'serious difficulty in finding enough lawyers who were of a social approach and actual contact with our social agencies.'[17]

The position of the Canadian Welfare Council, set out in the Archambault brief (1938c) and embraced so enthusiastically by Whitton, was not the one presented by W.L. Scott to the Canadian Supreme

Court three months later, however. On the contrary, the council's factum (1938b) made a convincing argument for the maintenance of the status quo, that is, for leaving the administration of family-welfare law in the magisterial system. A major reason for this reversal was the continued lack of unanimity within the social-welfare constituency about how to tackle the repercussions of *Clubine*. By no means was there uncritical acceptance of the family-court policy set out in the council's Archambault submission. Indeed, the divergent responses Whitton received to her request for comments, as much as events themselves, forced a reappraisal of the CWC position on courts in social causes.

Assessment of the Archambault brief by the people who had originally been charged with producing the document was quite negative, for example. Understandably so, since it appears that Whitton took the original draft memorandum submitted by the committee and unilaterally changed it.[18] After reading the revised version, Richard Hosking, deputy judge of the Toronto Family Court, quickly informed Whitton that he did not want his name used to endorse one particular section since he was unsure of its implications.[19] Subsequently, Kenneth Rogers, general secretary of the Big Brother Movement, Toronto, sent Whitton detailed comments on behalf of the committee initially appointed to prepare the Archambault submission, which included himself, Judge Hosking, and the superintendent of the Bowmanville Training School, Mr A.R. Virgin. The committee response clearly reveals that the long-time differences between Whitton and personnel working in or associated with the existing family courts about how such tribunals ought to be constituted had merely been papered over rather than eliminated through the years.

Rogers launched his critique of the council's Archambault brief by asserting that the name, 'court in social causes,' was 'relatively meaningless' and, more important, 'would damn the Court' in the eyes of the legal profession before it was even established. 'We must recognize the fact that among lawyers there is still considerable opposition to social work procedures.' Furthermore, he continued, the proposal that courts in social causes be restricted to judicial functions contradicted the concomitant emphasis in the document on creating a probation department within each court. Was the latter not 'a specialized social service' or 'family service' and did it not include 'those investigatory procedures which are an essential part of any treatment process'?[20]

Rogers and his colleagues who were actively involved in the administration of socialized justice were particularly concerned that, in practice, the proposed court in social causes might be 'incidental' to family-welfare services, constituted through provincial authority but placed under the direction of social-welfare services with no appeal from decisions of the latter. The implication seemed to be that the existing (family) court practice whereby probation officers mediated informal settlement of cases as 'occurrences' would be done away with. While the 'court' expert may sometimes handle these poorly 'because of a lack of knowledge of social work techniques,' Rogers argued, 'experience suggests that the average social worker (*a woman, remember*) could with difficulty do as well [my emphasis].' He concluded by emphasizing that, since it was the community social agencies who referred most of the 'occurrence' cases to the court, they, in fact, were reliant upon the continuation of 'this court procedure.'[21]

With specific reference to *Clubine*, then, what the Toronto Family Court personnel and their system allies wanted was a legitimation of the status quo, not the creation of a new set of courts in social causes from whose operations lay personnel and social-work services would be excluded. As previous discussion revealed, they felt the immediate solution was to obtain confirmation of the family-court judges' provincial appointments from the federal Department of Justice, a standard practice in the early days of juvenile courts that had petered out during the interwar years. As Robert E. Mills reported to Charlotte Whitton: 'Mott and Hosking feel that the only hope is with the Minister of Justice.'[22] Indeed, Hosking saw nothing problematic about this proposed solution to *Clubine*. Since the justice department had never questioned any provincial appointments of juvenile-court judges in the past, he said, why would they start now?[23]

Other responses to the council's Archambault submission also contained reservations about the courts in social causes envisaged by Charlotte Whitton. Vera Parsons, Mrs Clubine's lawyer in the appeal to the Ontario Supreme Court, agreed that any such tribunals should have county-court status and be presided over by lawyer-judges, but she thought the family court ought to have 'a staff of trained social workers' to carry out investigations, advise people, and so on.[24] In his reply, Justice Middleton wondered if 'the effect of the decision of the *Clubine* case [had] not been somewhat exaggerated.' So far as social courts were concerned, he was 'firmly convinced' that it would not be 'desirable' to try to establish a separate tribunal to deal with cases under the various Ontario welfare statutes, which had always been administered by 'the one Juvenile Court, a Family Court.' At the same time, he could not 'yet see any solution of the matter.'[25] As for the federal justice department, Deputy Minister Stuart Edwards declined to comment on the CWC

Archambault brief until the Penal Commission had issued its final report (Canada 1938).[26]

Even Robert E. Mills, director of the Toronto Children's Aid Society, who was usually in accord with Whitton about strategy, admitted that he found the proposal in the Archambault memorandum to seek a cooperative arrangement between the Ottawa government and the provinces that would allow the creation of courts in social causes 'a little difficult to visualize.' Furthermore, he said, it was not simply a matter of a federal-provincial accord. It was essential to 'satisfy the legal profession as well,' and there continued to be strong opposition within the legal community to the practice of conferring the powers of a superior-court judge on county-court judges in the establishment of various commissions. Whitton wanted county-court status for the judges who would preside over the proposed courts of social causes, he said, but there were some doubts about the authority of the existing federally appointed county-court judges in relation to alimony and custody since jurisdiction over these questions resided with the superior courts at the time of Confederation. Mills apparently preferred the English system of handling domestic cases within the magistrates' courts that had been implemented following the report of the Harris Committee (Great Britain 1936). Now, he noted approvingly, the courts of summary jurisdiction handled judicial separation, custody of children, adoptions, child-protection cases, and maintenance for wives and children up to a maximum of two pounds a week in desertion cases.[27]

Notwithstanding this pressure from the Toronto Family Court personnel and their allies for council support in the quest to have their appointments confirmed by the federal justice department, both Whitton and W.L. Scott continued to search for an alternative to a defence of the status quo. Scott, however, was willing to accept an interim arrangement whereby the justice department would appoint juvenile-court judges and amend the Juvenile Delinquents Act to give them jurisdiction under the various welfare statutes.[28] C.V. McArthur made a similar proposal. Pending a permanent arrangement, he said, if the provincial welfare laws made provision for hearings before either a county judge or a family-court judge appointed by Ottawa, that might 'settle the difficulty for the time being.'[29]

Responding to Judge Hosking's observation that the federal government had never opposed provincial appointments of juvenile-court judges, W.L. Scott said it was for the courts, not the justice department, to say whether a juvenile-court judge whose appointment was not confirmed by a federal order-in-council was a 'judge' within the meaning of the *Clubine* ruling.[30] Scott also conceded, however, that, despite the provision in the Federal Judges Act (R.S.C., 1927, c. 105, s. 4) requiring judges of superior, circuit, county, or district courts to have been at least ten years at the bar, Ottawa could enact legislation creating an exception to the rule as had been done with the Juvenile Delinquents Act, and 'could, of course, be done in the case of a Family Court, established by the Province presided over by a judge appointed by the Dominion.'[31] None the less, Scott did not favour such a course of action as a long-term solution to *Clubine*.

Nor did Charlotte Whitton, who even opposed the suggestion from her own honorary counsel that the CWC support the interim designation of juvenile- and family-court judges by Ottawa. She doubted, 'with the present attitude to lay judges,' that the council would get 'a sympathetic receipt to this proposal' unless there were a proviso that such judges would be appointed from the bar of the provinces. Indeed, she was 'quite sure that the [necessary legislative] amendment would be opposed by many of the lawyers in the House, even if we could get it past the Department of Justice.' Whitton also felt there was little chance that the provincial attorneys general would support the proposal, 'though Ontario might endorse it in respect to existing judges.'[32] This assessment of the situation was obviously correct. In a subsequent report to Kenneth Rogers of the Big Brother Movement, Toronto, Whitton said that, on the basis of the inquiries made by the council, it seems 'that we are not going to be able to get these extended jurisdictions federally confirmed for Juvenile Courts ... it would have to be for some other type of Court on a broader basis.'[33]

However, given her personal conviction that such matters ought to be handled by lawyer-judges who were legal professionals, Whitton would not likely have pressed very hard for Ottawa to legitimate the extended jurisdiction that the provinces had granted juvenile- and family-court judges. Both she and W.L. Scott clearly shared a certain contempt for the non-professionals presiding over courts of any type. Despite the fact that Whitton had cultivated close relations with the Toronto Family Court, then, her disapproval of lay judges remained very close to the surface.

Her reaction to a comment made by Richard Hosking is typical. In his report to her on the December 1937 meeting where the Ontario attorney general instructed the family-court judges to start sending all cases under the Children's Protection Act, the Children of Unmarried Parents Act, and the Adoption Act to the county courts, Hosking said: 'No one [in attendance] raised the question as to a County Court Judge who is not a Superior Court Judge, having any more authority than a Juvenile Court Judge under these *Acts*.'[34] It was the same point Robert Mills had previously raised with Whitton; to wit, the doubt about the authority of county-court judges to decide questions of custody and alimony since they had not possessed such powers in 1867. When Mills stated his concern, Whitton made no retort, but Hosking was not so fortunate. In a letter to W.L. Scott, Whitton confided that Hosking's observation about county judges seemed 'a little slow on the uptake.' Scott replied in kind: 'It is surprising how long it takes with some people for an obvious point to sink in.'[35]

None the less, despite her oft-stated preference for lawyer-judges of county-court status, at the end of December 1937 Whitton finally focused on Robert Mills's reference to the Harris report (Great Britain 1936). Indeed, with revisionist hindsight, she claimed, in a letter to Justice Middleton, that her objective in the council's Archambault memorandum had been to develop an idea parallel to the British procedures, 'which, within certain definitions and limitations, assign these social causes to the Courts of Summary Jurisdiction.'[36] On the same day, Whitton asked W.L. Scott for technical legal advice, both on the Canadian situation vis-à-vis the *Clubine* Judgment and on the British legislation implemented in the wake of the Harris report.[37] In his analysis, Scott concluded that the English developments were only indirectly helpful in formulating a resolution to the Canadian problem because the ongoing issue of jurisdiction generated by the federal-provincial division of powers in Canada was irrelevant in the British context. Moreover, since he believed that provincially designated justices of the peace and magistrates could not be part of the solution to *Clubine*, Scott proposed either to transfer jurisdiction over family-welfare law to the county courts on a permanent basis or to establish provincial family courts with authority over the various social acts and federally appointed judges.[38]

As Scott was quick to point out, both his suggested alternatives would require more federally appointed and paid judges because, although it was possible for an arrangement to be made whereby Ottawa selected the appointees and the provincial government assumed responsibility for their salaries, 'I should imagine that the Province would be chary of setting a precedent of that nature.'[39] At the same time, Scott remained adamant that the way out of the *Clubine* dilemma did not lie in the lower courts. While the question of whether the provinces had the power to appoint 'judges' under the Juvenile Delinquents Act had never been addressed by any court, Scott said, the issue raised by *Clubine* was not whether a juvenile court was a superior, district, or county court but, rather, if the court's function was judicial or merely ministerial. It was an appreciation of this fact that led Scott to conclude that 'the right of the Province to make the appointments [is] more doubtful than I formerly thought.' Admittedly, the *Clubine* Judgment laid down no rule for distinguishing one type of function from the other, yet 'clearly anything that was previously dealt with by the civil courts would be "judicial."' Consequently, Scott said, although police magistrates exercised jurisdiction and thus performed judicial functions in criminal matters, the *Clubine* decision deemed that, in non-criminal matters, 'the Provincial Legislature is powerless to make use of them.'[40]

Scott's legal analysis formed the basis of another council memorandum, circulated for comment by Whitton at the beginning of January 1938. The earlier emphasis of the Archambault brief, on acquiring judges of county-court status to administer family-welfare law, was retained. There were two alternatives: either federally appointed juvenile-court judges with extended jurisdiction over 'such causes' as the province might assign or county-court judges who would be designated under the Juvenile Delinquents Act and work in special divisions of the county courts that would sit in circuit outside their home communities. The first alternative would require the federal justice department to confirm the extended jurisdiction of sitting judges who had been appointed only under the JDA, and Whitton reiterated her earlier opinion that Ottawa would refuse to do so because many of the judges were non-lawyers and thus ineligible for appointment to 'these county courts.' The second option was more viable, she felt, in that it allowed for 'special consideration of the continuance of existing judges in Juvenile Courts who are lay men [*sic*].'[41]

However, the new council memorandum did not forge any more unanimity within the social-welfare constituency than the Archambault brief. Family-court personnel and their allies could undoubtedly see that the latest CWC proposal would accommodate them temporarily, but ultimately only lawyer-judges would preside in social cases. Moreover, the alternatives worked out by Whitton and Scott were formulated in terms of their primary concern – child protection – whereas they were more interested in the issues of desertion and non-support. Indeed, Whitton found it worrisome that 'the Ontario [attorney general] and Toronto Court people are disposed to resolve this whole thing about the matter of maintenance, whereas we are most gravely concerned about the administration of the *Children's Protection Act*, the *Children of Unmarried Parents Act* and the *Adoption Act* going solely to the [unadapted] County Courts.'[42] Such a policy would be feasible in Toronto and Ottawa, where county courts were located, but a big problem outside the larger urban areas.[43] Thus, although Whitton wanted judges of county-court status to administer family-welfare law, she did not advocate a simple transfer of jurisdiction to the county courts as they were, without the necessary adaptations.

While he shared Whitton's focus on child protection, Robert Mills remained dubious about the council's continued insistence on acquiring judges of county-court status. He seemed to fear that adopting this stance would facilitate a permanent transfer of jurisdiction over child-protection legislation to the county courts, as they were, because the possibility of special adaptations being implemented was very remote. Thus, Mills proposed that the Canadian Welfare Council 'give all the publicity we can, especially in the right quarters, to the need for usable Courts for domestic cases whether magistrates courts or family courts, emphasizing accessibility in terms of location, procedures, cost, etc., as well as special skill.'[44] His comments to Whitton in early January 1938 revealed the dissension that continued to plague the social-welfare constituency in the wake of *Clubine*. They also coincided with mounting apprehension about the seriousness of the situation. Feeling it was vital for the CWC to formulate a representative position on the issue, Whitton called a special board meeting for 24 January 1938 to discuss how that objective might be achieved, and to consider the possibility of the council participating in the Reference to the Supreme Court of Canada, which had been granted at the request of the Ontario attorney general.

'A Bird in the Hand'

Viewed retrospectively, the emergency board meeting clearly marked the turning-point in terms of the CWC position on the *Clubine* case and family courts. The participants accomplished two things. First, they selected a special committee to discuss whether, and under what circumstances, the council might seek to be heard on the Supreme Court Reference initiated by the Ontario attorney general. The committee comprised three lawyers – W.L. Scott; C.V. McArthur, honorary counsel to the council; and J.T. Hackett of Montreal, past president of the organization – as well as Whitton, in her capacity as executive director of the CWC, and Robert Mills, chair of the council's division of child care and protection.[45] Conspicuously absent was any representation from the Family Division of the CWC.

It seems surprising that the committee did not include at least one specialist in domestic affairs, given that the substantive focus of the *Clu-*

bine decision was the administration of the Ontario desertion legislation by the Toronto Family Court. However, the committee reflected the overwhelming focus of the CWC on child protection vis-à-vis husband–wife problems. Moreover, the Family Division of the CWC was very weak. It was not organized until the early 1930s, and, in 1938, still lacked the financial resources to hire a full-time coordinator; these additional factors may explain its lack of input on the *Clubine* issue.[46]

The second, and major, accomplishment of the special board meeting was to hammer out the council position on the family-court question. Everyone in attendance agreed that 'what was desired for the effective use of the Courts as instruments in social adjustments was accessibility and flexibility in procedure, specialization of the presiding officer of the Tribunal in these fields, and unity in the hearing of children's and family cases and cases in the fields of child protection and juvenile and youthful delinquency.' But how were these objectives to be reached? Some participants argued that, if the Supreme Court of Canada upheld the *Clubine* Judgment and, as a result, there were special adaptations of existing county-court facilities for social hearings, 'we might be better served in a few years than at present.' This, of course, was the position presented by Whitton and Scott in the two council memoranda circulated in December and January.

However, others at the meeting felt that 'we might lose something that we knew had worked and not acquire a fully workable system.' Ultimately, the 'bird in the hand' philosophy prevailed. As Whitton subsequently explained to C.V. McArthur, it seemed best 'to argue for the retention of these various powers in the Magistrates' Courts as at present' and, if this strategy was unsuccessful, to explore the possible alternatives at that point (CWC 1938a).[47] In short, the decision reached at the special board meeting was a complete reversal of the one put forth by Scott and Whitton over the previous two months.

So far as council representation at the Supreme Court Reference was concerned, the special committee of five debated the question for a week following the board meeting and had still not reached a decision. In a report to Robert Mills, Whitton revealed that Mr Hackett and Mr Scott were 'of two minds as to whether we really ought to go before the Supreme Court,'[48] and the committee finally agreed that Scott should try to meet privately with the chief justice, Sir Lyman Duff, to ascertain his reaction to the idea of council participation. Since the latter was amenable to having the CWC file a factum, the decision was made to do so.[49]

Although there is no extant correspondence explaining why the council was so hesitant, a major cause of anxiety among the special committee members was likely the question of whether an appearance by the CWC, together with the legal representatives of the attorney general of Canada and the attorneys general of several provinces, would be more of a hindrance than a help to the cause. With a few exceptions (Kanigsberg 1936, 1937/8), lawyers were not particularly receptive to socialized justice. Indeed, Whitton had previously been in contact with the attorneys general of the provinces and found that some of the responses were 'not too good.' She suspected there was 'a fair agreement in some of the provinces to put an end to the Juvenile Court "judges", and a tendency to get all of this into the [unadapted] County Courts.'[50]

For a legal representative from a social-welfare organization to appear at the same hearing as a group of government lawyers was a precedent-setting move, and the Canadian Welfare Council gambled that it would have positive consequences. While she still felt 'we would be better off if the social causes could be routed through the County Courts,' Whitton accepted the agreement reached at the emergency board meeting to fight for retention of the status quo.[51] In a pragmatic turn-about, those charged with preparing the council's factum elaborated a position that stressed the administrative as opposed to the judicial functions exercised by magistrates and family-court judges under the provincial social statutes; emphasized the continuity between magistrates and family-court judges; avoided any hint that lawyers were not socially minded; and refrained from mentioning American innovations while simultaneously playing up English practices.

On the question of the ministerial versus judicial functions of provincial courts, Charlotte Whitton reported to Robert Mills at the end of January 1938 that W.L. Scott felt 'the only hope is the one I have advanced ... in respect to the pre-Confederation jurisdiction in the Magistrates' Courts': to argue the derivation of these powers, 'as from an administrative function, of the Poor Law Guardians' and, then, try 'to establish that the Juvenile Court judges are magistrates under the Federal law [JDA], analogous to magistrates under the *Criminal Code.*'[52] Mills, too, was very keen to adopt this line of argument. Since the theory of 'public interest' was now the distinguishing characteristic of 'custody' and 'alimony' in the lower courts, he maintained, the social statutes enacted by the provinces were representative of a new kind of law where neither crime nor punishment was prominent. Thus, for example, commitment action taken under the Children's Protection Act was indirectly action by the crown, which, in the past, had entailed a quasi-criminal procedure. Although Judge Mott had 'done everything possible to have it recognized as a civil one,' Mills and other like-minded people did not want the commitment action to be designated 'as purely civil' because they might 'thereby force it into the higher courts, or at least out of the courts in which we are interested.'[53]

It was also important that the council factum not alienate the legal community. Accordingly, after discussion with several knowledgeable persons, Whitton made some changes in the memorandum, being prepared for public distribution, which explained the reasons for and implications of the Reference to the Supreme Court. She felt it was crucial 'to avoid any statement or implication of too definite a nature as to the improbability of getting "socially minded" action from members of the Bar.' There was 'quite a feeling on this point,' she said, and it would be a bad tactic to do anything to 'irritate it.'[54] For the same reason, she had 'dragged in the reference to British Adaptations' to accommodate the 'very strong tide running in the Supreme Court against "American innovations or practices", possibly aggravated because of Mr Roosevelt's troubles and attacks on the Supreme Court of the United States.'[55]

Concomitantly with the preparation of its factum (CWC 1938b), the Canadian Welfare Council formulated contingency plans in the event an adverse decision was handed down. If the Canadian Supreme Court reaffirmed the *Clubine* Judgment, Whitton felt the CWC 'must move immediately in [the] direction of County Court status [for judges administering family-welfare law].'[56] She also attempted to arrange a conference in Ottawa at the time of the hearing in the hope that 'we might be agreed among us all – provincial and municipal officials, counsel and social agency executives – as to appropriate action which might be set under way in the respective provinces, looking to this automatic implementing of any possible remedies or safeguards at once, if necessary.'[57] In short, if the Supreme Court upheld *Clubine*, it would be crucial to validate all past adoption, maintenance, commitment, and other orders made by family and magistrates' courts. However, Whitton encountered considerable resistance to such a conference among the attorneys general and even among some of the social agencies. Consequently, only a few people met in Ottawa after the Reference hearing in March 1938.[58]

The policy reversal of the Canadian Welfare Council on the appropriate solution to the *Clubine* dilemma seemingly helped rejuvenate the rapport with family-court personnel and their allies, which had been damaged by the position adopted by the CWC in its Archambault submission. When she sent a copy of the council memorandum on the Supreme Court Reference to Kenneth Rogers, for example, Whitton said she felt all opinions were reconciled in the document. She also took the opportunity to emphasize that the Toronto situation was different from that in every other city because agencies like the Big Brother Movement operated 'practically as part of the Court' while, in other centres, 'the amount of social work done by different agencies in Toronto is absorbed or neglected in the Court itself.'[59]

Whether the family-court personnel shared Whitton's opinion is unknown, since they were apparently excluded from participating in the preparations leading up to the Reference. Whitton later explained that she did not advise the family-court judges in Toronto and Ottawa about the council's plan to be heard on the Reference because of their official positions.[60] Given her long-time antipathy towards Judge McKinley, Whitton's decision was quite understandable. She had never had much contact with him over the years, despite the fact they were both based in Ottawa. Judge Hosking, however, was the central figure in the drama inasmuch as he had issued the original order against Ivan Clubine. He might reasonably have expected Whitton to notify him about the council's plans with regard to the Reference. None the less, family-court personnel had finally received strong CWC support for maintaining the status quo in the administration of provincial social legislation; assistance for which they had been pleading since the initial *Clubine* appeal in the spring of 1937.

The Ontario Attorney General and the Supreme Court Reference

Family-court advocates also obtained vital support from the Ontario government when Gordon Conant unexpectedly requested a Reference before the Supreme Court. In December 1937, the attorney general was forced to reconsider, and ultimately abandon, the interim plan for the administration of family-welfare law adopted by his predecessor the previous summer (see chapter 5). This position shift was the result of a combination of circumstances and reflected several ongoing concerns of the government: to keep welfare expenditures to a minimum; to protect its constitutional rights against federal encroachment; and to alienate as few members of the voting public as possible in the process.

Unfortunately for the province, welfare costs had increased, and were continuing to rise, under its interim policy. Magistrates and family-court judges found it was not nearly as easy to adjudicate cases of wife desertion, using section 242 of the Criminal Code rather than the DWCMA, because the former required a wife to demonstrate that her husband's non-support would cause destitution (see appendix C). Conant himself was still the Oshawa crown attorney when the interim policy was introduced and had experienced firsthand the difficulties posed by the 'destitute and necessitous circumstances' requirement under section 242, although, at the same time, he admitted it was 'the only thing we can fall back on.'[61] Six months later, as attorney general, he had proof to support his earlier misgivings. The results of *Clubine* were 'more serious and widespread than [was] generally realized,' he said, and although magistrates and family-court judges were using the relevant Criminal Code sections in cases of wife desertion, it was 'with less satisfactory results.'[62]

The problem did not lie solely with the use of the Criminal Code to handle new cases of non-support, however. There was also the matter of enforcing all the maintenance orders previously issued by magistrates and family-court judges under the DWCMA. It seems clear that husbands were refusing to pay, default was increasing, and what the municipalities had feared would happen, did. Their costs for maintaining deserted families were beginning to spiral upward by December 1937. Early in the month, York Township Council heard a report from their welfare commissioner about the 'alarming' situation created by the number of deserted families on the relief rolls and the fact that there was no way of forcing husbands and fathers to support their families.[63]

Later that month, the commissioner revealed in a special report that the township was paying six thousand dollars a month for the support of 105 deserted families. Moreover, the numbers were still rising, despite his stipulation that all deserted wives who applied for relief take out a warrant for the arrest of their husbands on desertion charges.[64] A similar situation had developed in East York. In a report to the East York Relief Committee, the relief administrator charged that Ontario laws lent themselves 'to a complete disregard of marriage vows.' There were forty-eight wives and families being supported by the township, most after warrants had been sworn against the husbands, but the warrants were usually ineffective because of a complete failure by police or the family court to enforce the law.[65]

Attorney General Conant agreed that the municipalities, already reeling under relief costs generated by the Depression, had legitimate cause for complaint. During the six months since the *Clubine* Judgment, he admitted, payments under the DWCMA had 'reached the vanishing point.' Wives and children were being 'forced to go on relief, thus disturbing the whole social fabric.'[66] This turn of events would not in itself have generated a complete reappraisal of the policy on the administration of family-welfare law, however. Indeed, the attorney general warned against what seemed to be the modern tendency of social services 'to develop the character of the snowball and to grow at every turn.' The taxpayer, he stressed, must not be burdened 'to the point of exhaustion and extinction.'[67] What really pressured the provincial government to rethink its position, then, was the same catalyst that had forced the Canadian Welfare Council to reappraise its policy – questions about the jurisdiction being exercised by magistrates and family-court judges under the Children's Protection Act, the Children of Unmarried Parents Act, and the Adoption Act.

In the immediate aftermath of the *Clubine* Judgment, the attorney general's department had apparently not anticipated that the authority of the lower courts over provincial social legislation similar to the DWCMA might also be threatened. However, a decision related to the Children's Protection Act, handed down in December 1937, 'further challenged' the powers of juvenile-court judges under social laws and confronted the Ontario government with the reality that, through a combination of 'conscience and convenience' (Rothman 1980), an entire welfare structure had been erected within the magisterial system, the legality of which was suddenly in serious doubt. Attorney General Conant acknowledged the budding crisis in a press release: any question of the jurisdiction of these officials is 'a serious matter [he said], as extensive machinery has been set up to deal with these cases, particularly in Toronto, Hamilton, Ottawa and other centres.'[68]

None the less, at this point Conant still seemed to think that transferring jurisdiction over all the legislation in question to the county courts was the only 'remedy apparent ... although it may mean setting up additional facilities and machinery.' Using an argument reminiscent of the 1920s (see chapter 3), the attorney general presented statistics indicating that, on average, county judges had tried only about one-third the number of cases handled by their counterparts in the superior courts in 1936. Thus, it was 'quite evident' to him that there had to be 'a redistribution of judicial duties ... even at the discomfiture of County Judges.'[69]

Four days after his public announcement of what the future government policy on the administration of family-welfare law would be, Conant contacted the federal Department of Justice to arrange a meeting. His specific objective was to discuss 'ways and means of resolving the difficulty and with a view to a reference to the Supreme Court of Canada on the points involved, if this is deemed necessary.'[70] Ottawa was amenable, and, on 16 December 1937, both Conant and his deputy, I.A. Humphries, reported to the federal officials on the 'serious situation' in

Ontario. Magistrates and juvenile- and family-court officials had made support orders 'running into the thousands,' they said, but, since the validity of those orders had been questioned, it was 'becoming impracticable to enforce them,' and many women and children were not receiving 'the alimony and maintenance payments to which they are entitled.'[71]

The Ontario attorney general's request for a Reference to the Supreme Court of Canada on the constitutional issues raised by the *Clubine* case thus seems to have been motivated primarily by a desire to learn what amendments to the provincial social laws would be required to transfer jurisdiction under those statutes to the county courts. It was not the government's intention to argue in favour of retaining the administration of family-welfare law within the lower courts. This explains Conant's response to the Toronto Family Court judges who had again been urging the attorney general to have their appointments confirmed by Ottawa. Following his December meeting with the justice department officials in Ottawa, Conant said he 'did not think it was necessary,'[72] presumably because the government had decided to shift the administration of family-welfare law out of the magisterial system. Indeed, once the justice department agreed to recommend a Reference, the attorney general was very persistent in his efforts to try to have it argued at the February 1938 sitting of the Supreme Court because he was 'most anxious to deal with any legislation that may be necessary' at the Ontario legislative session scheduled to begin on 23 February.[73]

Ironically, however, the provincial government, like the Canadian Welfare Council, ultimately found itself defending the status quo in the administration of family-welfare law. Although there are no extant documents explaining this strategy reversal, several factors were likely very important. First, the resistance of county-court judges to adjudicating welfare cases, so evident during the 1920s, had probably not diminished a decade later. Thus, just as the Ferguson government had failed in its efforts to shift the administration of social legislation to the county courts following the 1927 Law Revision, so the Hepburn Liberals faced similar opposition from county-court judges in 1937.

A second consideration that undoubtedly pushed Gordon Conant to fight for the continued administration of welfare statutes by the magistrates' and family courts was the increasing acrimony between Premier Hepburn and Prime Minister King. Throughout his political tenure, the former fought tenaciously against any federal proposals that would expand the province's fiscal responsibility in the welfare arena (see chapter 5). Moreover, by 1938, Hepburn was locked in mortal combat with

Ottawa over what he perceived as a direct threat to provincial autonomy, namely, the ongoing deliberations of the Rowell-Sirois Commission (McNaught 1982: 256–7). From his perspective, it was likely preferable to defend and entrench the welfare status quo, which in the main was still heavily financed by the municipalities, before the commission released a report recommending that the provinces relieve local governments of their crushing monetary burden for maintaining the poor.

Still, W.B. Common, who presented the case for the Ontario attorney general at the hearing on the Reference, initially shared the view of departmental solicitors that the *Clubine* Judgment handed down by the provincial Supreme Court would be upheld by its federal counterpart. It was only as the day for the hearing drew near that Common suddenly became 'very optimistic' about his chances of success. He apparently felt that the Supreme Court justices in Ottawa might tend to defend the status quo 'because a change would require more judges and ... because they would fear that the Province might lose interest in the whole business and dump it on their doorstep.'[74] As it turned out, his growing confidence was well-founded.

Judgment Day

Although specifically linked to the questions raised by the Ontario Supreme Court in the *Clubine* decision, the Reference clearly had broad implications for other provinces with similar welfare legislation. Ultimately, the Canadian Supreme Court handed down a unanimous judgment but the unanimity was only slowly achieved. For one thing, the justices had to read and weigh a voluminous amount of material, much of it contradictory. There were the factums of the participants in the Reference; previous cases related to the division of judicial and administrative powers between the federal government and the provinces; and all the family-welfare statutes from the various provinces. In addition, they had to determine which courts in each province had exercised jurisdiction over such matters at the time of Confederation (Williams 1984: 200; see also Dunn 1938).[75]

Most important, however, the Supreme Court had been asked to determine whether the socialization of magisterial justice, which had been in the making since the late nineteenth century in Ontario and other provinces, was legitimate. Two years earlier, with only the chief justice dissenting, the court had declared the Employment and Social Insurance Act, part of then–Prime Minister Bennett's 'new deal' legislation, unconstitutional (Snell & Vaughan 1985: 166; Williams 1984: 186), a decision later upheld by the Judicial Committee of the Privy Council (Struthers 1983: 161). It is understandable, then, why the justices did not reach a unanimous decision on the *Clubine* Reference without considerable debate. Indeed, W.L. Scott, who had presented the factum on behalf of the Canadian Welfare Council, revealed as much in a letter to Robert E. Mills of the Toronto Children's Aid Society in early June 1938. Scott had been 'told privately, [he said] that the judges had been in conference over this case but the discussion had disclosed such sharp differences of opinion between the judges as precluded the possibility of a decision at that time.'[76]

The hearing had been held on 8 March 1938; the fractious discussion described by Scott took place at the beginning of May; and the court finally released its Judgment on 23 June 1938. The Judgment was delivered by the chief justice, Sir Lyman P. Duff, who considered it one of his two greatest judicial achievements (Williams 1984: 180, 199–202). Adopting the same position as the New Brunswick Supreme Court had assumed in *Rex* v. *Vesey*, the justices said that, in the *Clubine* case, the Ontario Court of Appeal had 'not given due weight to the special character of the jurisdiction vested in the courts of summary jurisdiction under the *Deserted Wives' and Children's Maintenance Act*, or to the close analogy between that jurisdiction and the jurisdiction exercised for centuries by Courts of summary jurisdiction in England and Canada.'[77] The DWCMA did not pertain to alimony, as Justice Middleton and his confreres seemed to think. On the contrary, the statute was based on assumptions about 'the obligation of the community and of the husband in the community,' placing the responsibility to care for the deserted wife and children 'on the shoulders of that [individual] ... whose duty it is to the community as well as to his family to bear the burden.'[78]

Turning their attention to the more general question of social-welfare, the Supreme Court justices observed that the 'relief of persons in circumstances in which the aid of the State is required to supplement private charity in order to provide the necessaries of life has become one of enormous importance; and that, primarily, responsibility for this rests upon the Province' since 'constitutional restrictions' made it 'exceedingly difficult' for the federal government to intervene directly in such matters.[79] Furthermore, continued the Judgment, it was entirely within a province's powers 'to put in effect a Poor Law system modelled upon that which prevails in England today' and although Ontario 'had not seen fit to do that ... in some important respects the statutes that we have to consider embody features of the Poor Law system.'[80]

On the issue of whether the province could establish family courts, the Supreme Court Judgment pointed out that the juvenile court was 'beyond all doubt recognized as a properly constituted Court' under the Juvenile Delinquents Act and was, therefore, not a court within the meaning of section 96 of the British North America Act (see appendix D). Moreover, the justices believed it would not be 'seriously disputed' by anyone that magistrates and justices of the peace remained outside the scope of section 96. Therefore, they concluded, a juvenile court did not suddenly become a section 96 type of court 'by virtue of the fact that the officers presiding over it are invested with further jurisdiction of the same character as is validly given to magistrates and justices of the peace.'[81] In short, the Supreme Court of Canada reaffirmed its tendency to support provincial rights and thereby upheld the status quo (Russell 1969, 1987; Snell & Vaughan 1985).

The decision, which the federal justice department did not appeal to the Privy Council (Bradford 1938: 1; Scott 1938b), was a historic one in several respects. It was the first time that counsel for a national welfare organization had appeared alongside government lawyers in a hearing before the Canadian Supreme Court. Although the participants in the Reference, including the Canadian Welfare Council, were not primarily interested in the family court per se, it did provide the substantive focus for the subsequent arguments about whether the lower courts could administer social legislation, particularly when the presiding officers were non-lawyers. More important, the Supreme Court Judgment was precedent-setting because it legitimated the piecemeal, ad hoc implementation of a 'poor law system' in Ontario and other provinces, thus setting the stage for the full development of the Canadian welfare state during the 1940s. At the same time, by settling a question 'of tremendous importance' to Ontario, and of almost equal importance at that time to the other provinces with similar legislation,[82] the high court placed a stamp of approval on the expansion of socialized justice within the magisterial system and set the future course of family-court development in Canada.

The Federal Justice Department and the Supreme Court Reference

The legitimation of the status quo in the administration of family-welfare law could not have occurred without the express cooperation of the federal government, however. Unless the prime minister and his cabinet had formally recommended it, the historic Reference before the Canadian Supreme Court would never have taken place. Thus, two crucial questions require analysis: why the federal government agreed to make such a recommendation, given their acrimonious relations with Mitch Hepburn and the Ontario Liberals, and why Ottawa did not appeal the adverse Judgment of the Supreme Court to the Judicial Committee of the Privy Council in London.

So far as the decision to support the Reference is concerned, the federal justice department not only agreed to plead Ontario's case for a hearing before the cabinet but also acceded to the urgings of the provincial attorney general's department to expedite matters as much as possible. In less than a month, an order-in-council authorizing the Reference was submitted to the registrar of the Supreme Court.[83] The order stated that the 'validity of the [provincial] Acts' was not at issue; the point of dispute centred on 'the authority of the Magistrates and Juvenile Court Judges to act under them without being appointed by the Governor General in Council.'[84]

The Mackenzie King Liberals had several reasons to be cooperative in arranging the Reference. First, they apparently felt that the jurisdictional issues raised by the *Clubine* case were clear-cut and that a Reference would be decided in their favour. Therefore, just as the Ontario attorney general's department initially hesitated to request a Reference because they felt they would lose, so the federal justice department agreed to recommend a hearing because they expected to triumph. Deputy Minister of Justice Stuart Edwards said as much in a draft report to council recommending the Reference, which he submitted to the prime minister: 'So far as the legal considerations are concerned the Dominion will not suffer any disadvantage by acquiescing in Mr Conant's proposal. I feel confident that the judgment of the Court will favour the view that appointments of the kind in question must be made by the Dominion.'[85]

Undoubtedly, Ottawa's willingness to facilitate a Reference also stemmed from the knowledge that, if they did win, they would not have to fear an appeal to the Privy Council by the Ontario attorney general. Conant had agreed that, if the federal cabinet were willing to allow the Reference, he was willing to abide by the decision of the Canadian Supreme Court 'whether favourable or unfavourable to the Province.' His only objective in seeking a hearing before the high court was to clear up the legal points so Ontario could 'bring its legislation into conformity with its constitutional powers.'[86] This guarantee, together with Ontario's agreement to pay for all the printing costs associated with the Reference, apparently convinced the federal government to go ahead.[87]

J.C. McRuer was hired to represent the attorney general of Canada and instructed to prepare a factum that elaborated one major argument: 'Generally speaking, the contention of the attorney general is that the Juvenile Court Judges, Magistrates and Justices of the Peace could not constitutionally be vested with the jurisdiction which the Legislature has purported to vest in them.'[88] However, while the Ontario law officers grew more optimistic over time that the Supreme Court would support the province, their federal counterparts became increasingly less confident that the court would concur with the factum of the attorney general of Canada. At a conference with Deputy Minister of Justice Stuart Edwards following the Reference hearing in March 1938, McRuer 'advised him that, in my opinion, based on remarks from the Bench, the Court would support the legislation' that conferred jurisdiction under social statutes on provincial appointees.[89] When McRuer's prediction proved to be correct, Edwards expressed 'great anxiety lest the result would extend the right of the Provinces to take jurisdiction from the Superior Court and County Court Judges and give it to their own officials, thereby violating the scheme of Confederation.'[90]

None the less, despite the fear articulated by Edwards and the existence of some support for an appeal to the Privy Council, Ottawa did not contest the Judgment of the Supreme Court. Considering the significance of this ruling for the future development of socialized justice, specifically the family court, it is essential to understand why the federal government did not appeal. The decision was not reached easily, taking over two months from the date that the Supreme Court handed down its Judgment. Evidently, the justice department officials gave very careful consideration to the advice of those who favoured an appeal to the Privy Council. The lawyer who had successfully represented Mr Kazakewich before the Alberta High Court, expressed strong support for a federal appeal: the Supreme Court Judgment, he contended, was 'erroneous and ... had been written in such language as will enable the Legislatures of the Provinces, if so disposed, to altogether circumvent the provisions of the *B.N.A. Act.*'[91]

Some members of the judiciary also pressed the federal government to go to the Privy Council. An Ottawa judge wrote Justice Minister Lapointe to stress the 'paramount importance' of the Supreme Court decision, since it dealt 'exhaustively with the competence of Provincial Governments to appoint judicial officers'; and while the Supreme Court Judgment could not interfere with the federal power of disallowance, it was still 'of great moment that the law should be well-defined by judicial authority.'[92]

However, the strongest argument for an appeal came from the man who prepared the factum for the attorney general of Canada and represented the federal government at the hearing on the Reference. A staunch traditionalist, J.C. McRuer was unalterably opposed to any tampering with the division of powers between Ottawa and the provinces under the British North America Act. He felt the Canadian Supreme Court had set a 'very dangerous' precedent because their decision left 'an opening for the Provinces to cut down the jurisdiction of the Dominion by clothing officers appointed by the Provinces, with authority to determine matters that heretofore had been determined by judges appointed and paid by the Dominion.' Thus, it was 'of manifest importance' that the situation not be left in a 'state of confusion' that would encourage the provinces to extend their authority over judicial matters. This was very likely to occur, McRuer emphasized, because Mr Conant had 'already announced in the press that they propose to extend the powers now conferred under these statutes.' To pre-empt such action on the part of the provinces, he called for an appeal by the federal government to the Privy Council to clarify the issues once and for all.[93]

Agitation for the justice department to launch an appeal of the Supreme Court Judgment was counterbalanced by doubt among the departmental lawyers. In July 1938, W.L. Scott informed Charlotte Whitton that, according to the acting deputy of justice, there was disagreement in the government ranks about the merits of an appeal.[94] Later in the month, Whitton told Robert E. Mills of the Toronto Children's Aid Society there was strong pressure on the justice department to appeal 'but we are told that the Minister of Justice [Ernest Lapointe] is himself opposed to it.'[95]

Despite a paucity of detailed information about the debate inside the federal government over the appeal issue, existing documents reveal that there were a number of motivating factors behind Ottawa's eventual decision not to go before the Privy Council. One was the expressed opposition of the Ontario attorney general to such a course of action. Early in July 1938, a justice department lawyer informed Gordon Conant that Mr McRuer was 'not satisfied' with the 'opinions' of the Supreme Court and would probably advise an appeal to the Privy Council. However, because Ontario had requested the Reference, Ottawa first wanted to discover whether the province wished to take the Judgment of the Canadian high court 'as final.' At the same time, the federal lawyer continued, since 'the Dominion also has an interest in the question involved ... the Minister of Justice may desire to appeal notwithstanding your opinion.'[96]

Attorney General Conant was quick to reply: 'We are naturally somewhat surprised and not a little disturbed' at the prospect of a federal government appeal, 'principally because of the delay and expense that would be involved.' While conceding that the final decision was the prerogative of the justice department, he urged the federal law officers to inform him of their decision 'at the earliest possible date.'[97] The attorney general's consternation stemmed no doubt from a realization that the delay caused by a Privy Council appeal would force the provincial government to continue indefinitely its interim, and demonstrably unsatisfactory, arrangements for the administration of social legislation. The attitude of the Hepburn administration on the appeal issue seems to have been a consideration in the eventual decision by the justice department not to contest the Supreme Court Judgment. In a memorandum to Justice Minister Lapointe, for example, F.P. Varcoe pointed out that, while it would be advantageous to obtain a judgment from the court of last resort on questions that had not been settled by the Canadian Supreme Court, Attorney General Conant did not 'consider it desirable' to appeal on this ground.[98]

A second, and probably more persuasive, reason for not challenging the Supreme Court Judgment was the possibility of losing again. Ottawa's own legal representative, J.C. McRuer, acknowledged that a judicial committee decision might be 'to the same effect,' although he also believed that it would be 'very much narrower in its scope and not leave the matter in the confusion that exists.'[99] In his memorandum to Justice Minister Lapointe on the advantages and disadvantages of a federal government appeal, F.P. Varcoe emphasized the potential for a second defeat. While the Privy Council might well agree that maintenance was the same as alimony, he said, the Lords might still decide it could be adjudicated by the lower courts. Moreover, Varcoe added, there would be a tendency for the Privy Council to uphold the various summary jurisdiction statutes relating to welfare because they had existed throughout Canada for several generations.[100]

A third consideration that influenced Ottawa's decision not to appeal the Judgment of the Canadian Supreme Court was the potentially negative consequences of winning. Such a victory might well turn out to be a Pyrrhic one. Thus, although the justice department lawyers firmly believed maintenance to be the equivalent of alimony, they did not really wish to pursue this argument too vigorously because, if successful, it would ultimately cost Ottawa money. What if the Privy Council decided that only federally appointed judges could exercise jurisdiction under statutes dealing with maintenance? Clearly, the justice department would be forced to appoint, and pay, more judges. Ottawa would also have to confront the resistance of higher-court judges to handling the domestic problems of poor people. Even J.C. McRuer, one of the chief proponents of an appeal, admitted that, in terms of the nature of jurisdiction involved in the welfare statutes, he quite agreed it was 'better exercised by the appointees of the province.'[101]

The final, and apparently decisive, factor in Ottawa's decision not to appeal was the disagreement between justice department lawyers and J.C. McRuer over the specific interpretation and implications of the Supreme Court Judgment. The dispute focused on the answers to four questions. First, were the Supreme Court justices saying that, if a court were not a superior or county court, the province might 'clothe it with any jurisdiction it pleases'? McRuer contended that this was the underlying principle of the decision. Justice department lawyers did not come to the same conclusion and pressed McRuer to refer to 'specific passages' in the Judgment that supported his interpretation. Although unable to comply, he remained convinced that the 'whole tenor of the judgment' was towards applying as a test the general character of the court and not whether the jurisdiction exercised was that of a superior court. After considerable deliberation, the justice department lawyers concluded that McRuer's argument would not be convincing to the Privy Council without more precise reference to statements in the Supreme Court ruling.[102]

The second major point of contention between McRuer and the justice department lawyers arose over the question of whether the Canadian Supreme Court Judgment on the Reference was inconsistent with or conflicted with appeal decisions of the Privy Council in previous cases.[103] McRuer asserted that it did. However, the justice department lawyers argued that, since the Supreme Court ruling made no mention of inconsistency or conflict with previous cases, they were very doubtful that such an interpretation could be 'reasonably inferred.' Moreover, the federal government obviously did not want to be placed in a position where they would have to appoint, and remunerate, lower-court officials. As C.P. Plaxton put it: 'I doubt if the Dominion would desire to contend that [magistrates and justices of the peace] must be appointed by the Dominion.'[104]

Still another point of dispute between McRuer and the federal government lawyers centred on the question of whether the jurisdiction exercised by the magistrates' courts at the time of Confederation could be increased. McRuer was inclined towards the view that the powers of these tribunals were permanently fixed in 1867. However, the justice department solicitors noted specific passages in the Supreme Court ruling that affirmed that the jurisdiction of the magistrates' courts could legitimately be expanded. 'This must be correct,' they argued, because almost every year magistrates were empowered 'to deal with new offences.' Moreover, the Deserted Wives' and Children's Maintenance Act merely penalized a husband for not supporting his wife if he could do so; it did not, therefore, extend magisterial powers. Thus, although the justice department lawyers agreed that it would be 'a serious matter' if all new rights and obligations created by legislation could be placed within the jurisdiction of courts presided over by provincial appointees, they did not think the question was 'so decided in this Reference.'[105]

The final contentious issue arising from the Supreme Court Judgment was whether the jurisdiction exercised by magistrates under the DWCMA was similar to the type of jurisdiction traditionally exercised by courts of summary jurisdiction as opposed to the type of courts governed by section 96 of the British North America Act. The Supreme Court said it was. McRuer strongly disagreed. As for the justice department lawyers, they felt the point was of no legal importance. The fact that magistrates elsewhere had exercised similar powers, as, for example, under the English Poor Law, was not 'strictly speaking' relevant in deciding the question of whether Ottawa ought to 'seek to have it held that this legislation is *ultra vires*.' However, after careful consideration, the justice department lawyers concluded that the Supreme Court was correct; the DWCMA was analogous to legislation like the Poor Law, and this was 'a reason for taking no further steps.'[106]

Justice Minister Ernest Lapointe obviously concurred with his departmental solicitors. Moreover, despite his advocacy of a Privy Council appeal, J.C. McRuer was not overly perturbed by Ottawa's official announcement at the end of August 1938 that the government had opted to accept the Supreme Court Judgment. If the provinces now tried to expand their jurisdiction in the way he predicted they would, McRuer said, 'the points in question [would] come before the courts in due course.'[107]

Clearly, as was the case with the Ontario attorney general and the Canadian Welfare Council, an interest in socialized justice or family courts per se played no role in the deliberations of justice department lawyers about a possible appeal. Their sole concern was the constitutional division of legal powers between Ottawa and the provinces and whether the latter had usurped powers not granted them under the British North America Act. None the less, the decision not to appeal the Supreme Court Judgment, which legitimated the status quo in the administration of family-welfare law, effectively entrenched both the principles and concrete manifestations of socialized justice.

CHAPTER SEVEN

Rehabilitating Deviant Families in Ontario: From Police Courts to Family Courts

> Reform movements tend to disown those movements which come before them. They depend in their appeal upon fostering the belief that what they advocate is new.
>
> W.L. Morton (1950: viii)

> The family is the basic unit of society and out from it flows the renewal of all social and national life. One can conceive of no more important task than the protection of little children through the safe-guarding of family life. This is the high mission of a Family Court.
>
> R.S. Hosking (1930: 3)

Social-welfare reformers always promote innovations aimed at the marginal with the intention of 'doing good' and as if the reforms they advocate are totally new and much superior to the status quo. Thus, family courts were touted as more humane, effective, and economical mechanisms than the traditional police courts for regulating those families who failed to meet middle-class standards of child-rearing and domestic life. However, an examination of how Ontario's socialized courts operated during the interwar years reveals that these tribunals failed to fulfil the promises of their advocates. Juvenile and family courts did not decriminalize domestic cases, nor did they produce a marked reduction in social problems and the cost of regulating marginal populations. On the contrary, socialized courts served the same clientele and performed the same functions as the police courts, continuing to act as moral watchdogs and debt collectors for a certain segment of the poor.

At the same time, socialized tribunals were very different from the police courts in the way that they reproduced, or attempted to reproduce, desired class and gender relations in deviant families. Juvenile and family courts formed the carceral core of an emergent private, technocratic justice system in which non-lawyer experts, particularly social workers, worked to 'normalize' intrafamilial relations among the marginal, using socialized legal coercion rather than direct repression. The major effect of the new system was to extend state control over a greater number of the working and dependent poor than was previously possible, albeit sometimes with the cooperation and to the benefit of those who were 'done to.' Thus, socialized justice turned out to be a more effective way of policing the underclasses in twentieth-century liberal democracies.

Family Courts as Police Courts in Another Guise

The analysis of Ontario's pioneer juvenile and family courts between 1920 and 1940 suggests that, in some ways, they were simply revamped versions of the police tribunals so far as the administration of family-welfare law was concerned. The question, then, is why socialized tribunals did not deliver the more humane, effective, and economical alternative to the traditional police courts reformers had envisaged. For example, advocates of socialized courts were convinced that these tribunals would decriminalize, and thereby humanize, domestic proceedings. They did not. Yet, for a number of reasons, this failure seems completely predictable.

First, most of the early juvenile and family courts were special divisions of existing magistrates' courts, where full-time police magistrates doubled as part-time judges. A 1942 report by the Canadian Welfare Council on the state of juvenile-court development in Canada noted that, of the nineteen Ontario juvenile- and family-court judges, twelve exercised other jurisdiction as police magistrates and four as stipendiary magistrates (Canadian Welfare Council [CWC] 1942: 19; see also Laycock 1943: 1). Even in Toronto and Ottawa where juvenile and family courts were independent of the police courts, they were still created through the extension of magisterial jurisdiction, and the judges were *ex officio* magistrates. This situation was problematic for the judge, continued the report, 'in that it requires a considerable adjustment after dealing with cases in an adult [criminal] court to handle children's cases in a court which calls for an entirely different approach' (CWC 1942: 41). Obviously, the same conflict would occur in domestic cases. It was unrealistic to expect a police magistrate to switch automatically from an adversarial to an inquisitorial frame of mind when he was handling family matters.

Moreover, many workers in the early juvenile and family courts had acquired an adversarial approach to social problems through their previous service in the police and/or the military. A good number of the court personnel hired in the 1920s and 1930s were veterans of the First World War. Indeed, this hiring pattern had not changed appreciably when war erupted again. For example, one of the judges appointed to the Toronto Family Court during the Second World War had previously sat as a military judge. Similarly, when the Toronto court began operations in 1929, all the police personnel attached to the women's court who had been handling maintenance collections under the Deserted Wives' and Children's Maintenance Act, including Sgt David Goodwin of the Morality Division, were simply transferred to the new court.[1]

The fact that most of the early juvenile and family courts were located in or near police departments also militated against the decriminalization of proceedings. The Canadian Welfare Council found that, by the early 1940s, only four socialized courts in Ontario had special accommodation entirely removed from the police court. Of the remainder, six courts met in separate rooms, either at the regular police court or in official municipal buildings; five conducted hearings in the judges' (usually police magistrates') chambers; three used the regular police courtroom at different hours from other hearings; and one used the local Children's Aid Society office (ibid: 18). On this issue, the CWC report commented: 'The letter of the law has been observed but too often the atmosphere of the police court remains. It is not necessary to spend money in order that juvenile court hearings may be held in a place where there is no police court associations [sic] whatsoever' (ibid: 39).

However, even if the desired personnel, facilities, and resources had been forthcoming, the nature and legislative mandate of socialized tribunals presented insurmountable obstacles to the decriminalization of family-welfare cases. No matter how hard court personnel tried to transform domestic cases into civil hearings, juvenile and family courts remained, at best, quasi-criminal tribunals. They exercised jurisdiction over several Criminal Code sections pertaining to family relations, and the provincial social legislation they administered was enforced through quasi-criminal procedures delineated in the Summary Convictions Act.

Under the Deserted Wives' and Children's Maintenance Act (DWMCA), for example, men were summonsed to the court; the summons was generally delivered by a police officer; and defaulters could be, and were, incarcerated. The Toronto Family Court increasingly issued maintenance orders with a jail threat attached for non-compliance. In 1936, there were 29 'pay or go to jail' orders issued; by 1945, partly because of the war, the number had jumped to 365 (Toronto Family Court [TFC] 1936, 1945).

Juvenile and family courts may not have decriminalized domestic hearings, but their proponents also expected them to be more effective and economical alternatives to the traditional police courts for the administration of family-welfare law. If effectiveness is gauged in terms of recidivism, however, the new tribunals did not produce a marked reduction or elimination of social problems. As the annual court reports attest, desertion, delinquency, and non-support continued to flourish during the interwar years, despite reformers' predictions that a community approach to deviancy and dependency would keep nuclear family units intact and thereby contribute to a diminution of such evils. For example, it seems clear from the Toronto Family Court reports that the slight drop in court hearings pertaining to non-support during the 1930s was more the result of economic depression than the application of socialized procedures or an emphasis on deinstitutionalization: 'The decrease in non-support cases is readily explained by the fact that so many men are unemployed through no fault of their own and *it is futile to charge them with non-support*' (my emphasis; TFC 1931: 17).

However, the claim of reformers that socialized courts would provide a more centralized and, therefore, more efficient system than the traditional police courts for collecting maintenance monies was borne out to some extent. The juvenile and family courts, whether independent of or socialized divisions within the police courts, amassed considerable sums of money, most of which was the result of support orders. During the 1920s, for example, Magistrate Margaret Patterson created an improved system of maintenance collection in the Toronto Women's Court; between 1922 and 1929, the number of support cases remained the same but the amount of money collected through the court increased fourfold.[2] In 1929, the Toronto Family Court inherited and continued her system. Indeed, Judge Mott continually emphasized the fact that the monies collected by the court exceeded the annual expenditures for running it (see table 1).[3]

None the less, in the absence of effective enforcement machinery, family courts were probably no more successful overall than the traditional police courts in preventing men from defaulting on support orders. During the interwar period, family-court officials constantly reiterated the need for more money 'to bring such criminals to justice'

TABLE 1

Monies collected by the Toronto Family Court, 1920–1940

(percentage of total in parentheses)

Year	Support[a]		Other[b]		TOTAL
1920	5,721.00	(66.0)	2944.60	(34.0)	8,665.60
1922	12,711.15	(74.3)	4405.66	(25.7)	17,116.81
1924	19,517.75	(82.4)	4171.68	(17.6)	23,689.43
1926	22,136.67	(84.4)	4101.40	(15.6)	26,238.07
1928	22,888.35	(82.4)	4896.62	(17.6)	27,784.97
1929[c]	99,830.88	(96.5)	3632.68	(3.5)	103,463.56
1930	179,806.00	(98.7)	2301.00	(1.3)	182,107.00
1932	155,956.27	(99.3)	1043.03	(0.7)	156,999.30
1934	170,264.87	(99.7)	425.09	(0.3)	170,689.96
1936	185,140.00	(99.0)	844.01	(1.0)	186,984.01
1938	207,932.00	(99.1)	1836.52	(0.9)	209,768.52
1940	225,222.21	(99.2)	1728.21	(0.8)	226,950.42

Source: Toronto Family Court, Annual Reports, 1920–40

a Wives, parents, children

b Includes industrial school fees, fines, restitution, bail, and appeal costs

c Family Court began operation on 1 July 1929.

(Balharrie 1929: 83), but the tepid state response to such pleas reflected the constant jockeying between the province and the municipalities to evade financial responsibility for deserted families. The trouble and expense of locating, bringing back, and prosecuting the deserter and the cost of maintaining dependents during the search and the period of adjustment were still regarded 'as the direct responsibility of private philanthropy' (Canadian Conference on Social Welfare 1928: 55).

Consequently, although local councils and relief officials constantly bemoaned the 'soft' treatment of deserting husbands and 'the appalling failure on the part of family court officials to enforce the law,' particularly during the Great Depression, they were unwilling to expend much money for tighter enforcement of the law.[4] Civic governments might at times provide small sums to help family-court officials trace deserters who were being sought for trial, but the funds allotted were a pittance.[5] Similarly, while the province amended the DWMCA in 1934 to make provincial funds available for enforcing the statute when a complainant was unable to pay, in practice the only funds for locating and returning the absconders came either from the complainant (rarely) or from private charities and social agencies. Moreover, even if a deserter was located, the only options open to the magistrate were jail or suspended sentence, and since offenders on probation frequently absconded, both options meant that the cost of maintaining the man's dependants was often borne by private-sector social-work organizations as well (Canadian Conference on Social Welfare 1928: 55).

None the less, despite the considerable success of both the provincial and local governments in evading fiscal responsibility for socialized courts during the interwar period, state expenditure for juvenile and family courts, over and above that entailed by the police courts, did increase, either directly or indirectly. For example, as a state-supervised child-welfare bureaucracy emerged in Ontario, the province assumed greater financial responsibility for the Children's Aid societies (Jones & Rutman 1981: 148). By 1927, the Children's Protection Act (S.O., 1927, c. 78, s. 3) specifically stated that the salaries not only of the superintendent of neglected and dependent children but also of 'such other officers and servants as may be deemed necessary' would be paid from money 'appropriated by the Legislature for that purpose, or partly out of money appropriated for children's aid work.' Since many of the local CAS superintendents acted as official probation officers for the juvenile and family courts, the government was clearly making indirect contributions to the payment of court expenses.

Moreover, the province contributed direct, albeit minimal, financial aid to the family courts in Ottawa, Toronto, and Hamilton. By 1942, the Ontario government was paying the salaries of two adult probation officers, attached to the Ottawa Family Court, as well as one-half of the judge's. Similarly, by 1944, the province was assuming the fiscal responsibility for three probation officers and a clerk working in the domestic-relations division of the Toronto Family Court. In Hamilton, the provincial government appointed the first adult probation officer in 1929 and added an assistant officer in 1936 when the court's jurisdiction was extended to the County of Wentworth.[6]

At the municipal level, local governments were always required to provide the attorney general with written acceptance of fiscal responsibility for a socialized court before the province would issue the requisite order-in-council (see chapter 4). However, civic administrations managed to keep costs down because police-court personnel frequently doubled as the juvenile-court staff without additional remuneration; some judges received only a small honorarium; many probation officers were paid by private social agencies such as the Big Brother Movement, and the Children's Aid Society; and Children's Aid Society shelters for neglected children were often used as detention homes for delinquent children (CWC 1942: 18–22; see also Brett 1953; Laycock 1943).

At the same time, municipalities did increasingly provide money, over and above their police-court expenditure, for the operation of socialized tribunals. By 1942, eight juvenile and family courts in Ontario had salaried probation officers unassociated with the local Children's Aid Society, although only the senior probation officers in the larger courts earned good salaries; six courts had paid judges; and five courts had special provision and staff for detention homes. Moreover, even when a CAS shelter or boarding home was used as a juvenile-court detention home, the municipality still had to compensate the Society at a per-capita per-diem rate (CWC 1942: 19).

Local governments also contributed to the maintenance costs of children who became CAS charges under the Children's Protection Act. After the act was amended in 1913 (S.O., 1913, c. 62, s. 13, ss. 2), the municipal corporation was able to recover those maintenance costs from the parents of the children involved but, if the parents would not or could not pay, the municipality was wholly liable for such maintenance. Thus, the CWC survey found that, while the amount of money expended on socialized courts was 'greatly below' the maximum permitted each district under Ontario's Juvenile and Family Courts Act, total court expenditure reached substantial, if modest, proportions for all the family courts as well as the London and Windsor juvenile courts (1942: 19, 22, 44).

Overall, then, the available evidence indicates that socialized tribunals did not constitute a dramatically more humane, effective, and economical alternative to the traditional police courts of the province for the processing of domestic cases. On the contrary, juvenile and family courts continued to serve the same clientele and functions as the police courts. With respect to the people being judged, for example, 'the respectable and wealthy classes rarely appeared' in the Toronto Police Court (Homel 1981: 176; see also Ontario 1921: 13) and this situation did not change with the establishment of juvenile and family courts. The new socialized tribunals were widely perceived as courts for the 'more unfortunate classes.'[7] The Judgment of the Ontario Supreme Court in *Clubine* was certainly based on this perception. Although they upheld the challenge to family-court powers on legal grounds, the justices also lauded the expertise of the Toronto Family Court judges in handling domestic disputes among people 'in ... the humbler walks of life, in which the element of expense has always proved a stumbling block' ([1937] 68 CCC 333).

Since those adjudicated under social laws in the juvenile and family courts were invariably from the lower social strata, questions related to alimony, guardianship, and adoption as they affected the working and dependent poor were increasingly decided in those courts, as they had previously been adjudicated in the regular police courts. Socialized tribunals thus perpetuated a dual system of family law, similar to that in England, in which the heirs to property were constituted as 'legal subjects' through the higher courts while the propertyless typically confronted the legal system through the magistrates' courts (Fitz 1981a, 1981b; Russell 1987: c. 9).

Juvenile and family courts also carried out the same activities as the traditional police courts with respect to domestic cases; that is, they continued to supervise the morality of and to operate as debt collection and enforcement agencies, particularly in relation to the DWMCA, for a certain segment of the working and dependent poor (Chunn 1987). The annual reports of all the family courts in Ontario during the interwar years clearly reveal that the majority of offences resulting in formal hearings for adults were either morality or support related. As table 2 shows, for example, most adults who appeared before the Toronto Family Court during that period were there for breaches of middle-class behavioural standards that made them 'bad' role models for children or because they had failed to maintain their dependents.

None the less, despite the obvious continuities between the traditional police courts and family courts, the two types of tribunal differed sharply in the way they attempted to inculcate the class and gender norms incorporated in the middle-class family model among the working and dependent poor.

Family Courts and Socialized Justice

Upholding the Cult of Domesticity

In contrast to police courts, the new domestic-relations courts were guided by an explicit emphasis on the rehabilitation of families when the reality of home life blatantly contradicted the middle-class ideal; specifically, where one or more members deviated from their 'natural' roles within the domestic unit and/or where the nuclear unit as such did not exist because the husband/father was absent through desertion, incapacitation, or death. Thus, the emphasis of family-court workers on policing morals and collecting support money for dependent women and children was directly linked to their conceptualization of the family as

TABLE 2

Offences bringing adults to Toronto Family Court, 1920–1940:
formal court hearings

Year	Contrib. drink M	Contrib. drink W	Contrib. other[a] M	Contrib. other[a] W	Contrib. truancy M	Contrib. truancy W	Non-support M	Non-support W	Assault M	Assault W	Other[b] M	Other[b] W	TOTAL
1920[c]	44		156		50		NC		NC		34		284
1922	32	10	149	82	62	47	103	8	NC		115	11	619
1924	84	16	220	70	19	19	99	6	NC		262	12	807
1926	120	21	203	83	73	72	78	15	NC		18	13	696
1928	150	19	189	78	237	225	73	7	NC		15	11	1004
1929[d]	172	17	353	165	112	156	376	12	NC		18	16	1397
1930	178	30	340	207	105	103	751	5	71	4	30	13	1837
1932	66	9	135	28	56	65	577	9	39	3	13	13	1013
1934	42	3	95	14	66	74	510	0	44	1	1	1	851
1936	62	9	107	13	78	56	456	1	54	1	2	0	839
1938	70	4	106	13	59	57	410	4	101	1	16	1	842
1940	65	4	86	2	17	0	728	0	84	0	29	0	1015

Source: Toronto Family Court, Annual Reports, 1920–40

a Contributing to neglect/delinquency through immorality, bad language, gambling, disorderly conduct, vagrancy

b Includes affiliation cases (1922–4), threatening, contributing to property offences, violation of suspended sentence or probation

c 1920 figures not broken down by sex.

d Toronto Family Court began operation on 1 July 1929.

one based on a biological division of labour that had led to the creation of separate, but equal, spheres inhabited by each member of the domestic unit (Gavigan 1988; Poster 1978; Thorne & Yalom 1982; Zaretsky 1976). In keeping with these assumptions about the family, Toronto Family Court personnel operated with an overriding belief that the monogamous, heterosexual nuclear family unit was the only appropriate environment for children. Thus, the sole guarantee children would turn out well (and that society would continue) was for them to grow up with two parents who were suitable role models.

The following comment by a probation officer is typical of those which appeared in the annual reports of the Toronto court: 'Everyone believes that a happy marriage and a wholesome family life is the very cement of our society. Too many broken homes and unhappy marriages

are a menace and if they become too great in proportion to the successful marriages our society is in grave danger of crumbling' (TFC 1937: 17).
'Successful' marriages were those in which husband and wife adhered
to the requirements of their respective roles and the family unit operated 'naturally,' that is, on the basis of consensus. Conflict in a family
developed only when members refused or were unable to carry out their
responsibilities.

It is hardly surprising, then, that probation officers and other workers in the Toronto Family Court placed inordinate emphasis on keeping parents together 'for the sake of the children.' The 'best interests'
of children were badly served if their mother and father separated, 'for
the moulding of a child's life, so that he will grow up to be a worthy
citizen, must receive the combined good influence of the parents' (TFC
1921: 18). Confronted with domestic conflict between a husband and
wife, probation officers in the Toronto Family Court invariably attempted to convince the parents to reconcile and to assume their 'proper' roles
for the future well-being of their offspring. The wife, however, was often viewed as more culpable than the husband in such situations. Probation officers seemingly believed that, if a woman were carrying out
her responsibility to maintain a good home, her husband would have
nothing to complain about. Thus, in the Toronto Family Court, workers concentrated a great deal of energy 'on preventing conditions becoming so serious in the home *that the man feels like deserting*' (my emphasis;
TFC 1934: 18).

The following case is illustrative of how family-court personnel operated. A woman complained to a Toronto court worker that her husband had locked her and the children out of their house. When contacted by the probation officer, the man lodged a counter-complaint that
his wife was not fulfilling her responsibilities because she worked eve-
nings outside the home, the children were being neglected, and he was
even forced to make his own dinner. Locking her and the children out
was a strategy, he maintained, to make his wife 'come to her senses, give
up her work and keep house for him and the children and to live hap-
pily together' (TFC 1920: 20). The officer responded by calling both the
husband and the wife to his office, where he underlined the negative impact of their quarrelling on the children and emphasized how detrimental their living apart would be for the son and daughter.

This approach effected what the probation officer considered a successful resolution of the case: 'My appeal seemed to touch the heart
string, and immediately there was a change of attitude towards each

other. The wife decided to give up her work and go home with her husband, the latter promising to treat his wife properly in the future and to make a nice home for her and the children' (ibid).

However, while conciliation and mediation were preferred methods of resolving domestic difficulties, Toronto Family Court personnel would, in the last resort, sanction those who failed to meet their moral–fiscal obligations. Indeed, moral supervision and debt collection were often intertwined. Thus, men who abandoned their economic obligation to the family through desertion were considered particularly reprehensible by court workers, despite their tendency to blame the wife for an absconding husband. They believed a deserter was 'usually a weak individual' unable to 'face his domestic responsibility,' who lacking 'the will power or strength of character to make a plan for his family [ran] away' (TFC 1934: 18).

The court, then, was principally concerned with forcing the male provider to engage in legitimate labour, avoid expensive habits, and maintain his dependents. After a deserted woman contacted the family court, the chief probation officer almost always acted as 'the complainant against the father.' Seemingly, many such cases were satisfactorily concluded and the home 'finally rehabilitated through the father finding out that he must meet his obligation' (TFC 1922: 8).

At the same time, so far as a wife was concerned, the court officials made their assistance contingent on her adherence to the monogamous, chaste stereotype of the 'good' wife. The morality clauses of the desertion and other family-welfare legislation were stringently enforced.[8] Thus, if a wife were deemed blameless in situations of desertion and non-support/default, the judge would readily issue a maintenance order, and, if necessary, probation officers would try to help her track the husband down and collect support monies. During the Second World War, for example, when there were many applications for maintenance orders from wives whose husbands were at war, the Toronto Family Court responded on the following basis: 'There would seem to be no good reason why, when a man elects to serve his country, his wife, *provided her conduct is not open to criticism*, should be debarred from receiving the usual amount of pay and separation allowances' (my emphasis; TFC 1941: 11). However, if a wife defied the double standard by committing 'uncondoned adultery,' either with a live-in lover after her husband's desertion or through extramarital affairs, court personnel considered that she 'had forfeited any right of support from her husband,' although they would try to obtain maintenance for dependent children (TFC 1923: 8).

In enforcing parental roles, court workers operated on the assumption that children were the future of the nation, and when parents did not carry out their responsibilities, children could be both threatening to and threatened by adults. When natural parents failed to provide material necessities, set appropriate moral standards, and otherwise follow middle-class standards of child-rearing, the court would step in. In most cases, probation officers first implemented a 'program of strict supervision' and parents were 'ordered by the Court to straighten up and fulfill their obligations' (TFC 1924). If they did not comply, charges were laid. The contributing clause of the Juvenile Delinquents Act gave the juvenile and family courts exceptionally wide latitude in their policing of morality among the lower orders. Thus, adults were sometimes hauled into court for contributing to delinquency by using bad language and by living in common-law relationships.

Enforcement of the contributing clauses of the Juvenile Delinquents Act took up a large portion of the court's time (see table 2), especially prior to 1929 when, of the adults brought to court, 'nearly all were fathers and mothers who were rendering their homes unfit for their children by habitual drunkenness, immorality or other vices' (TFC 1925; see also 1922: 16).[9] Men and women were prosecuted for somewhat different (e.g., gender-based) reasons, however. Women who drank too much, had frivolous or corrupting habits, or were actively sexual outside a marriage relationship were censured for not adhering to their asexual homemaker/caregiver role within the family. It is noteworthy, for example, that mothers were brought before the Toronto Family Court almost as frequently as fathers during the interwar years for contributing to the truancy of their children, probably because truant children were perceived to be evidence that they were flouting their maternal function and allowing the children to run wild. Since it was a mother's proper place to be at home, she had the major responsibility for making sure her children attended school. In contrast, men who gambled or were habitually drunk or promiscuous were sanctioned by the court primarily because they frittered away their money and could not provide for their families who thereby ended up as state charges; personal immorality was an important but secondary factor.

As table 3 reveals, parents also found themselves in court for violations of the neglect–dependency clauses in the Children's Protection Act (CPA). Toronto Family Court officials acknowledged the difficulty of making wardship decisions, especially when 'parents [were] anxious to retain their children.' However, if parents continued to place their children at risk, the latter were taken away from them and placed in an appropriate foster home under the supervision of a Children's Aid So-

TABLE 3

Disposition of neglected-child cases by the Toronto Family Court, 1920–1940

Year	Permanent wards	Temporary wards	Temporary wards made permanent	Withdrawn/ adjourned dismissed	Other	Total
1920	130	NC[a]	NC	52	31	213
1922[b]	268	NC	NC	51	0	319
1924	273	NC	NC	20	0	293
1926	371	NC	NC	38	0	409
1928[c]	155	97	0	73	0	325
1929	74	112	40	93	0	319
1930	91	238	30	73	3	435
1932	142	232	67	56	21	518
1934	153	170	86	30	13	452
1936	69	158	23	34	35	319
1938	55	138	17	10	12	232
1940	62	129	29	31	9	260

Source: Toronto Family Court, Annual Reports, 1920–40

a NC = not a category

b Figures for permanent wards 1921–8 include children adopted as well as those placed under the jurisdiction of the Children's Aid Society.

c Revision of Children's Protection Act in 1927 included creation of 'temporary ward' and 'temporary ward made permanent' categories.

ciety. Following the 1927 revision of the CPA, such a wardship might initially be temporary and could end with the child being returned to his or her natural home if the parents mended their ways. But, in cases where the biological parents remained wholly inadequate in the opinion of court officials, either the CAS wardship became permanent or the child was put up for adoption.

When children directly threatened the morality and property of middle-class society through delinquency (e.g., theft, truancy, sexual promiscuity), juvenile and family courts would act to ensure the future protection of society by focusing on the resocialization of juvenile offenders in their proper roles. This resocialization might entail placing a child on probation or providing substitute or supplementary adult role models such as probation officers, Big Brothers, or Big Sisters. As a last resort, children would be placed in training schools or sent to farms for their own good and that of society.

In general, attempts to rehabilitate delinquents involved persuading them to adapt themselves to society by adhering to the class and gender values incorporated in the Protestant ethic and familial ideology and accepting their status as 'forced dependents': 'While on probation, the boy must report regularly, be in at regular hours at night and bring report cards of his school work and conduct to his Probation Officer. It is not a punishment, nor is it letting the boy off. It is an earnest effort on the part of the Probation Officer to stimulate the good in the boy so that the bad will disappear' (TFC 1934: 19). For personnel in the Toronto court, a successful case was one where the delinquent became 'neat and tidy ... and clean,' attended school regularly, and received 'excellent reports' from teachers and guardians or parents (TFC 1924).

Overall, the early family courts in Ontario worked hard to repair and maintain nuclear family units in danger of disintegration, using mediation and conciliation if possible and reserving overt coercion for the 'incorrigible' cases. Through moral supervision and debt collection, family-court officials attempted to buttress the ideology of 'the family' among that section of the population most immune to it. Indeed, some Toronto court personnel almost seemed grateful for the 1930s Depression because it made their work easier. Mass unemployment meant lower desertion rates. Consequently, there was 'a definite swing back to the accepted standards of morality and family life,' which had been abandoned in the 'period of high wages and luxurious living' following the First World War when 'all the old standards were questioned and new ideas of companionate marriage, unfaithfulness to the marriage vow, etc., were advocated' (TFC 1931: 17).

In upholding the cult of domesticity, then, juvenile and family courts helped reproduce the class and gender divisions that make up the status quo in Western market societies. At the same time, the socialized methods and procedures employed by juvenile- and family-court personnel in their work ultimately created a new private, technocratic justice system for the administration of family-welfare law in Ontario.

The Emergence of Private Technocratic Justice

The traditional police courts did not process domestic cases any differently from other cases. Magistrates operated on the basis of open hearings, adversarial procedures, and, in the larger urban centres, some legal training. In contrast, socialized tribunals emulated the privacy of the family; justice was dispensed at closed hearings, often by non-legal, 'expert' personnel utilizing inquisitorial procedures. The result was the genesis of a 'tutelary complex' (Donzelot 1980) or 'welfare sanction' (Garland 1981) during the interwar years in Ontario. The emergent private, technocratic justice system followed two lines of development: the socialization of personnel and procedures *within* the juvenile and family courts and the establishment of a relationship *between* the courts and outside organizations concerned with child and family-welfare among the working and dependent poor.

Socialization within juvenile and family courts was linked to a conception of such tribunals as the public equivalent of the private family. Court personnel assumed that, since members of healthy families experienced no fundamental conflicts of interest, when families were troubled, litigious hearings rooted in an adversarial model of criminal justice would be counter-productive to the rehabilitation process (Hosking 1930: 2). Thus, a de-emphasis on clients' legal rights and a focus on decriminalized proceedings were required.

In regard to the former, the family courts administered social legislation that curtailed the legal rights of the nineteenth-century patriarchal husband/father within the privacy of the home; that is, he no longer enjoyed complete freedom in law to regulate internal family relations (Ursel 1986; see also chapter 2). Instead, various state representatives, including juvenile- and family-court judges, probation officers, and social workers, were accorded the legal prerogative to intervene directly in family life under certain circumstances.[10]

It is hardly surprising, then, that socialized courts were increasingly private and inquisitorial in their operations or that clients' legal rights were deemed to be irrelevant, even impediments, to the satisfactory resolution of domestic cases. Justice may well have been done within the new tribunals, but it was more and more invisible. During hearings, closed to the media and general public, defendants almost never had counsel, applicants were generally not fully aware of their legal rights, and decisions were not open to review (Allard 1972: 6).

So far as the attempt to decriminalize proceedings was concerned, Ontario family-court personnel transformed what was a clear-cut exercise of criminal jurisdiction by police magistrates into a more subtle exercise of quasi-criminal authority. Throughout most of the nineteenth century, the police courts had sanctioned members of deviant families only when they committed specific criminal offences. In the Toronto Police Court, for example, although Magistrate George Denison frequently expressed his moral censure of defendants through overt racial or political comments, he never meted out punishment for immoral behaviour unless it was the direct result of a criminal transgression. Indeed, Denison strongly opposed 'moral reform campaigns to curb the lower orders' and accused perpetrators of such actions 'of trying to force cruel and drastic punishment upon certain classes of the criminal population who offended their tender susceptibilities' (Homel 1981: 182).

Family-court personnel took a very different approach, however. In Toronto, as in other Ontario jurisdictions, many people were brought to court because they had violated particular middle-class mores incorporated in the federal Juvenile Delinquents Act and the various pieces of provincial social legislation administered by socialized tribunals. Thus, children were strenuously prosecuted for status offences such as truancy and adults for contributing to delinquency. Men were prosecuted for desertion and non-support, under the provincial Deserted Wives' and Children's Maintenance Act rather than the relevant Criminal Code sections. None the less, since the JDA and provincial social statutes carried criminal penalties, by attempting to decriminalize proceedings, family courts succeeded only in obscuring the civil–criminal distinction without eliminating it. The blunting of the differentiation between criminal and non-criminal in socialized tribunals meant that growing numbers of children and adults were subject to criminal sanctions for the commission of acts with which they could or would not have been charged by magistrates in the traditional police courts.

More important, many children and adults never appeared at a formal hearing before a family-court judge. Why was this so? First, informal processing of domestic cases was one way for court personnel to decriminalize proceedings, that is, to ignore the reality that the domestic-relations court was at best a quasi-criminal tribunal. Second, court workers saw as their task not only the diagnosis and treatment of troubled families to restore harmony but also the prevention of potential problems through early detection. The backbone of this preventive work, and indeed of the entire system of socialized justice, was the informal, out-of-court settlements mediated by the probation departments of the various courts, which were known as 'occurrences.'

Over the years, as table 4 reveals, the number of occurrences processed by the Toronto Family Court increased to the point where they constituted the bulk of work done by probation officers and social workers. By 1936, the Probation Department estimated that about 50 per cent of occurrences involved the unofficial settlement of domestic problems (TFC 1936: 15). Probation officers believed that the 'mere recounting of trouble to a sympathetic person [was] a help' and that of the couples advised by them 'reconciliations and settlements were reached in 89 per cent of these cases' (ibid). By 1940, about 2,300 people a month on average were approaching the court for this informal type of assistance (TFC 1940: 10).

TABLE 4

Occurrences processed by Toronto Family Court, 1920–1940

| Year | Adults | | | | | Children | Total |
	Contrib-uting[a]	Non-support[b]	Desertion/neglect	Domestic problems	Assault[c]		
1920	7	39	125	57	40	687	955
1922	244	272	93	74	2	1068	1753
1924	195	129	60	61	68	730	1243
1926	143	100	39	48	108	1198	1636
1928	153	120	49	58	110	1147	1637
1929[d]	224	851	128	449	220	1499	3371
1930	267	1197	158	912	248	1345	4127
1932	185	766	179	1119	242	1530	4021
1934	217	687	234	822	297	1705	3962
1936	343	881	208	805	303	2240	4780
1938	310	1116	115	1027	271	3699	6538
1940	209	1468	63	1001	216	3943	6900

Source: Toronto Family Court, Annual Reports, 1920–40

a Contributing to neglect/delinquency/truancy through immorality, bad language, gambling, disorderly conduct, vagrancy
b Includes cases of default, parents' maintenance, and orders varied or rescinded
c Occurrences not broken down by sex or age; includes assault cases involving child perpetrators.
d Toronto Family Court began operation on 1 July 1929.

The erosion of clients' legal rights allowed the new socialized tribunals to scrutinize the morality and internal family relations of the working and dependent poor with a freedom and in such detail as had been inconceivable within the parameters of the traditional police courts. Indeed, the very administration of social legislation by juvenile and family courts required that 'clients' open their doors to state representatives with absolutely no guarantee that any assistance would be forthcoming. Socialized tribunals increasingly became the private preserve of growing numbers of 'experts' who ferreted out 'defective' homes, prescribed the appropriate treatment, and placed the family unit under supervision, with a heavy emphasis on inducing the deviants to accept the ideology of 'the family.' The essence of the probation system, in fact, was 'regular supervision of the home by one of the Court Officers' until a 'house divided against itself [could be] united and conditions made safe under which the children could live' (TFC 1922: 16).[11]

This system of home visits allowed in-depth inspection of individuals who might never have come to official attention in the traditional police courts and provided opportunities for proactive, preventive work. For example, probation officers and social investigators commonly used breaches of the law by juveniles as a pretext for investigating the habits of their parents or, as the probation officers put it, 'to ascertain the facts regarding the family life' (Hamilton, Ont., Probation Office 1945: 5). Court personnel would also act on information from informants. In one case where a drinking husband had been placed on probation by the Toronto Family Court, his wife complained to the probation officer during home visits that her spouse had not reformed, yet the man was never drunk in the presence of the court worker. The situation was finally resolved after the probation officer received 'an anonymous phone call' to the effect that a surprise visit to the family would provide 'some evidence.' Finding the husband 'badly under the influence of liquor,' the officer was legitimately able to intervene (TFC 1934).

Court workers also actively recruited assistance from one family member, usually the wife/mother, to help in the rehabilitation of another. In 1935, a Toronto Family Court probation officer described a 'successful' case in which his alliance with the mother and sister of a delinquent boy had produced such positive changes in the boy's behaviour that the officer was confident that 'the little lad [would] be able to adjust himself in the community and grow to be a respected citizen' (TFC 1935: 24; see also 1923: 20–1). In cases where a husband/father drank and gambled his salary away, Toronto court personnel frequently tried to implement an arrangement whereby the man handed over all wages to his wife, who would, in turn, dole out an allowance to him (TFC 1934).

Although they exercised enormous powers over their clients with little accountability, probation officers remained oblivious to the potential for abuse provided by the occurrence system. On the contrary, imbued with the notion of 'doing good,' they were exceedingly proud of their innovation: 'There is no part of our work that gives more pleasure than the field of occurrences. Here we try to adjust the problems of life unofficially, using, of course, all our resources' (TFC 1928).

These resources increasingly included mental-health 'experts.' Thus, socialized courts not only infiltrated the homes of the working and dependent poor but also gained growing access to their heads, particularly in Toronto. Reflecting the general trend towards the medicalization of deviance and dependency after the First World War, the Toronto Family Court Clinic, established in 1920, became more and more pivotal in the treatment of family problems. Initially, the emphasis was on

rehabilitating children. After 1929, however, the clinic was used more and more by the adult division of the court when there was 'any suggestion of psychopathic personalities involved in a domestic problem' (TFC 1943: 30; see also 1940: 18). The court psychiatrist also produced a study of marital discord, isolating factors leading to 'disintegration of the family,' which had a strong impact on the marriage-counselling work of probation officers (TFC 1939: 28-9).

In retrospect, it seems clear that socialization within Ontario's juvenile and family courts during the interwar years helped consolidate the foundations of a private, technocratic justice system. However, the courts did not operate in a vacuum. The development of the new system was predicated not only on the increasing use of non-legal personnel, methods, and discourse by the courts themselves but also on the forging of close links between socialized tribunals and outside organizations such as the police and other justice-system personnel, schools, churches, municipal social-service departments, and community social agencies concerned with child and family-welfare among the working and dependent poor. All these organizations referred cases to and many received referrals from the juvenile and family courts. As table 5 indicates, police diversion of juvenile and domestic cases to the Toronto Family Court and referrals from the various 'normalizing' (Foucault 1980a) agencies and institutions guaranteed a steady stream of clients.

The same interlocking structure of socialized courts and outside organization can be discerned, to a greater of lesser degree, in all the cities and towns that established juvenile and/or family courts prior to the Second World War, but it was most expansive and observable in Toronto, where a social-service network was in place by the mid-1920s. The report of the Children's Aid Society for 1924/5 emphasized the 'mutual interdependence of the social agencies of Toronto' and lamented how few people realized 'the wonderful progress that has been made in the last decade in the organization and coordination of the community's social resources' (p. 10). The cooperation between the city's social agencies was also a source of pride to juvenile-court officials during the 1920s. In his yearly reports, Judge Mott never failed to mention the 'splendid cooperation' accorded the court by outside organizations, especially 'the Chief Crown Attorney and his assistants, the Chief of Police and the various other members of the force, the Big Brother Movement and Big Sister Association, the two Children's Aid Societies, and the Superintendent and Matron of the Observation Home' (TFC 1928).

When the children's court became a family court in 1929, the existing network simply expanded to accommodate adult family members.

For example, in solving husband–wife disputes, the court sometimes used social agencies to supervise couples. A probation officer always tried to effect a reconciliation without a formal hearing and, if successful, would ask a social agency to oversee the couple rather than having a court officer do so.[12] Moreover, although it had 'specialists' on staff, the family court frequently sought the knowledge and assistance of 'a wide group of social workers from the family agencies, Children's Aid Societies, visiting house-keepers, public health nurses, etc.' when making decisions about domestic cases (Hosking 1930: 2).

It should be noted that some organizations had especially tight relationships with the Toronto Family Court, and presumably the same was true in other areas where socialized tribunals existed. All the established churches, for example, had designated social-service workers who attended court sessions, conferred with the judge or a probation officer, and were provided with the names and addresses of probationers who claimed affiliation with their respective churches. Thus, in 1933 the social-service worker for the United Church received information about 379 cases within a six-month period (United Church of Canada 1933). Moreover, in some cases the church worker did probation supervision at the request of the court, which he felt frequently created a better understanding between the parents and greater cooperation in relation to child training (ibid 1931: 35).

The Big Brother Movement of Toronto had an even closer relationship with the court, having been founded with the express objective of helping delinquent boys. The juvenile-court judge was a director of the BBM from its inception in 1912, and 'his membership became mandatory when the agency was incorporated' (Brett 1953: 43). Furthermore, between 1919 and 1938, the central office of the Toronto BBM was located on the same premises as the court (ibid: 42, 185); and, until the mid-1930s, the BBM received almost all its referrals from the court. Even after the agency began to concentrate more on 'preventive' cases where they felt they might have more likelihood of success, the relationship with the family court remained tight.[13] The former continued to make extensive use of the court clinic and to discuss boys referred to the BBM with the court psychiatrist (Brett 1953: 185–8).

Juvenile and family courts also had exceptionally close ties to the local Children's Aid societies. The CASs frequently provided volunteer probation officers for the courts, and many court personnel were members of the society and/or had held executive positions prior to their court appointments. The first juvenile-court commissioner in Toronto had previously been a Children's Aid agent as well as a board member, and, during the interwar years, Judge Mott continued the alliance between the court and the society. As a member of the Children's Aid Society of Toronto (CASOT), he frequently addressed board meetings where he emphasized 'the close relationship existing between the [family] court and the Children's Aid Society.'[14] At annual meetings, he invariably and 'in his usual happy vein' nominated the Board of Management for the CASOT for the ensuing year. As late as 1939, a newly appointed judge of the Toronto Family Court who handled Children's Aid cases had to resign from the CASOT board, to which he had recently been added, because the society was 'frequently a litigant' in the court.[15]

Whatever the intentions of its architects, the interlocking structure of social-service organizations and the juvenile and family courts created a huge potential for systematic surveillance of the working and dependent poor that had not existed in the nineteenth century. Such was even more true in cities like Toronto, which had established a Social Service Index. This index constituted a central file containing the names of all clients processed by each participating agency, which could be accessed by member organizations. The benign objective of the index was to avoid duplication of social-work services, but it had the unintended consequence of facilitating the erosion of legal rights and guarantees of those same clients. Information about families and family members was disseminated among index members, and decisions made about the families, without their consent or even knowledge, which were presumed to be in their 'best interests.'

Indeed, confidentiality had been an issue when the Toronto Juvenile Court was invited to become a member of the index in 1916. Although personally in favour of such a move, the commissioner was unsure of his authority to provide information about the people processed by the court because of the ban on publicity that was the basis of the children's tribunal. In soliciting the advice of the attorney general, he mentioned the problem of privileged information but, none the less, strongly recommended that the juvenile court begin to supply the index with the names and circumstances of the individuals it handled. In addition to delinquencies, he argued, the court handled many cases under the Children's Protection Act 'where a good deal of evidence is obtained as to facts of home life, which would be of great service to social agencies dealing with families.'[16] For whatever reasons, the attorney general concurred with the commissioner and extended his express approval of the venture.[17]

Certainly, from the perspective of member organizations, the Social Service Index was a success. In 1934, after 21 years of operation, there were 137 private agencies, public-welfare departments, and churches represented. That same year, the central file contained 176,899 name cards; 40,958 'identifications' were made by the index and 67,122 mail and telephone inquiries cleared (Toronto Social Service Index 1935: 39). Considering Toronto had a total population of 631,207 in 1931 (Canada 1931, table 8), it would seem that the Social Service Index could track a considerable proportion of the city's inhabitants. This was an accomplishment far beyond the scope of nineteenth-century charity organizations, or even scientific philanthropy, and a reflection of the ascendancy of a socialized vis-à-vis a rights model of justice in Ontario.

However, the extensive cooperation between juvenile and family courts and outside organizations was not the only indicator of an ascendant private, technocratic justice system in the province. Outside organizations were increasingly involved in the actual decision making by the courts. Thus, socialized tribunals essentially emerged as the carceral component of a 'welfare sanction' in which non-legal experts and expertise came to dominate. In Toronto, the judge discussed 'boy problems' with workers from the Big Brother Movement on a daily basis, frequently 'adjusting conditions' so a boy would be spared a court appearance. This assistance from the court was viewed as one of the elements contributing to success in the work of BBM workers: 'To have the backing of the Judge when endeavouring to make social adjustments has been of great value' (BBM Toronto 1928: 12; see also 1943: 4). The BBM was also represented at a monthly conference with the superintendent of Bowmanville Training School and the family-court psychiatrist to discuss the boys being discharged from the institution into the care of the BBM (Brett 1953: 187).

In addition to consultations and joint decision making with individual agencies, the Toronto Family Court increasingly operated on the basis of a 'clinic' concept. Children found delinquent were placed in the Observation Home where they were examined by a medical doctor and a psychiatrist. At the same time, 'a careful social study' based on reports from home, school, and 'other persons having particular contact' was made (Mott 1933: 46). Then, a 'clinic' composed of the doctor, psychiatrist, superintendent of the Observation Home, teachers, and social workers from the court or 'any other Agency that has had any contact with the child or who might be expected to assist' met to 'formulate a plan of treatment to assist the child and its home to overcome the delinquency' (ibid).

After the establishment of the Toronto Family Court in 1929, the 'clinic' expanded to cover family units rather than individual delinquents. Thus, while family-court officials were careful to emphasize that they had no intention of usurping the functions of existing social agencies, they stressed the necessity of cooperating with them to provide 'a unified plan for the families who appeal to the Court for assistance' (Hosking 1932: 27). By 1932, fifteen agencies in child and family work were collaborating with the court; conferences with all the agencies involved with a specific case were routinely called before the court made a decision. With difficult cases, in particular, the court would adjourn; the 'clinic' did its work; a plan for the family was drawn up and put into operation '*with the sanction of the Court and the understanding that should the parties concerned fail to co-operate they would be brought back to the Court for further treatment* [my emphasis].'[18]

In Ontario, what the growing reliance on experts and expertise both inside and outside the juvenile and family courts entailed was the progressive exclusion of the lay public not only from attending court hearings but also from exercising any control over the operations of the socialized tribunals. The clearest indicator of this trend was the decline of juvenile-court committees during the interwar years. Initially mandatory under the Juvenile Delinquents Act, the committees were conceived as the mechanism for community input and control of the new courts. Although they seemed to function well for several years after the passage of the JDA, most had been discontinued by the mid-1920s because of 'a tendency to friction between the judge and the committee' (Scott 1927: 11).

Their decline also seems to have been the direct result of the creation of social-service networks. In Toronto, the court committee was abandoned altogether with the development of family work and conference arrangements. The judge felt that the conference system continued in principle but improved upon the committee.[19] The report of the Canadian Welfare Council on juvenile and family courts in Canada made the same argument: the committees, it said, were 'disappointing' in practice; 'their failure to gain in strength arises from the fact that it is a delicate matter to advise courts, and since the social work side of the picture was being handled more and more by expanding social services, the committees found their purpose hard to define' (1942: 44). By 1942, only five of Ontario's juvenile and family courts maintained a court committee (ibid: 21) and there was no uniformity either in terms of how members were appointed or in relation to functions served. Moreover, even the existing committees did not meet regularly and were used primarily in discussions 'on broad questions of policy' (ibid).

By 1940 the new system of private, technocratic justice was operational, albeit not fully developed, in Ontario's juvenile and family courts.

However, it is important to stress that socialized legal coercion did not displace but, rather, transformed the existing legal framework for handling domestic matters among the working and dependent poor through the incorporation of alternative principles and ideologies. Thus, it actually entailed an expansion of law and legal rule while, at the same time, disguising the carceral nature of the coercion through a blurring of the social and legal spheres so rigidly differentiated in nineteenth-century legal ideology and structures. Consequently, juvenile and family courts might not have fulfilled the expectations of their advocates, but they turned out to be more suitable mechanisms than the traditional police courts for reinforcing middle-class standards of domestic life among deviant families under conditions of industrialization, urbanization, and mass democracy.

CHAPTER EIGHT

The Family Court
as a Reform:
A Concluding Note

> We wish to argue that the law is not in fact a unity ... Our
> argument is that it is important to distinguish betwen the
> law and the *effects* of law and legal processes in order to
> identify the contradictions which allow space for change.
>
> J. Brophy and C. Smart (1985: 17)

Since the 1960s, the socialized system of family-welfare law that was established during the emergence of the Canadian welfare state has itself undergone a fundamental reordering. During this period, various law reform commissions, mandated to examine existing legislation governing family relations, issued reports that, while differing in specifics, explicitly rejected the paternalism inherent in such statutes as the Deserted Wives' and Children's Maintenance Act. As a result, both the federal and the provincial governments implemented reforms that collectively shifted the rationale for family law from an emphasis on difference and fault to an emphasis on formal legal equality (Klein 1985; Mossman & MacLean 1986). Concomitantly, the tribunals charged with responsibility for administering this gender-neutral law, including a number of pilot unified family courts, were now governed by the ideology of legal formalism based on the principles of individual rights and procedural guarantees.

For reform advocates, however, the reorganization of family law along liberal egalitarian lines has been disappointing in practice. A growing number of studies on the impact of gender-neutral legislation indicate that the targets of reform, particularly women experiencing marital separation or divorce, obtain legal settlements that leave them no better off under the new laws than they were under the old statutes (Boyd 1989; Brodsky & Day 1989; Manitoba Association of Women and the Law [MAWL] 1988; Martin & Mahoney 1987; Morton 1988; Mossman & MacLean 1986; Smart & Sevenhuijsen 1989). Indeed, many feminists now make a direct link between contemporary family-law reforms and the worsening economic position of women as evidenced by the 'feminization of poverty' (ibid). Similarly, contemporary reformers have been no more successful than their historical counterparts in attempts to create a national system of unified family courts with comprehensive jurisdiction over all family-related matters. The same constitutional obstacles continue to pre-empt the emergence of the 'co-operative federalism' that is necessary for such a development in Canada (Russell 1987: 226).

As the negative effects of contemporary family-law reforms are documented, feminists and other reformers have begun to express increasing pessimism about the utility of legal strategies for achieving substantive change, that is, change that has positive consequences for the objects of reform (Brodsky & Day 1989; MAWL 1988; Martin & Mahoney 1987; Smart 1989). But is this pessimism warranted? Do legal innovations, specifically those concerned with family-related issues, inevitably generate more harm than good? If so, reformers should obviously either vacate the legal arena and direct their attention to institutional sites that may be more amenable to change than law or abandon reform initiatives altogether.

At first glance, the historical study of socialized justice and family courts in Ontario seems to provide support for this gloomy assessment of the reform enterprise. The preceding discussion about the impact of socialized courts during the interwar years (see chapter 7) conveyed a clear instrumentalist image of an ever-expanding system of socialized legal coercion that impinged on a passive, homogeneous clientele. However, this picture merely reflects the reality that, in researching the effects of social-welfare reforms, it is always easy to find the voices of reformers and difficult to find the voices of the reform targets among the working and dependent poor. Furthermore, despite a paucity of data on the latter, there is still enough extant information about how Ontario's pioneer family courts operated prior to 1940 to affirm the revisionist conceptualization of reform as an inherently dualistic phenomenon – one that will always generate both positive and negative consequences.

In short, socialized legal coercion was not a uniform system of oppression conceived and used by the capitalist, patriarchal state in a direct, instrumentalist fashion to control the marginal but, rather, a system characterized by contradictions that had a differential impact on its clients relative to social class and gender. Thus, poor families and, in particular, poor women were both empowered and oppressed, active and acted upon, by the new domestic-relations tribunals. With regard to the social-class issue, for example, the transition from laissez-faire to welfare state did entail direct state intervention into working-class family life. At the same time, contrary to what Lasch (1979) argues, this development did not represent a simple straightforward shift from familial autonomy to state surveillance. Marginal families in market societies were subject to outside supervision throughout the nineteenth century. As Donzelot (1980) demonstrates, the right to privacy has always been class-based, reserved for those families with the resources to sustain the home as a haven.

What changed so markedly during the emergence of the welfare state, then, was the unprecedented degree and the particular mode of state intervention in the working-class family (Smart 1982: 130–1). Moreover, the reformulation of the relationship between the social and legal, public and private, realms that occurred actually disguised the nature and implications of this development. Thus, when family-court personnel emphasized privacy in the processing of domestic cases, they obscured the reality that the state – in the form of socialized legal coercion – was more intrusive than ever before in regulating the intrafamilial relations of the working and dependent poor. To paraphrase McBarnet (1981: 191), it was a paradox that family-court cases were deemed too personal for public adjudication but not too personal for state intervention; too personal for due processes of law but not too personal for the intercession of law in the person of the judge and the probation officer.

None the less, it also seems clear that juvenile and family courts were not part of any organized state conspiracy to oppress the poor. On the contrary, the subtlety of socialized legal coercion makes it more appropriate to speak of regulation rather than control, which is 'a much more rigid and direct manifestation of power' (Smart 1984: 18). More important, a conception of social control being imposed on hapless victims by arbitrary state agents ignores the awkward fact that the new socialized form of policing could not have been entrenched in Ontario, or other jurisdictions (Gordon 1988a), without the active support of those who were 'done to.' Toronto Family Court officials constantly exhorted people to report problem situations: 'We wish our Court to be a moral clinic, diagnosing cases and assisting parents to guide their children, thus saving the child from committing delinquencies. We, therefore, earnestly suggest that parents come to us with difficulties so that we may be able to thus assist' (1924: 8).

And, while the evidence is scant, it does confirm that some individuals accepted the invitation of the court. Admittedly, the majority of referrals came from institutional sources such as the police and schools, but not a few court hearings were the result of complaints by citizens, wives, husbands, and parents (see chapter 7, table 5). Moreover, although the Toronto court records do not indicate the number of 'occurrences' that were initiated by individuals, it is probably safe to assume that as formal court hearings declined relative to 'occurrences,' an increasing percentage of the latter were launched by the people affected. That is certainly the impression conveyed by the annual reports of the court's Probation Department: 'There is, however, the bright aspect of our Court and that is, to wit: the large number of parents who come with their difficulties for assistance, not waiting for some matter that needs judicial determination to settle, both in the Family and Juvenile Departments of our Court' (TFC 1938: 9).

So far as the individual members of client families were concerned, socialized legal coercion had the same contradictory and differential impact. On the one hand, a segment of men and women among the working and dependent poor were targeted for supervision on the basis of deviation from class and gender norms associated with the middle-class family. On the other hand, husbands/fathers and wives/mothers were also empowered through the socialized administration of family-welfare law. Thus, the former were subject to sanctions for failing to support their dependents yet were simultaneously reinforced in their dominant position as family breadwinner and protector. In Ontario at least, family courts did not transform the husband/father into the pathetic creature, depicted by Donzelot (1980), Lasch (1979), and others, whose dominion within the family was wholly usurped by representatives of a patriarchal state.[1]

Donzelot, for example, attributes the frequent absence of the husband/father from juvenile-court hearings to the 'actual fact there is no role for him to play,' his traditional authority as family patriarch having been appropriated by judge and probation officer (1980: 103–4). Yet, Toronto Family Court personnel saw a central role for the husband/father in the resolution of domestic conflicts. They believed his presence at both formal hearings and 'occurrence' discussions with probation officers was vital to successful rehabilitation of deviant families. Annual reports lamented the fact that husbands/fathers often could not come to court because their employers threatened to fire them if they took time off work and that some were dismissed for doing so: 'Surely employers have sufficient regard for the welfare of society, generally, to permit employees to attend the Family Court and afford the Court an opportunity of settling domestic difficulties. The efficiency of employees will often improve once their family affairs have been settled' (TFC 1941: 12–13).

In a similar way, socialized courts sanctioned women for being 'bad' wives and mothers and reinforced the sexual division of labour, yet, at the same time, gave them new powers vis-à-vis men within the family. By upholding the cult of domesticity, for example, family-court personnel clearly helped to reproduce the economic (and psychological) dependency of the wife/mother on her male provider. When the latter was absent from the family unit, probation officers, social workers, and other state-designated officials stepped into the breach. Thus, 'successful' case resolution frequently meant that women quit their jobs in the paid labour force and/or did work for money at home under exploitative conditions. Moreover, the clear lesson for a woman who had no male breadwinner was to find another man as soon as possible.

None the less, in contrast to some research on other jurisdictions (Ehrenreich & English 1978), the Ontario family-court study shows that women were not completely at the mercy of male judges, probation officers, and other experts, nor of their husbands. Much of the family-welfare legislation administered by domestic-relations courts improved the position of married women in the family. For example, they gained rights to property, custody of children, and maintenance that they did not have for most of the nineteenth century. Moreover, women's increased power in the private sphere was real, notwithstanding the fact that it was gained at the expense of equality in the public realm, was contingent on adherence to middle-class morality, and was tied to their motherhood role (Brophy & Smart 1981; Brophy 1982; Gordon 1988a; Smart 1982, 1984; Ursel 1986).

Thus, it is not surprising that, in Ontario, as in other locales (Donzelot 1980; Gordon 1988a), the majority of those who voluntarily sought the assistance of the family courts and allied social agencies were women. After all, the new social-service networks provided substantive aid to working-class women that had not been forthcoming from the traditional police magistrates' courts: with the collection of maintenance or relief, difficult children, abusive husbands, and other problems that might otherwise have been insurmountable. For many of Ontario's working and dependent poor, then, the family court was perceived as a considerable improvement upon the old-style police court, despite the cost of the services rendered – infiltration of their homes, and increasingly their heads, by the state – and, for women, perpetuation of their restricted and subordinate role outside the domestic realm.

APPENDIX A

Primary Data Sources

Archival Collections

Archives of Ontario

Association of Children's Aid Societies of Ontario, Papers
Local Council of Women, Toronto, Papers
Ontario, Department of the Attorney General, Papers and Correspondence
Ontario, Prime Minister's Office: Ferguson Papers, Henry Papers, Hepburn Papers
Ontario, Provincial Secretary's Department, Papers and Correspondence
Provincial Council of Women, Ontario, Papers

Public Archives of Canada

Canadian Council on Social Development Papers
J.J. Kelso Papers
National Council of Women of Canada Papers
W.L. Scott Papers
C.E. Whitton Papers

Ottawa Municipal Archives

Local Council of Women, Ottawa, Minute Books

Toronto Municipal Archives

Children's Aid Society of Toronto, Papers
Toronto, Board of Control, Correspondence and Minutes
Toronto, City Clerk's Department, Miscellaneous Subject Files

Newspapers

Hamilton Spectator
Ottawa Citizen; *Ottawa Journal*
Toronto *Globe*; *Toronto Daily Star*; Toronto *Telegram*

Legislation Administered by the Toronto Family Court

An order-in-council dated 13 June 1929 granted the judge and deputy judge of the Toronto Juvenile Court joint and exclusive jurisdiction over the following legislation:

Children's Protection Act (R.S.O., 1927, c. 279) and amendments
Deserted Wives' and Children's Maintenance Act (R.S.O., 1927, c. 184)
Minors' Protection Act (R.S.O., 1927, c. 259)
Parents' Maintenance Act (R.S.O., 1927, c. 185)
Married Women's Property Act (R.S.O., 1927, c. 182, s. 14 – dealing with orders of protection)
Criminal Code (R.S.C., 1927, c. 36, s. 238, ss. (b); s. 239; s. 242, ss. 3(a) and (b), ss. 4; s.291)

The judge was also granted non-exclusive jurisdiction over the following legislation:

Adoption Act (R.S.O., 1927, c. 189)
Children of Unmarried Parents Act (R.S.O., 1927, c. 188)

Sources: Archives of Ontario, Dept. of the Attorney General, RG4 Series C-3, 1929, file 1917, Order-in-Council 13 June 1929; Hosking (1930: 1).

Criminal Code Sections Related to Family Welfare

238. Every one is a loose, idle or disorderly person or vagrant who,
- (b) being able to work and thereby or by other means to maintain himself and family, wilfully refuses or neglects to do so ...

239. Every loose, idle or disorderly person or vagrant is liable, on summary conviction, to a fine not exceeding fifty dollars or to imprisonment, with or without hard labour, for any term not exceeding six months, or to both.

242. Every one who as parent, guardian or head of a family is under a legal duty to provide necessaries for any child under the age of sixteen years is criminally responsible for omitting, without lawful excuse, to do so while such child remains a member of his or her household, whether such child is helpless or not, if the death of such child is caused, or if his life is endangered, or his health is or is likely to be permanently injured, by such omission.

3. Every one is guilty of an offence and liable upon indictment or on summary conviction to a fine of five hundred dollars, or to one year's imprisonment, or to both, who,
- (a) as a husband or head of a family, is under a legal duty to provide necessaries for his wife or any child under sixteen years of age; or
- (b) as a parent or guardian, is under a legal duty to provide necessaries for any child under sixteen years of age; and who, if such wife or child is in destitute or necessitous circumstances, without lawful excuse, neglects or refuses to provide such necessaries.

4. Upon any prosecution under this section
- (a) evidence that a man has cohabited with a woman or has in any way recognized her as being his wife shall be *prima facie* evidence that they are lawfully married;
- (b) evidence that a man has in any way recognized children as being his children shall be *prima facie* evidence that they are his legitimate children;

(c) evidence that a man has, without lawful cause or excuse, left his wife without making provision for her maintenance for a period of at least one month from the date of his so leaving, or for the maintenance for the same period of any child of his under the age of sixteen years, shall be *prima facie* evidence of neglect to provide necessaries under this section.

291. Every one who commits a common assault is guilty of an indictable offence and liable, if convicted upon an indictment, to one year's imprisonment, or to a fine not exceeding one hundred dollars, and on summary conviction to a fine not exceeding twenty dollars and costs, or to two months' imprisonment, with or without hard labour.*

* Family-court jurisdiction was limited to cases where a husband assaulted a wife, a wife assaulted a husband, or parents assaulted their children.

Source: R.S.C., 1927, c. 36

The British North America Act
VII Judicature

Appointment of Judges
96. The Governor General shall appoint the Judges of the Superior, District and County Courts in each Province, except those of the Courts of Probate in Nova Scotia and New Brunswick.

Selection of Judges in Ontario, etc.
97. Until the Laws relative to Property and Civil Rights in Ontario, Nova Scotia, and New Brunswick, and the Procedure of the Courts in those Provinces, are made uniform, the Judges of the Courts of those Provinces appointed by the Governor General shall be selected from the respective Bars of those Provinces.

Selection of Judges in Quebec
98. The Judges of the Courts of Quebec shall be selected from the Bar of that Province.

Tenure of Office of Judges of Superior Courts
99. The Judges of the Superior Courts shall hold office during good Behaviour, but shall be removable by the Governor General on Address of the Senate and House of Commons.

Salaries, etc., of Judges
100. The Salaries, Allowances, and Pensions of the Judges of the Superior, District and County Courts (except the Courts of Probate in Nova Scotia and New Brunswick), and of the Admiralty Courts in cases where the Judges thereof are for the time being paid by Salary, shall be fixed and provided by the Parliament of Canada.

General Court of Appeal, etc.

101. The Parliament of Canada may, notwithstanding anything in this Act, from Time to Time provide for the Constitution, Maintenance, and Organization of a General Court of Appeal for Canada, and for the Establishment of any additional Courts for the better Administration of the Laws of Canada.

Source: Varcoe (1954: 241–2)

Notes

Chapter 1

1 The terms 'marginal populations,' 'working and dependent poor,' 'deviant and dependent' are used interchangeably to denote those strata of people in Western market societies who historically have been perceived as a potential threat to social order because they will not or cannot adhere to bourgeois norms and who are thus targeted for reform measures – criminal-justice, mental-health, welfare – aimed at coercing compliance.

2 Archives of Ontario (AO), Dept. of the Attorney General, RG4 Series C-3, 1929, file 1917, Order-in-Council 13 June 1929. *Reference as to Constitutionality of the Adoption Act, the Children's Protection Act, the Children of Unmarried Parents Act, and the Deserted Wives' and Children's Maintenance Act* ([1939] 71 CCC 110).

3 There was an important difference between the United States and Canada with respect to the constitution of domestic-relations vis-à-vis family courts. In the former, domestic-relations courts dealt solely with adults and were usually part of the lower-court system but the full-time family courts with jurisdiction over all family members, as well as the more established juvenile courts, were 'part of the Superior Court system' (Allard 1972: 2). In Canada, both domestic-relations courts and family courts developed as integral parts of the magisterial or lower-court system.

4 The lack of detailed attention to the legal transformation that marked the emergence of the Canadian welfare state is curious since there is an extensive literature on other aspects of this period. See Allen (1971), Brown and Cook (1974), Strong-Boag (1976, 1988), Sutherland (1976), Cross and Kealey (1983), Bacchi (1983) Struthers (1983), McLaren (1990), McLaren and McLaren (1986), Moscovitch and Albert (1987).

5 See appendix A for a list of primary data sources used in the study.

6 The reference to Canada/Ontario at various places in the text is meant

to emphasize the point that, although this book focuses on Ontario, similar developments were taking place elsewhere in the country.

7 It is necessary to distinguish between the ideology of privacy and separate spheres and actual practice. In fact, the state has always intervened differentially in the family (Donzelot 1980).

8 Patriarchal relations did not disappear. Law reform gave married women new rights (e.g., custody, maintenance) within the family that were linked to their motherhood role. But most wives remained economically dependent upon a male breadwinner.

Chapter 2

1 The proliferation of large-scale industrial enterprises in the first three decades of the twentieth century was remarkable. There were 200 mergers, involving approximately 440 firms, between 1900 and 1920, and another 315 between 1924 and 1930 (Palmer 1983: 139, 186; see also Goff & Reasons 1978; Traves 1979). A similar concentration of finance saw the number of banks drop from a high of 51 in 1874 to 11 in 1925 and by 1927 the three largest banks accounted for about 70 per cent of banking resources (ibid).

2 In 1881, 70 per cent of the total population was rural and 30 per cent urban ($N = 1,926,922$); in 1941, 67.5 per cent was urban and 32.5 per cent rural ($N = 3,787,655$) (Urquhart & Buckley 1965, Series A2-14: 14). The sex ratio in such cities as Toronto, Hamilton, and Ottawa also shifted during the nineteenth century, with women increasingly outnumbering men (Cohen 1988: 120–2, 162–4).

3 The population of Hamilton increased from 35,961 (1.9 per cent of the provincial total) in 1881 to 166,337 (4.4 per cent) in 1941, and the population of Ottawa rose from 27,412 (1.4 per cent) in 1881 to 154,951 (4.1 per cent) in 1941 (Canada 1931, table 8; Canada 1941, table 16; Leacy 1983, Series A2-14).

4 The Unemployment Insurance Act of 1940 was arguably the first state-subsidized, non-means-tested social-security scheme and has been designated as a milestone in the development of the Canadian welfare state (Struthers 1983: 202–4; see also Guest 1980: 106–8; Herman 1971: 136).

5 The ideological ascendancy of professionalism among social-welfare workers was reflected in the school's name changes from the original to the Department of Social Science in 1929, to the School of Social Work in the 1940s.

6 Between 1924 and 1926, the Social Service Council of Canada lost five affiliated secular organizations, including the National Council of Women and the Canadian Conference of Public Welfare (Allen 1971: 288). In contrast, the 1926 Conference of the Canadian Council on Child Welfare noted a 100 per cent increase in membership over the previous year (Castell Hopkins 1927: 633).

7 The federal Department of Health was founded in 1919 and the Children's Division a year later, under the direction of Dr Helen MacMurchy (1923; see also Sutherland 1976: 229–30). When she retired in 1932, her position was offered to Whitton who, in turn, suggested absorption of the division by the CCCW (Hareven 1969: 92). The Canadian Association of Child Protection Officers (CACPO), founded in 1921, was an attempt to form a national association of Children's Aid societies and juvenile-court workers. When it foundered in 1935, many members, if they had not already done so, joined the CCCFW. See Public Archives of Canada (PAC), Scott Papers, MG30 C27, v. 12, file 45, W.L. Scott to H. MacMurchy, 22 October 1920; v. 12, file 46, CACPO 1927–35.

8 PAC, Canadian Council on Social Development (CCSD) Papers, MG28 110, v. 30, file 150, C.E. Whitton to W.A. Weston, CAS of Winnipeg, 19 April 1929

9 PAC, CCSD Papers, v. 1, file 33, University of Toronto Social Services Department. See correspondence between Whitton and Agnes McGregor, director of field work, about cooperation between the CCCW and the university.

10 In Toronto, some of the more notable individuals drawn into the Whitton orbit included: Frank Stapleford, holder of an MA degree in sociology from Chicago, who was appointed general secretary of the Toronto Neighbourhood Workers' Association in 1918 (Allen 1971; Bator 1979; Stapleford 1938); Robert E. Mills, with an MA in political economy from the University of Toronto, who was appointed director of the Toronto Children's Aid Society in the early 1920s (Jones & Rutman 1981: 149–50, 165–6; Sutherland 1976: 64); Frank Sharpe, a graduate of the Social Service Department at the University of Toronto, who was hired in 1922 as general secretary of the Big Brother Movement of Toronto (Brett 1953: 82; and Ethel G. Cameron-Parker, who was secretary of the Toronto Child Welfare Council in the mid-1920s and president of the Canadian Association of Social Workers from 1930 to 1934 when Whitton was convener of Social Work Recruitment and Training (Maines 1959: 14).

11 AO, Dept of the Provincial Secretary, RG49 I-7-E, R.E. Mills to L. Goldie, 3 January 1924

12 None the less, she wrote a laudatory article about Kelso when he retired (Whitton 1934). Kelso, who was quite aware of how the professionalizers viewed him, thanked Whitton for her comments and added: 'You know I thought for a time that you were like the little girl who spent a year at the Social Service class and remarked to a friend "Isn't it too bad that Mr Kelso is not a trained worker for he is such a nice man."' See PAC, CCSD Papers, v. 19, file 79, J.J. Kelso to C.E. Whitton, 10 March 1934.

13 The movement towards a monopoly over the social-welfare field is reflected in the council's name changes from the original Canadian Council on Child Welfare to the Canadian Council on Child and Family welfare in 1929, to the Canadian Welfare Council in 1935. Whitton's

influence in the welfare arena peaked around the mid-1930s. Thereafter, she experienced increasing resistance to her views from professional social workers who advocated the implementation of social security programs based on universality, and she finally resigned as executive director of the CWC in 1941 (Rooke & Schnell 1987).

14 The greatest proliferation of institutions for both adults and children took place from the 1870s to the 1890s. During that period, using primarily voluntary means, social-welfare leaders managed to double the number of institutions for neglected and dependent children and the number of children in care (Sutherland 1976: 12; see also Houston 1982: 136).

15 The movement towards increased state control of children was not entirely linear. For example, the 1927 Law Revision led to the creation of a new category of temporary wards under the Children's Protection Act (R.S.O., 1927, c. 279, s. 7, ss. 8). The idea was to reduce the number of children who became permanent state wards.

16 In 1912, the federal government enacted a Criminal Code section that made it mandatory for men to provide for their dependents (see appendix C), but the section was rarely used by the courts.

17 In 1918, the number of Family Welfare associations was negligible. Ten years later, 28 of 192 (14.6 per cent) Canadian Association of Social Workers members were employed in such family agencies and, by 1943, 136 of 720 (18.9 per cent) CASW members were so engaged (CASW 1943: 20–1).

18 See PAC, CCSD Papers, v. 22, files 99, 489; CCCW 1925, 1930, 1940, 1940–1, 1941.

19 The Adoption Act (S.O., 1921, c. 54); the Children of Unmarried Parents Act (S.O., 1921, c. 54); the Parents Maintenance Act (S.O., 1921, c. 52)

Chapter 3

1 Archives of Ontario (AO), Dept of the Attorney General, RG4 Series C-3 1916, file 1087, A.N. Middleton to I.B. Lucas, 14 March 1916

2 Public Archives of Canada (PAC), Scott Papers, v. 19, file 58, W.L. Scott to Sir William Van Horn, 25 October 1912. See also W.L. Scott to the federal Minister of Justice, 17 October 1912.

3 Ibid, J.J. Kelso to W.L. Scott, 6 August 1914

4 'Children's Aid Societies,' *Toronto Sentinel*, 18 July 1918

5 PAC, Canadian Council on Social Development (CCSD) Papers, v. 13, file 64, C.E. Whitton to D.B. Harkness, 12 January 1923

6 AO, Provincial Council of Women, MU2342 Series A-1, *Minutes* of the Annual Meeting of the Provincial Council of Women of Ontario, 1929

7 PAC, Whitton Papers, MG30 E256 v. 18, Canadian Conference on Child Welfare, 4th, 1923, *Proceedings and Papers* (Ottawa 1925)

8 Ibid, 53

9 PAC, CCSD Papers, v. 12, file 64, D.B. Harkness to C.E. Whitton, 3
    January 1923
10 Ibid, C.E. Whitton to D.B. Harkness, 26 May 1923
11 Ibid, v. 6, file 30, C.E. Whitton to R.S. Hosking, 2 June 1930
12 This is a pervasive point in the literature. See Social Service Council of
    Canada (1923); Harkness (1924); Hosking (1930); County of York, Special
    Committee on Juvenile and Domestic Relations Courts (1931: 81); Mott
    (1933).
13 AO, Association of Children's Aid Societies of Ontario, MU5081, Box 10,
    Proceedings of Conference, 31st, 1–2 June 1945: 20–1; Box 16, 'Editorial,'
    The Bulletin 6/2 (1946); AO, Dept of the AG, Series A-2, Box 24.3,
    Secretary, Assn of CASs to L.E. Blackwell, 9 June 1945
14 PAC, Whitton Papers, v. 18, Canadian Conference on Child Welfare, 4th,
    1923, *Proceedings and Papers*, 53 (Ottawa 1925)
15 PAC, CCSD Papers, v. 5, file 12, Social Service Council of Ontario, Child
    Welfare Conference, *Minutes* of Meeting, 28 December 1928
16 AO, Dept of the PS, RG3 Appx E, the Rev. H. Ferguson, secretary, Assn
    of CASs of Ontario, to Premier Ferguson, 23 September 1925. See also
    AO, Dept of the AG, Series C-3 1926, file 1608.
17 AO, Dept of the AG, Series C-3 1929, file 3027, D.B. Harkness to W.H.
    Price, 21 September 1929
18 AO, Dept of the AG, Series C-3 1921, file 2023, the Rev. G. Agar to W.E.
    Raney, 9 February 1921
19 PAC, CCSD Papers, v. 5, file 18. The committee, which held its first
    meeting on 28 December 1925, initially consisted of the Child Welfare
    Committee of the Social Service Council of Ontario, the Association of
    Children's Aid Societies of Ontario, and the Child Welfare Council of
    Toronto. Later, both the CCCW and the CACPO added representatives.
    AO, Dept of the PS, RG49 I-7-E, Proposed Legislation and Precedents, Box
    2, Dr James T. Daley, 'The Revision of the CPA,' Paper presented at the
    Annual Conference of the Assn of CASs, May 1926, and expanded for
    submission to the Law Reform Commission. Rev. H. Ferguson to F.V.
    Johns, 27 July 1926
20 Commissioner Boyd's tenure was a stormy one. There had been previous
    complaints about the Toronto Juvenile Court, which he survived, but the
    1919 uproar was the end of his administration. Hawley Sanford Mott was
    appointed judge of the Toronto Juvenile Court by an order-in-council
    passed on 10 December 1919, and he assumed his duties on 1 January
    1920. See Toronto Board of Control, *Minutes*, no. 12, 14 January 1920.
21. AO, Dept of the AG, Series C-3 1921, file 1684, H.S. Mott to W.E. Raney,
    13 December 1920
22 Ibid
23 AO, Dept of the PS, RG8 I-7-E, Proposed Legislation and Precedents 1922–
    4, H.S. Mott to F.V. Johns, 14 December 1922

24 AO, Dept of the AG, Series C-3 1921, file 1684, H.S. Mott to W.E. Raney, 13 December 1920

25 Ibid, 1924, file 942, H.S. Mott to W.F. Nickle, 11 October 1923

26 Ibid, 1928, file 3034, F. Sharpe to W.H. Price, 2 February 1928

27 Ibid, 1921, file 1684, Judge Archibald to W.E. Raney, 20 November 1920

28 Ibid, Judge Archibald to W.E. Raney, 8 December 1920

29 The women felt that a young, unmarried man was hardly a suitable person to handle delinquent girls or the parents of delinquent children. See 'Juvenile Judge,' *Ottawa Journal*, 17 February 1922; 'Wants Woman Judge in Juvenile Court,' *Ottawa Citizen*, 3 March 1922. For positive reactions to the appointment, see 'The Juvenile Court Judge,' *Ottawa Citizen*, 5 April 1922; 'Ottawa's Juvenile Court,' *Ottawa Citizen*, 30 September 1922.

30 AO, Dept of the PS, RG8 I-I-B-5, Box 2, file 1000-12, F.V. Johns to L. Goldie, 23 November 1923

31 PAC, Scott Papers, v. 12, file 45, D.B. Harkness to C.E. Whitton, 30 January 1924. It should be noted that Harkness wrote the pamphlet for the CCCW prior to his appointment to the SSC of Ontario. In later years, he was not only at odds with Whitton but also one of the strongest advocates of a province-wide system of juvenile courts.

32 Ibid

33 PAC, Whitton Papers, v. 18, CCCW, *The Council's Objectives 1925–1930, Being the Statement of Resolutions Adopted at the Ottawa Conference 1925* (Ottawa 1925)

34 PAC, CCSD Papers, v. 31, file 151, H.S. Mott to C.E. Whitton, 16 August 1928

35 PAC, Scott Papers, v. 9, file 32, W.L. Scott to Ethel MacLachlan, 27 February 1928

36 AO, Dept of the AG, Series C-3 1920, file 133, J.J. Kelso to W.E. Raney, 7 January 1920

37 Ibid, J.J. Kelso to A.N. Middleton, 15 January 1920; A.N. Middleton to W.E. Raney, 12 January 1920

38 It is important to emphasize that the British model of legal education, based on apprenticeship, rather than the American model, based on university education, was dominant in Ontario until the 1940s. Moreover, the Osgoode Hall Law School, established by the Benchers of the Law Society of Upper Canada, was ranked very low despite the fact that it was the largest school in the country (Bucknall, Baldwin, & Lakin 1968: 186). The conviction that lawyers were superior to non-lawyers by virtue of their training must, therefore, be weighed against the fact that in 1918, law was the 'easiest profession to enter' in Ontario and that, following the armistice, 'a great number of men were allowed into the profession with almost no training at all as a reward for their war service' (ibid: 190–1; see also Honsberger 1972).

39 AO, Dept of the AG, Series C-3 1921, A. Dymond to W.E. Raney, [undated] February 1921

40 Ibid

41 Ibid

42 AO, Dept of the AG, Series C-3 1921, file 1684, W.E. Raney to A. Dymond, 15 December 1920

43 Ibid, 1922, file 1427, H.S. Mott to A. Dymond, 24 February 1922

44 Ibid, Laura Denton to W.E. Raney, [undated] February 1922

45 Ibid, W.E. Raney to J. McNamara, MPP, 28 February 1922

46 Ibid, H.S. Mott to W.E. Raney, 22 March 1922. See also H.S. Mott to W.E. Raney, 14 March 1922, and W.E. Raney to H.S. Mott, 20 March 1922.

47 Ibid, 1924, file 942, A. Dymond to W.F. Nickle, 24 October 1923

48 Ibid, 1925, file 404, Dr G.V. Harcourt, MPP, to W.F. Nickle, 26 August 1924; W.F. Nickle to Judge Powell, 11 September 1924; A.N. Middleton to Judge Powell, 19 December 1924; Judge Powell to A.N. Middleton, 14 January 1925

49 Ibid, A.N. Middleton to W.F. Nickle, 28 August 1924

50 Ibid, J.J. Kelso to L. Goldie, 19 September 1924. See also J.J. Kelso to L. Goldie, 14 October 1924, 21 October 1924.

51 Ibid, A.N. Middleton to W.F. Nickle, 25 September 1924

52 Ibid, Judge Hewson to A.N. Middleton, 24 November 1924; A.N. Middleton to Judge Hewson 26 November 1924; A.N. Middleton to J.J. Kelso 26 November 1924

53 Ibid, 1921, file 679, W.E. Raney to A. Dymond, 28 February 1921

54 PAC, CCSD Papers, v. 5, file 18, W.G. Middleton to C.E. Whitton, 2 January 1926

55 Ibid

56 Ibid

57 Ibid

58 Ibid

59 AO, Dept of the AG, Series C-3 1927, file 682, W.G. Middleton to W.H. Price, 9 February 1927

60 Ibid, A.M. Dymond to C.E. Whitton, 28 January 1926. See also PAC, Kelso Papers, MG30, C97, v. 33, file 145; AO, Dept of the PS, RG49 I-7-E, Proposed Legislation and Precedents, Box 2; RG3 Appx E, Box 80, Child Welfare file.

61 AO, Dept of the AG, Series C-3 1928, file 3034, D.B. Harkness to W.H. Price, 13 February 1928

Chapter 4

1 The enabling legislation was the Magistrates' Jurisdiction Act (S.O., 1929, c. 36). See also 'To Make Survey of Institutions in Province,' *Ottawa Journal*, 20 March 1929, P. 11; 'New Court Sworn for Family Spats,' *Toronto Daily Star*, 19 June 1929, p.1; 'Family Court Opens to Mark Milestone of Justice in City,' *The Globe*, 20 June 1929, pp. 1, 4.

2 Archives of Ontario (AO), Dept of the Attorney General, Series A-2, Box 1.31, W.H. Price to the BBM of Toronto, 21 January 1929
3 AO, Dept of the AG, Series C-3 1929, file 3027, W.H. Price to F. Sharpe, 24 September 1929, thanking Sharpe 'for the very great assistance you have given in getting a Domestic Relations Court established in Toronto'
4 Ibid, 1928, file 3034, F. Sharpe to W.H. Price, 2 February 1928
5 AO, Dept of the AG, Series A-2, Box 1.34, W.H. Price, 26 April 1929
6 AO, Ontario Assn of Children's Aid Societies, Conferences, MU5081 Box 10, 'Address on Domestic Court and Probation Act,' presented to Annual Conference of the Assn of CASs of Ontario, 15–16 May 1929
7 'Domestic Relations Court Established for the City,' *Toronto Telegram*, 15 June 1929, pp. 1, 4. See also 'Judge Hawley S. Mott to Head New Court of Domestic Relations,' *Toronto Daily Star*, 15 June 1929, p. 1.
8 'Judge McKinley Senior Officer: Heads Probationary Court for Newly Formed Ottawa District,' *Ottawa Journal*, 13 February 1931, p. 2; 'Wider Scope of Duties Falls to Judge McKinley,' *Ottawa Citizen*, 12 February 1931. See also 'J.P. Balharrie Given Promotion,' *Ottawa Journal*, 13 February 1931, p. 1; 'J.P. Balharrie Is Deputy Judge of Juvenile Court,' *Ottawa Citizen*, 13 February 1931, p. 1; 'Judge McKinley's Work' (Editorial), *Ottawa Citizen*, 14 February 1931.
9 On the name issue, Price initially referred to the new tribunals as 'domestic relations courts.' Five years later, he said he 'frowned on the title "Domestic Relations Court" now applied to tribunals in the larger cities,' and was, therefore, amending the Juvenile Courts Act to change the name to 'family court.' See the Juvenile and Family Courts Act (S.O., 1934, c. 25); 'Government Overdraft without Note Issue,' *The Globe*, 8 February 1934.
10 AO, Dept of the AG, Series C-3 1929, file 1008, W.H. Price to Mayor McBride, 1 June 1929
11 Ibid
12 Ibid, A.N. Middleton to W.H. Price, 2 April 1929. See also A.N. Middleton to W.H. Price, 26 March 1929.
13 AO, Dept of the AG, Series C-3 1929, file 3027, D.B. Harkness to W.H. Price, 21 September 1929
14 'H.A. Burbidge Will Succeed Magistrate,' *Hamilton Spectator*, 26 June 1929, pp. 5, 24; 'Court at Hamilton to be Reorganized, Price Announces,' *The Globe*, 27 June 1929, p. 6; Burbidge 1950: 4.
15 AO, Dept of the AG, Series C-3 1929, file 2517, W.W. Denison to I.A. Humphries, 1 December 1931; I.A. Humphries to W.W. Denison, 8 December 1931
16 Ibid, 1936, file 1231, Order-in-Council, 20 May 1936
17 Ibid, 1929, file 1917, Order-in-Council, 13 June 1929. See also W.H. Price to Judge E. Coatsworth, 10 June 1929.
18 AO, Dept of the PS, RG8 I-I-U, Box 3, no. 206.2262, Order-in-Council, 28 January 1931. See also AO, Dept of the AG, Series C-3 1931, file 491, I.A. Humphries to W.H. Price, 26 January 1931.

19 AO, Dept of the AG, Series C-3 1931, file 491, I.A. Humphries to W.H. Price, 26 January 1931
20 Ibid, J. Sedgwick to I.A. Humphries, 20 February 1931
21 Ibid, 1929, file 2517, A.N. Middleton to W.H. Price, 28 June 1929. See also Public Archives of Canada (PAC), Canadian Council on Social Development (CCSD) Papers, v. 86, file 1854, H.A. Burbidge to C.E. Whitton, 22 February 1938.
22 AO, Dept of the AG, Series C-3 1931, file 1821, I.A. Humphries to W.H. Price, 12 March 1931; I.A. Humphries to W. Keith, 24 April 1931; I.A. Humphries to W. Keith, 11 June 1931
23 Toronto City Council, *Minutes*, Appx A, no. 133, 26 January 1920
24 The Toronto Police Court still managed to dispose of 30,170 cases in 1919 as opposed to the 978 handled by the higher criminal courts (Coatsworth 1920: 20; Denison 1920: 7).
25 Some of the more important statutes included: the Police Magistrates Extended Jurisdiction Act, 1921 (S.O., 1921, c. 42); the Toronto and York Crown Attorneys Act, 1921 (S.O., 1921, c. 40); the Magistrates' Jurisdiction Act, 1929 (S.O., 1929, c. 36); the Magistrates Act, 1934 (S.O., 1934, c. 28); the Magistrates Act, 1936 (S.O., 1936, c. 35); the Magistrates Act, 1941 (S.O., 1941, c. 28).
26 'Consecrated Common-Sense Is Quality New Magistrate Will Bring to Bench,' *The Globe*, 5 January 1922, p. 14
27 AO, Dept of the AG, Series C-3 1925, file 315, Order-in-Council, 7 February 1925. See also Toronto Police Dept 1926: 9.
28 'Cut Crime at Roots by Social Prevention Pleads Coatsworth' *The Globe*, 28 January 1931, p. 11
29 County of York Municipal Council, *Minutes*, 25 January 1929, p. 14. Keith had chaired a county committee that looked into the administration of justice and made recommendations for its rationalization. See County of York, Special Committee Re the Administration of Justice, Report to the Council ..., in *Minutes* of the Council of the Corporation of the County of York (Newmarket 1923), pp. 282–3.
30 'H.A. Burbidge Will Succeed Magistrate,' *Hamilton Spectator*, 26 June 1929, pp. 15, 24. See also 'Court at Hamilton to be Reorganized, Price Announces,' *The Globe*, 27 June 1929, pp. 1, 3.
31 'Strong Opposition to Act Foisting Probation Official on Toronto,' *The Globe*, 5 April 1922; 'Province Pays Probation Men,' *The Globe*, 2 May 1922; County of York Probation Dept (1923: 7)
32 For specific mention of this policy, see AO, Dept of the AG, Series C-3, 1924, file 1738, W.F. Nickle to W.H. Harrington, 14 January 1926; Series C-3 1931, file 2519, I.A. Humphries to Magistrate Calnan, 16 January 1933; Series C-3 1930, file 2096, I.A. Humphries to W.H. Elliott, MLA, 8 September 1932.
33 AO, Dept of the AG, Series C-3 1920, file 133, J.J. Kelso to W.E. Raney, 7 January 1920
34 It was not until 1968, following the recommendation of the McRuer

Commission (Ontario 1968: 564), that the Ontario government finally assumed financial responsibility for juvenile and family courts.

35 AO, Dept of the AG, Series C-3 1929, file 3027, W.H. Price to F. Sharpe 24 September 1929. See also Series C-3 1929, file 2814, I.A. Humphries to L.E. Jamieson, 9 November 1929.

36 Ibid, 1929, file 1338, A.N. Middleton to J.J. Kelso, 5 January 1929

37 'Wider Scope Proposed for Juvenile Court,' *Mail & Empire*, 18 January 1928; 'Recommendations of the Grand Jury' (Editorial), *Mail & Empire*, 18 January 1928

38 AO, Dept of the AG, Series C-3 1929, file 2419, W.H. Price to H.S. Mott, 18 January 1928; H.S. Mott to W.H. Price, 21 January 1928

39 Ibid, A.N. Middleton to W.H. Price, 6 February 1928

40 Ibid, 1926, file 3301, H.S. Mott to A.N. Middleton, 9 December 1926; A.N. Middleton to W.H. Price, 13 December 1926; A.N. Middleton to H.S. Mott, 20 December 1926

41 Ibid, 1929, file 1406, W.H. Price to A.N. Middleton, 7 January 1929

42 AO, Dept of the AG, Series A-2, Box 1.31, W.H. Price, 26 April 1929

43 'New Era in Dealing with First Offenders Is Pictured by Price,' *The Globe* (City News), 1 July 1929, pp. 13–14

44 Ibid

45 AO, Dept of the AG, Series C-3 1929, file 2814, I.A. Humphries to Laura E. Jamieson, 9 November 1929

46 Ibid, 1931, file 491, I.A. Humphries to N. Campbell, 16 April 1931

47 Ibid, 1929, file 1338, A.N. Middleton to W.H. Price, 13 December 1928

48 Ibid, 1929, file 3406, W.H. Price to A.N. Middleton, 7 January 1929

49 Ibid, A.N. Middleton, 21 January 1929

50 Ibid, 1921, file 1649, J.E. Jones to W.E. Raney, 18 March 1921; 1925, file 957, F.W. Wilson to W.F. Nickle, 25 February 1925

51 Ibid, 1934, file 3910, G.D. Conant to I.A. Humphries, 27 November 1934; I.A. Humphries to A. Sorsoleil, 5 December 1934; J. Sedgwick to B.W. Heise, [undated] January 1936

52. Ibid, W.W. Denison to J. Sedgwick, 20 February 1936

53 Ibid, A.N. Middleton to W.F. Nickle, 25 September 1924

54 Ibid, 1927, file 2050, Judge Hopkins to W.H. Price, 26 May 1927

55 Ibid, A.N. Middleton to W.H. Price, 19 May 1927

56 Ibid

57 AO, Dept of the PS, RG8 I-1-U, Box 3, no. 206.1971, Hamilton CAS to L. Goldie, 16 April 1927

58 AO, Dept of the AG, Series C-3 1927, file 2050, A.N. Middleton to W.H. Price, 19 May 1927

59 Ibid, Order-in-Council, 26 May 1927; Series A-2, Box 3.6, F.V. Johns

60 'Domestic Relations Court Established for the City,' *Toronto Telegram*, 15 June 1929, pp. 1, 4.

61 AO, Dept of the PS, RG8 I-7-E, Proposed Legislation and Precedents, 1922–4, H.S. Mott to F.V. Johns, 14 December 1922

62 Ibid, J.J. Kelso to F.V. Johns, 19 October 1922
63 AO, Dept of the PS, RG8 I-I-U, Box 3, no. 206.1971, L. Goldie to the Lieutenant Governor in Council, 13 April 1927
64 AO, Dept of the P.S., RG8 I-I-B-5, Box 2, file 1000-12, F.V. Johns to L. Goldie, 23 November 1923
65 See also PAC, CCSD Papers, v. 85, Juvenile Courts – Returns from Ontario, 1938–41, J.F. McKinley to the CWC, 1 April 1940; v. 50, file 455, Judge A.J. Fraser to M. Wieber, 26 August 1943; Balharrie (1929: 83).
66 AO, Dept of the PS, RG8 I-I-U, Box 1, no. 206.108, Order-in-Council, 4 February 1927; Order-in-Council, 12 January 1932. See also 'Judge McKinley Parole Chairman,' *Ottawa Citizen*, 12 January 1932, p. 1. Like Mott's designation as head of the Adult Probation Department for York County, McKinley's appointment to the Parole Board placed him in a clear conflict-of-interest position, which contradicted the government emphasis on the rationalization of magisterial justice.
67 Toronto Board of Control, *Minutes*, no. 455, 19 August 1926
68 Ibid, no. 482, 3 March 1927
69 PAC, CCSD Papers, v. 5, file 18, C.E. Whitton to R.E. Mills, 29 January 1927
70 AO, Dept of the AG, Series C-3 1930, file 1609, I.A. Humphries to W.H. Price, 16 June 1930
71 Ibid, W.H. Price to I.A. Humphries, 18 June 1930
72 AO, Dept of the AG, Series A-2, Box 30.6, H.H. Donald to L.E. Blackwell, 25 November 1943
73 AO, Dept of the AG, Series C-3 1931, file 491, J.F. McKinley to I.A. Humphries, 19 January 1931
74 AO, Dept of the PS, RG8 I-I-U Box 5, no. 206.2262, Order-in-Council, 28 January 1931; AO, Dept of the AG, Series C-3 1931, file 491, I.A. Humphries to J.F. McKinley, 16 February 1931
75 *Toronto Daily Star*, 5 January 1922, p. 3
76 AO, Dept of the AG, Series C-3 1929, file 1917, Dr Margaret Patterson, *The Women's Court*, a report submitted to Judge Coatsworth, [undated] June 1929
77 Ibid, J. Netterfield, Adult Probation Officer, Toronto, *Report for His Honour Judge Coatsworth*, submitted 10 June 1929
78 AO, Toronto Local Council of Women, MU6362, *Minutes* of the Sub-Executive Meeting, 11 December 1928; *Minutes* of the Sub-Executive Meeting, 28 December 1928; *Minutes* of Annual Meeting, 31 January 1929
79 PAC, National Council of Women, MG28 I25 v.38, *Minutes* of Sub-Executive Meeting, 18 January 1929
80 AO, Toronto Local Council of Women, MU6362, *Minutes* of the Sub-Executive Meeting, 5 February 1929
81 Toronto City Council, *Minutes*, no. 186, 11 February 1929, p. 48, Toronto Diocesan Board of the Women's Auxiliary of the Church of England to the Mayor and Members of Council; 'Ministers Protest against Changes

in Women's Court,' *The Globe* (City News), 6 March 1929, p. 1; Toronto Board of Control, *Communications*, 1929, no. 816, Toronto West Presbyterial of the Women's Missionary Society, United Church of Canada, to Mayor McBride, 18 March 1929; ibid, no. 770, Rutherford Women's Christian Temperance Union to Mayor McBride, 18 March 1929

82 'Board Sends Protests to Attorney-General,' *Toronto Daily Star*, 21 March 1929, p. 2

83 'Deputation Urges Cabinet Positions for Ontario Women,' *The Globe* (City News), 7 March 1929, p. 1

84 AO, Toronto Local Council of Women, MU6362, *Minutes* of Special Meeting, 12 March 1929

85 AO, Dept of the AG, Series C-3 1929, file 1917, I.A. Humphries to W.H. Price, 8 June 1929

86 Ibid, Dr Margaret Patterson, *The Women's Court* submitted to Judge Coatsworth [undated] June 1929; a report.

87 Ibid, I.A. Humphries to W.H. Price, 8 June 1929

88 'Judge Hawley S. Mott to Head New Court of Domestic Relations,' *Toronto Daily Star*, 15 June 1929, p. 1

89 Ibid. See also Stewart (1971).

90 'Family Court Opens to Mark Milestone of Justice in City,' *The Globe*, 20 June 1929, pp. 1, 4

91 'Domestic Relations Court Established for The City,' *Toronto Telegram*, 15 June 1929, pp. 1, 4. Magistrate Patterson was finally forcibly removed from the Bench in 1934. See 'Woman CADI Is Removed,' *Border Cities Star*, 22 November 1934; 'Sex Not of First Importance in Appointment to Women's Court' (Editorial), *Toronto Telegram*, 23 November 1934; Gordon (1980, 1984); Chunn (1988a).

92 See also AO, Dept of the AG, Series A-2 Box 4.28, W.H. Price to the Annual Meeting, Junior Conservative Club, St Thomas, Ontario, 3 October 1933; Box 4.29, W.H. Price to Niagara Falls Kiwanis Club, 13 October 1933; Series C-3 1930, file 2964, I.A. Humphries to Council of Social Agencies, Sault Ste Marie, 20 September 1930; 'Price Tells of Work in Crime Prevention,' *Mail & Empire*, 7 December 1932.

93 AO, Dept of the AG, Series A-2 Box 4.28, W.H. Price to the Annual Meeting, Junior Conservative Club, St Thomas, Ontario, 3 October 1933

94 Ibid

Chapter 5

1 Public Archives of Canada (PAC), Canadian Council on Social Development (CCSD) Papers, v. 86, file 1854, W.G. Middleton to C.E. Whitton, 24 December 1937

2 Ibid, C.E. Whitton to R.S. Hosking, 28 December 1937; C.E. Whitton to H.A. Burbidge, 3 January 1938

3 Ibid, C.E. Whitton to Canadian High Commissioner, London, 20 January 1938

4 Ibid, C.E. Whitton to B. Heise, 18 December 1937
5 Ibid, C.E. Whitton to R.E. Mills, 23 December 1937. See also C.E. Whitton to W.F. Nickle, KC, 24 February 1938.
6 PAC, CCSD Papers, v. 10, file 85, *Minutes* of Meeting of Governing Board, 1 May 1933; *Correspondence* with Executive Board, H.S. Mott to C.E. Whitton, 23 May 1933; C.E. Whitton to H.S. Mott, 26 May 1933; H.S. Mott to C.E. Whitton, 30 May 1933
7 PAC, Scott Papers, v. 13, files 47-49, C.E. Whitton to the Rev. H.D. Raymond, 25 April 1933
8 PAC, CCSD Papers, v. 5, file 18, C.E. Whitton to R.E. Mills, 28 January 1927
9 Ibid, C.E. Whitton to Mrs G. Cameron Parker, 28 March 1927
10 PAC, CCSD Papers, v. 86, file 1854, C.E. Whitton to R.E. Mills, 27 December 1937
11 Ibid, v. 45, E. King, 'The Necessity of Case Work in Child Protection,' an address presented at the Social Welfare Conference under the auspices of the Social Service Council of Canada, North Bay, Ontario, 14 October 1929
12 PAC, Scott Papers, v. 14, file 50, H. Atkinson to W.L. Scott, 16 October 1936
13 Ibid, W.L. Scott to H. Atkinson, 20 October 1936
14 Ibid, 'Memo for Miss Whitton Re. the Submission to the Royal Commission,' W.L. Scott, [undated] December 1937
15 Ibid, Secretary, CWC, to W.L. Scott, 3 December 1937
16 Ibid, C.E. Whitton to W.L. Scott, 18 December 1937. See also PAC, CCSD Papers, v. 86, file 1853, 'Delinquency and Juvenile Courts: Consideration of a Social Nature Indicating the Advisibility of a Re-Examination of the Existing Situation.'
17 PAC, CCSD Papers, v. 86, file 1854, C.E. Whitton to V. Parsons, 20 December 1937. Some of the other recipients of the Archambault submission were: W.G. Middleton, Ontario Supreme Court judge and author of the Clubine Judgment; Stuart Edwards, deputy minister of justice, Ottawa; C.V. McArthur, KC, honorary counsel to the CWC; Vera Parsons, counsel to Mrs Clubine in the appeal to the Ontario Supreme Court; H.A. Burbidge, magistrate and family-court judge in Hamilton; and, of course, the Toronto Family Court judges, Robert Mills of the Toronto CAS and W.L. Scott.
18 Archives of Ontario (AO), Dept of the Attorney General, Series C-3 1926, file 221, W.L. Scott to H.S. Mott, 3 February 1926
19 Ibid, H.S. Mott to W.F. Nickle, 5 February 1926
20 Ibid, E. Bayly, Deputy Attorney General, to H.S. Mott, 21 April 1926
21 Ibid, 1937, file 264, H.S. Mott to A.W. Roebuck, 19 March 1937
22 Ibid, A.W. Roebuck to I.A. Humphries, 3 April 1937
23 Ibid, R.S. Hosking to I.A. Humphries, 15 April 1937; I.A. Humphries to R.S. Hosking, 20 April 1937
24 Ibid, I.A. Humphries to Cochrane & MacRae, 22 April 1937; I.A.

Humphries to W.S. Gray, 3 April 1937; I.A. Humphries to J.W. McFadden, 4 May 1937. See also J.W. McFadden to I.A. Humphries, 29 April 1937. McFadden, the crown attorney for Toronto and York County, wrote to say: 'Judge Mott is very anxious in view of this constitutional question that someone from your department should be present at the hearing [before County Court Judge Barton].'

25 Ibid, I.A. Humphries to W.S. Gray, 22 April 1937
26 Ibid, W.S. Gray to I.A. Humphries, 21 May 1937. See also W.S. Gray to I.A. Humphries, 28 April 1937.
27 Ibid, I.A. Humphries to W.S. Gray, 26 May 1937
28 Ibid, S.A. Caldbick, Crown Attorney, Timmins, to P. Leduc, 2 July 1937
29 Ibid, W.S. Gray to I.A. Humphries, 21 July 1937
30 Ibid, W.B. Common to W.S. Gray, 29 July 1937
31 Ibid, I.A. Humphries to W.S. Gray, 4 August 1937
32 AO, Dept of the AG, Series C-3 1937, file 1902, W.B. Common to J.S. Allan, KC, 18 October 1937; W.B. Common to Hough & Hough, Windsor, 20 October 1937
33 PAC, CCSD Papers, v. 86, file 1854, R.E. Mills to C.E. Whitton, 22 February 1938
34 Canada, Dept of Justice, file C.1329 137572, Reference to Supreme Court of Canada, W.B. Common to F.P. Varcoe, KC, 17 January 1938
35 AO, Dept of the AG, Series C-3, 1937, file 264, J.F. McKinley to C.R. Magone, 29 July 1937
36 'Court Appointment Not Confirmed, Non-Support Charge Is Quashed,' The Globe, 15 June 1937, p. 4
37 AO, Dept of the AG, Series C-3 1937, file 264, W.E. MacDonald to Premier Hepburn, 14 July 1937
38 Ibid, G.D. Conant to C.R. Magone, 10 July 1937
39 Ibid, C.R. Magone to P. Leduc, 2 July 1937
40 Ibid, C.R. Magone to W.E. MacDonald, 21 July 1937
41 Ibid, C.R. Magone to G.D. Conant, 12 July 1937
42 Ibid, C.R. Magone to P. Leduc, 2 July 1937
43 Ibid, I.A. Humphries to J.F. McKinley, 14 June 1937
44 Ibid, C.R. Magone to H.S. Mott, 9 July 1937; C.R. Magone to J.F. McKinley, 9 July 1937
45 Ibid, C.R. Magone to G.D. Conant, 12 July 1937; C.R. Magone to W.E. MacDonald, 21 July 1937
46 Ibid, C.R. Magone to G.D. Conant, 12 July 1937

Chapter 6

1 Reference as to Constitutionality of the Adoption Act, the Children's Protection Act, the Children of Unmarried Parents Act, the Deserted Wives' and Children's Maintenance Act ([1939] 71 CCC 110). Factums in

support of the Ontario attorney general were presented by the attorneys general of Manitoba, British Columbia, Prince Edward Island, Saskatchewan, and Alberta (ibid: 111). See also 'The Questioning of Jurisdiction in Certain Social Causes,' *Child and Family Welfare* (Suppl., March 1938): 1.

2 Public Archives of Canada (PAC), Canadian Council on Social Development (CCSD) Papers, v. 86, file 1937–38, R.S. Hosking to M. Bradford, 17 June 1937

3 Ibid, M. Bradford to W.L. Scott, 28 June 1937; M. Bradford to C.E. Whitton, 28 June 1937; M. Bradford to R. Hosking, 26 June 1937; C.E. Whitton to M. Bradford, 24 August 1937

4 Ibid, C.E. Whitton to H.A. Burbidge, 20 December 1937. See also 'Court Change in Three Acts May Be Made,' *Globe and Mail*, 11 December 1937, p. 2.

5 PAC, CCSD Papers, v. 86, file 1854, C.E. Whitton to W.G. Middleton, 27 December 1937

6 Ibid, R.E. Mills to C.E. Whitton, 21 December 1937

7 Ibid, R.E. Mills to C.E. Whitton, 23 December 1937

8 Ibid, C.E. Whitton to C.V. McArthur, KC, 20 December 1937

9 Ibid, C.E. Whitton to B. Heise, 18 December 1937

10 Ibid, C.E. Whitton to R.E. Mills, 23 December 1937

11 Ibid, R.E. Mills to C.E. Whitton, 21 December 1937

12 Ibid, C.E. Whitton to R.E. Mills, 28 December 1937

13 Ibid, C.E. Whitton to B. Heise, 18 December 1937; C.E. Whitton to R.E. Mills, 18 December 1937; C.E. Whitton to W.L. Scott, 27 December 1937

14 Ibid, R.S. Hosking to C.E. Whitton, 27 December 1937; C.E. Whitton to R.E. Mills, 28 December 1937; C.E. Whitton to R.S. Hosking, 28 December 1937

15 Ibid, C.E. Whitton to W.G. Middleton, 20 December 1937

16 Ibid, C.E. Whitton to C.V. McArthur, 20 December 1937

17 Ibid, C.E. Whitton to B. Heise, 18 December 1937

18 PAC, Scott Papers, v. 14, file 50, M. Bradford to W.L. Scott, 25 September 1937. Bradford sent Scott a draft memorandum prepared by Harry Atkinson and the other two members of the special committee, R.S. Hosking and K.H. Rogers.

19 PAC, CCSD Papers, v. 86, file 1854, R.S. Hosking to C.E. Whitton, 27 December 1937

20 Ibid, K.H. Rogers to C.E. Whitton, 4 January 1938

21 Ibid

22 Ibid, R.E. Mills to C.E. Whitton, 21 December 1937

23 Ibid, R.S. Hosking to C.E. Whitton, 27 December 1937

24 Ibid, V. Parsons to C.E. Whitton, 21 January 1938

25 Ibid, W.G. Middleton to C.E. Whitton, 24 December 1937

26 Ibid, S. Edwards to C.E. Whitton, 22 December 1937

27 Ibid, R.E. Mills to C.E. Whitton, 23 December 1937

28 Ibid, C.E. Whitton to R.E. Mills, 27 December 1937
29 Ibid, C.V. McArthur, 6 January 1938
30 Ibid, W.L. Scott to C.E. Whitton, 29 December 1937. See also C.E. Whitton to R.S. Hosking, 31 December 1937
31 Ibid, W.L. Scott, 'Memorandum dealing with Mr Mills' comments on my memo dated January 5, 1938,' 11 January 1938
32 Ibid, C.E. Whitton to R.E. Mills, 27 December 1937
33 Ibid, C.E. Whitton to K.H. Rogers, 8 January 1938
34 Ibid, R.S. Hosking to C.E. Whitton, 6 January 1938. See also R.S. Hosking to C.E. Whitton, 10 January 1938.
35 Ibid, C.E. Whitton to W.L. Scott, 7 January 1938; W.L. Scott to C.E. Whitton, 8 January 1938
36 Ibid, C.E. Whitton to W.G. Middleton, 27 December 1937
37 Ibid, C.E. Whitton to W.L. Scott, 27 December 1937
38 Ibid, W.L. Scott, 'Memorandum as to the Legal Situation which has arisen because of the decision of the Court of Appeal in *Clubine v. Clubine*, reported [1937] Ontario Reports, page 636,' 29 December 1937
39 Ibid
40 Ibid, W.L. Scott, 'Memorandum dealing with Mr Mills' comments on my memo dated January 5 1938,' 11 January 1938
41 Ibid, 'Re. Jurisdiction and Status of Juvenile and Family Courts.' See also C.E. Whitton to C.V. McArthur, 11 January 1938
42 Ibid, C.E. Whitton to W.L. Scott, 11 January 1938
43 Ibid, C.E. Whitton to R.S. Hosking, 7 January 1938; C.E. Whitton to H.A. Burbidge, 8 January 1938
44 Ibid, R.E. Mills to C.E. Whitton, 10 January 1938
45 Ibid, C.E. Whitton to C.V. McArthur, 3 February 1938; C.E. Whitton to J.T. Hackett, 11 February 1938
46 PAC, CCSD Papers, v. 21, file 85, Executive Correspondence 1931, C.E. Whitton to H. Atkinson, 1 May 1931. Whitton told Atkinson she had been authorized at the annual meeting of the council to appoint a family-welfare secretary 'sufficiently *au fait* with the whole field' to relieve her of technical work for several months, but there was no money to hire a permanent worker. This situation did not change in the years that followed. See Executive Correspondence 1932, 'CCCFW Proposed Re-Organization of the Council and Working Relations,' 18 May 1932.
47 PAC, CCSD Papers, v. 86, file 1854, C.E. Whitton to C.V. McArthur, 3 February 1938
48 Ibid, C.E. Whitton to R.E. Mills, 31 January 1938
49 Ibid, C.E. Whitton to C.V. McArthur, 7 February 1938
50 Ibid, C.E. Whitton to R.E. Mills, 31 January 1938
51 Ibid, C.E. Whitton to C.V. McArthur, 12 February 1938
52 Ibid, C.E. Whitton to R.E. Mills, 31 January 1938
53 Ibid, R.E. Mills to C.E. Whitton, 10 February 1938. See also R.E. Mills to C.E. Whitton, 7 February 1938.

54 Ibid, C.E. Whitton to R.E. Mills, 4 February 1938. The memo was titled 'The Why and Wherefore of the Supreme Court Reference on the Jurisdiction of County, Magistrates' and Juvenile Courts in Certain Social Causes,' February 1938.
55 Ibid
56 Ibid, C.E. Whitton to V. Parsons, 3 February 1938
57 Ibid, C.E. Whitton to H.A. Burbidge, 18 February 1938
58 Ibid, C.E. Whitton to Director, Children's Aid Society of Vancouver, 8 March 1938
59 Ibid, C.E. Whitton to K.H. Rogers, 11 February 1938
60 Ibid, C.E. Whitton to R.S. Hosking, 14 February 1938; C.E. Whitton to J.F. McKinley, 16 February 1938; C.E. Whitton to H.A. Burbidge, 18 February 1938
61 AO, Dept of the AG, Series C-3 1937, file 264, G.D. Conant to C.R. Magone, 10 July 1937
62 'Court Dispute Adds to Relief, Is Claim,' *Toronto Daily Star*, 11 December 1937, p. 21
63 'To Ask Ontario "Put Teeth" in Deserted Wives' Statute,' *Toronto Daily Star*, 2 December 1937, p. 6
64 '105 Families in York Deserted, on Relief,' *Globe & Mail*, 21 December 1937, p. 7
65 'Deserted Wives Can't Get Aid from Courts, Relief Head Charges,' *Globe & Mail*, 23 December 1937, p. 4
66 'Court Change in Three Acts May be Made,' *Globe & Mail*, 11 December 1937, p. 2
67 'Warns Lest Social Service be Used as Political Glory,' *Toronto Daily Star*, 15 December 1937, p. 15
68 'Court Change in Three Acts May be Made', Globe & Mail, 11 December 1937, p. 2
69 Ibid
70 Canada, Dept of Justice, file C.1329 137572, Reference to Supreme Court of Canada, G.D. Conant to E. Lapointe, KC, 14 December 1937
71 Ibid, S. Edwards to W.L. MacKenzie King 11 January 1938
72 PAC, CCSD Papers, v. 86, file 1854, R.S. Hosking to C.E. Whitton 31 December 1937
73 Canada, Dept of Justice, file C.1329 137572, Reference to Supreme Court of Canada, G.D. Conant to E. Lapointe, 10 January 1938. At this time, the Ontario legislature met only once a year, in the spring.
74 PAC, CCSD Papers, v. 86, file 1854, R.E. Mills to C.E. Whitton, 1 March 1938
75 Canada, Dept of Justice, file C.1329 137572, Reference to Supreme Court of Canada, S. Edwards, Deputy Minister of Justice, to the attorneys general of Prince Edward Island and of the other provinces, 10 March 1938. He said the chief justice of the Supreme Court had asked the justice department counsel to obtain information about all the courts

having jurisdiction in the respective provinces at Confederation and refer-
ences to any statutes constituting the courts or effecting the jurisdiction.

76 PAC, CCSD Papers, v. 86, file 1854, W.L. Scott to R.E. Mills, 14 June 1938

77 *Reference as to Constitutionality of the Adoption Act, the Children's Protection Act, the Children of Unmarried Parents Act, the Deserted Wives' and Children's Maintenance Act* ([1939] 71 CCC 110 at 130)

78 Ibid, 129

79 Ibid, 112

80 Ibid, 113

81 Ibid, 122, 131–2

82 'Power of Ontario Courts Confirmed,' *Toronto Daily Star*, 23 June 1938, p. 1

83. At a meeting with Attorney General G.D. Conant and his law officers on 16 December 1937, the federal minister of justice, E. Lapointe, agreed to recommend a Reference to his cabinet colleagues. By 1 January 1938, federal and provincial lawyers had hammered out the terms of the proposed Reference. The latter was presented to the federal cabinet on 11 January 1938 and an order-in-council issued the following day (PCI11). See Canada, Dept of Justice, file C.1329 137572, Reference to Supreme Court of Canada, G.D. Conant to E. Lapointe, KC, 14 December 1937; G.D. Conant to E. Lapointe, 23 December 1937; W.B. Common, Acting Deputy AG, to F.P. Varcoe, KC, 23 December 1937; S. Edwards, Deputy Minister of Justice, to W.B. Common, 30 December 1937; S. Edwards to W.B. Common, 3 January 1938; G.D. Conant to E. Lapointe, 10 January 1938; S. Edwards to W.L. Mackenzie King, 11 January 1938; S. Edwards to J.F. Smellie, KC, Registrar, Supreme Court, 13 January 1938.

84 Ibid, S. Edwards to W.B. Common, 30 December 1937

85 Ibid, S. Edwards to W.L. Mackenzie King, 11 January 1938

86 Ibid

87 Ibid, S. Edwards to J.C. McRuer, KC, 21 January 1938

88 Ibid

89 Ibid, J.C. McRuer to C.P. Plaxton, Acting Deputy Minister of Justice, 25 June 1938

90 Ibid

91 Ibid, S.J. Helman to J.C. McRuer, 18 July 1938

92 Ibid, Judge Constantineau to E. Lapointe, 12 July 1938

93 Ibid, J.C. McRuer to C.P. Plaxton, 28 June 1938; J.C. McRuer to C.P. Plaxton, 10 August 1938

94 PAC, CCSD Papers, v. 86, file 1854, W.L. Scott to C.E. Whitton, 16 July 1938

95 Ibid, C.E. Whitton to R.E. Mills, 20 July 1938

96 Canada, Dept of Justice, file C.1329 137572, Reference to Supreme Court of Canada, C.P. Plaxton to G.D. Conant, 2 July 1938

97 Ibid, G.D. Conant to C.P. Plaxton, 8 July 1938; F.P. Varcoe to G.D. Conant, 11 July 1938

98 Ibid, F.P. Varcoe to E. Lapointe, 24 August 1938

99 Ibid, J.C. McRuer to C.P. Plaxton, 10 August 1938

100 Ibid, F.P. Varcoe to E. Lapointe, 24 August 1938

101 Ibid, C.P. Plaxton to J.C. McRuer, 9 August 1938; J.C. McRuer to C.P. Plaxton 10 August 1938; J.C. McRuer to C.P. Plaxton, 29 August 1938

102 Ibid, C.P. Plaxton to J.C. McRuer, 13 August 1938; F.A. Brewin to C.P. Plaxton, 16 August 1938

103 McRuer was specifically concerned about inconsistency between the Supreme Court Judgment on the Reference and the decisions by the Judicial Committee of the Privy Council in the cases of *City of Toronto* v. *Corporation of the Township of York* ([1938] AC 415) and *Martineau & Sons Limited* v. *Montreal City* ([1932] AC 113). The Privy Council had upheld a strict division of judicial and administrative powers; the former could be exercised only by federal appointees and the provinces had no mandate to bestow judicial powers on their appointees.

104 Ibid, F.P. Varcoe to S. Edwards, 8 August 1938; C.P. Plaxton to J.C. McRuer, 9 August 1938; F.P. Varcoe to E. Lapointe, 24 August 1938

105 Ibid, F.P. Varcoe to S. Edwards, 8 August 1938; C.P. Plaxton to J.C. McRuer, 9 August 1938

106 Ibid, C.P. Plaxton to J.C. McRuer, 9 August 1938

107 Ibid, C.P. Plaxton to J.C. McRuer, 26 August 1938; C.P. Plaxton to G.D. Conant, 26 August 1938; J.C. McRuer to C.P. Plaxton, 29 August 1938

Chapter 7

1 'Judge Hawley S. Mott to Head New Court of Domestic Relations,' *Toronto Daily Star*, 15 June 1929, p. 1. Although most of the illustrations and statistics in this chapter pertain to the Toronto Family Court, all the larger socialized courts in Ontario operated in similar ways and had the same general impact.

2 Archives of Ontario (AO), Dept of the Attorney General, Series C-3 1929, file 1917, Dr Margaret Patterson, The Women's Court, a report submitted to Judge Coatsworth, [undated] June 1929

3 AO, Dept of the AG, Series A-2, Box 53.3, H.S. Mott to D. Porter, 1 September 1949

4 'Deserted Wives Can't Get Aid from Courts, Relief Head Charges,' Globe & Mail, 23 December 1937, p. 4

5 The Ottawa Board of Control, for example, authorized expenditure of up to $100 by the juvenile-court judge to trace men who had deserted their wives and children and were being sought for trial. See Ottawa Board of Control, *Minutes*, 28 June 1928, p. 5806

6 Public Archives of Canada (PAC), Canadian Council on Social Development (CCSD) Papers, v. 50, file 455, J.P. Balharrie, *Report on the Ottawa Court*, 1942; AO, Dept of the AG, Series A-2, Box 24.4, H.S. Mott to L.E. Blackwell, 17 October 1944; Series C-3 1929, file 2517, Order-in-Council,

29 July 1929; ibid, 1936, file 1231, Order-in-Council, 20 May 1936

7 AO, Dept of the AG, Series C-3 1931, file 1821, W.E. MacDonald to I.A. Humphries, 19 May 1931

8 Every version of the provincial desertion legislation stipulated that maintenance orders would be denied to deserted women who were adulterous and would also be rescinded on the same grounds.

9 After the official proclamation of the Toronto Family Court in June 1929, the court spent most time on cases of desertion and non-support, although the policing of morality was still a big concern.

10 The argument that individual men simply relinquished their familial powers to the 'patriarchal' state is addressed below.

11 See also AO, Dept of the AG, Series C-3 1929, file 2814, I.A. Humphries to L.E. Jamieson, 9 November 1929.

12 PAC, CCSD Papers, v. 50, file 455, R.S. Hosking to J.I. Wall, 4 September 1935

13 Of 803 new cases received by the BBM in 1924, 395 were referrals from the Toronto Juvenile Court; of 929 new cases received by the BBM in 1943, 80 were court referrals. See BBM, Toronto (1924, 1943).

14 Children's Aid Society of Toronto, Board of Directors, *Minutes* of Meeting, 18 March 1920. See also *Minutes* of Meeting, 20 January 1921; 18 February 1932; 21 March 1935.

15 Children's Aid Society of Toronto, Board of Directors, *Minutes* of Meeting, 23 November 1938; 18 December 1939

16 AO, Dept of the AG, Series C-3 1916, file 2277, Commissioner Boyd to I.B. Lucas, 9 December 1916

17 Ibid, I.B. Lucas to Commissioner Boyd, 19 December 1916

18 PAC, CCSD Papers, v. 13, file 64, C.E. Whitton to W.A. Weston, 26 November 1932

19 Ibid

Chapter 8

1 For a detailed critique of both Donzelot and Lasch, see Barrett and McIntosh (1982).

References

Allard, H.A. 1972. Family courts in Canada. In D. Mendes da Costa, ed., *Studies in Canadian Family Law*, vol. 1, 1–43. Toronto: Butterworths

Allen, R. 1968. The social gospel and the reform tradition in Canada, 1890–1928. *Canadian Historical Review* 49 (Dec.): 381–99.

– 1971. *The Social Passion: Religion and Social Reform in Canada, 1914–1928*. Toronto: University of Toronto Press

Anon. 1927. Toronto experiments in applied psychology. *Canadian Child Welfare News* 3 (1): 29

– 1935. The Canadian Welfare Council. *Child and Family Welfare* 12 (1): 1–2

– 1949. Historical highlights. *Canadian Welfare* 24 (7): 42–3

Ariès, P. 1962. *Centuries of Childhood: A Social History of Family Life*. New York: Vintage Books

Arnup, K. 1986. Education for Motherhood: Government Health Publications, Mothers and the State. Presented at the CSAA Meetings, June

Bacchi, C. 1983. *Liberation Deferred? The Ideas of the English-Canadian Suffragists, 1877–1918*. Toronto: University of Toronto Press

Balharrie, J.B. 1929. Child delinquency in relation to family problems. *Social Welfare* 11 (4): 83–4

Banks, M.A. 1983. The evolution of the Ontario courts 1788–1981. In D.H. Flaherty, ed., *Essays in the History of Canadian Law*, vol. 2, 492–572. Toronto: The Osgoode Society

Barrett, M. 1988. *Women's Oppression Today*, rev. ed. London: New Left Books

Barrett, M., and M. McIntosh. 1982. *The Anti-Social Family*. London: Verso Editions/New Left Books

Bator, P.A. 1979. 'The struggle to raise the lower classes': Public health reform and the problem of poverty in Toronto, 1910 to 1921. *Journal of Canadian Studies* 14 (1): 43–9

Bellamy, D. 1965. Social welfare in Canada. In *Encyclopedia of Social Work*, 36–48. New York: National Association of Social Workers

Big Brother Movement, Inc., Toronto. *Annual Report* (various years). Toronto

Boushy, T.F. 1950. The Historical Development of the Domestic Relations Court. PhD diss., University of Oklahoma

Boyd, S.B. 1989. Child custody, ideologies and employment. *Canadian Journal of Women and the Law* 3 (1): 111–33

Bradford, M. 1938. Dominion will not appeal judgment affecting juvenile and family courts. *Canadian Welfare Summary* 14 (3/Sept.): 1

Brett, F.W. 1953. A History of the Big Brother Movement of Toronto, Inc., 1912–1939. MSW diss., University of Toronto

Briggs, A. 1961. The welfare state in historical perspective. *European Journal of Sociology* 11 (2): 221–58

Brodsky, G., and S. Day. 1989. *Canadian Charter Equality Rights for Women: One Step Forward or Two Steps Back?* Ottawa: Canadian Advisory Council on the Status of Women

Brophy, J. 1982. Parental rights and children's welfare: Some problems of feminists' strategy in the 1920s. *International Journal of the Sociology of Law* 10: 149–68

Brophy, J., and C. Smart. 1981. From disregard to disrepute: The position of women in family law. *Feminist Review* 9/Oct.: 3–16

– 1985. *Women-in-Law.* London: Routledge and Kegan Paul

Brown, R.C., and R. Cook. 1974. *Canada, 1896–1921: A Nation Transformed.* Toronto: McClelland and Stewart

Bryce, P. 1922. Family desertion. *Social Welfare* 4 (4): 82

Bucknall, B., T. Baldwin, and J. Lakin. 1968. Pedants, practitioners and prophets: Legal education at Osgoode Hall to 1957. *Osgoode Hall Law Journal* 1 (2): 139–229

Burbidge, H.A. 1950. The Juvenile and Family Court in Association with the Public Welfare Department. An address presented in Hamilton, Ontario, 21 October 1950

Burnet, J.R. 1974. The urban community and changing moral standards. In M. Horn and R. Sabourin, eds., *Studies in Canadian Social History,* 447–75. Toronto: McClelland and Stewart

Canada. Dominion Bureau of Statistics. 1931. *Census of Canada, Seventh, 1931.* Ottawa: King's Printer

Canada. Royal Commission to Investigate the Penal System. 1938. *Report.* Chair: Hon. Mr Justice Archambault. Ottawa: King's Printer

Canadian Association of Social Workers (CASW). 1926a. Charter membership list. *Social Welfare* 9 (2/Nov.): 303

– 1926b. Official announcement in respect to the organization of the Canadian Association of Social Workers. *Social Welfare* 9 (1 Oct.): 284–6

– 1943. Agency affiliations of CASW members in 1928 and 1943. *The Social Worker* 12 (1/Sept.): 20

Canadian Conference on Child Welfare. 1920. *Proceedings and Papers of Annual Meetings.* Ottawa: Canadian Council on Child Welfare

Canadian Conference on Social Welfare. 1928. *Proceedings*, vol. 1. Ottawa

Canadian Corrections Association. 1960. *The Family Court in Canada*. Ottawa

Canadian Council on Child and Family Welfare. 1930. *Deserted Wives' and Children's Maintenance* (mimeo). Ottawa

– 1931. *Report on Child Protection and Family Welfare Services for the City of Kingston*. Ottawa

Canadian Council on Child Welfare. 1925. *Problems in Family Desertion*. Papers presented by G.B. Clarke, W.L. Scott, and J. Woolf at the Canadian Conference on Child Welfare, Ottawa, 1925 (CCCW Pubn no. 27). Ottawa

Canadian Welfare Council. 1935. *Canadian Cavalcade 1920–1935: A memorandum*. Prepared by C.E. Whitton, Executive Director. Ottawa

– 1938a. *Fundamental Requirements in the Adjustment of the Situation Re Jurisdiction of the Lower Courts in Certain Social Causes*. Ottawa

– 1938b. *Factum of the Canadian Welfare Council*. In the Supreme Court of Canada: In the Matter of Four Acts Passed by the Legislative Assembly of the Province of Ontario: Adoption Act, Children's Protection Act, Children of Unmarried Parents Act, Deserted Wives' and Children's Maintenance Act. sl: sn

– 1938c. The problem of the juvenile and youthful offender. *Child and Family Welfare* 13 (5/Jan.): 49–56

– 1938d. The questioning of jurisdiction in certain social causes. *Child and Family Welfare* (Supplement, March)

– 1940. The problem of family desertion. *Canadian Welfare* 16 (7): 27–9, 36

– 1940–41. *The Problem of Family Desertion*. Ottawa

– 1941. *Some Problems in Family Maintenance, Desertion, etc., together with Summaries of Relevant Dominion and Provincial Legislation: A memorandum*. Ottawa

– 1942. *Juvenile Courts in Canada* (CWC Pubn no. 121). Ottawa

Castell Hopkins, J. 1927. *Canadian Annual Review of Public Affairs*. Toronto: The Canadian Annual Review Ltd

Chan, J.B.L., and R.V. Ericson. 1981. *Decarceration and the Economy of Penal Reform*. Toronto: Centre of Criminology, University of Toronto

Children's Aid Society, Hamilton. 1929. *Report of a Special Committee on the C.A.S. of Hamilton*. Technical Advisers: C.E. Whitton, R.E. Mills, and E. King. Hamilton

Children's Aid Society of Toronto. 1920–. *Annual Report*. Toronto

Chunn, D.E. 1982. Doing good in the twentieth century: The origins of family courts in the United States. *Canadian Criminology Forum* 5: 25–39

– 1987. Regulating the poor in Ontario: From police courts to family courts. *Canadian Journal of Family Law* 6 (1): 85–102

– 1988a. Maternal feminism, legal professionalism and political pragmatism: The rise and fall of Magistrate Margaret Patterson, 1922–1934. In W. Pue and B. Wright, eds., *Canadian Perspectives on Law & Society*, 91–117. Ottawa: Carleton University Press

– 1988b. Rehabilitating deviant families through family courts: The birth of 'socialized' justice in Ontario, 1920–1940. *International Journal of the Sociology of Law* 16 (2): 137–58

Chunn, D.E., and R.C. Smandych. 1982. An interview with David Rothman. *Canadian Criminology Forum* 4 (2/Spr.): 152–62

Clark, S.D. 1942. *The Social Development of Canada.* Toronto: University of Toronto Press

– 1968. *The Developing Canadian Community,* 2d ed. Toronto: University of Toronto Press

Clarke, G.B. 1928. Goals in family social work. *Social Welfare* 10 (7): 151–2

Cleverdon, C.L. 1974. *The Woman Suffrage Movement in Canada,* 2d ed. Toronto: University of Toronto Press

Coatsworth, E. 1920. *Report on the Administration of Criminal Justice and Treatment of Prisoners in New York, Chicago, Detroit, and Toronto.* (Ontario Sess. Paper no. 56). Toronto: King's Printer

Cohen, M.G. 1988. *Women's Work, Markets, and Economic Development in Nineteenth-Century Ontario.* Toronto: University of Toronto Press

Cohen, S. 1979. The punitive city: Notes on the future of social control. *Contemporary Crises* 3 (4): 339–63

– 1983. Social control talk: Telling stories about correctional change. In D. Garland and P. Young, eds., *The Power to Punish,* 101–29. London: Heinemann Educational Books

– 1985. *Visions of Social Control.* Cambridge: Polity Press

Cohen, S., and A.T. Scull, eds. 1983. *Social Control and the State.* Oxford: Martin Robertson

Comack, E. 1987. Theorizing on the Canadian state and social formation. In R.S. Ratner and J.L. McMullan, eds., *State Control: Criminal Justice Politics in Canada,* 225–40. Vancouver: University of British Columbia Press

County of York. Adult Probation Dept. *Annual Report for County of York (including Toronto)* (various years). Toronto

– Building Committee. 1929. Final Report of Building Committee – York County Building. In *Minutes of the Council of the Corporation of the County of York,* 327–32. Newmarket

– Juvenile and Domestic Relations Court. Annual Report (various years). In *Minutes of the Council of the Corporation of the County of York.* Newmarket

– Juvenile Court Committee. 1931. Report to the Warden and Council, 17 June 1931. Chairman: W.E. MacDonald. In *Minutes of the Council of the Corporation of the County of York,* 337–45. Newmarket

– Special Committee on Juvenile and Domestic Relations Courts. 1931. Report to the County Council, 29 January 1931. Chairman: W.E. MacDonald. In *Minutes of the Council of the Corporation of the County of York,* 78–83. Newmarket

Craven, P. 1983. Law and ideology: The Toronto Police Court, 1850–1880. In D.H. Flaherty, ed., *Essays in the History of Canadian Law,* vol. 2, 248–307. Toronto: The Osgoode Society

Cross, M.S., and G.S. Kealey, eds. 1983. *The Consolidation of Capitalism, 1896–1929*. Toronto: McClelland and Stewart

Crysdale, S. 1961. *The Industrial Struggle and Protestant Ethics in Canada*. Toronto: Ryerson Press

Curtis, B. 1987. Preconditions of the Canadian state: Educational reform and the construction of a public in Upper Canada, 1837–1846. In A. Moscovitch and J. Albert, eds., *The Benevolent State: The Growth of Welfare in Canada*, 47–67. Toronto: Garamond Press

Dahl, T.S., and A. Snare. 1978. The coercion of privacy: A feminist perspective. In C. Smart and B. Smart, eds., *Women, Sexuality and Social Control*, 8–26. London: Routledge and Kegan Paul

Dangerfield, G. 1961. *The Strange Death of Liberal England*. New York: Capricorn

Denison, G.T. 1920. *Recollections of a Police Magistrate*. Toronto: Musson

Dingman, F. 1948. The Story of the Wellington Family Court. MSW diss., University of Toronto

Donzelot, J. 1979. The poverty of political culture. *Ideology and Consciousness* (5): 73–86

– 1980. *The Policing of Families*. New York: Pantheon

Dunn, N. 1938. Constitutional law – jurisdiction of domestic relations courts – interference with jurisdiction of superior courts. *Canadian Bar Review* 16: 644–53

Dymond, A.M. 1923. *The Laws of Ontario Relating to Women and Children*. Toronto: Clarkson W. James

Ehrenreich, B., and D. English. 1978. *For Her Own Good*. Garden City, NY: Anchor Press

Eichler, M. 1985. Family policy in Canada: From where to where? In *Justice beyond Orwell*. Montreal: Les Editions Yvon Blais

– 1988. *Families in Canada Today*, 2d ed. Toronto: Gage

Ericson, R.V. 1987. The state and criminal justice reform. In R.S. Ratner and J.L. McMullan, eds., *State Control: Criminal Justice Politics in Canada*, 21–37. Vancouver: University of British Columbia Press

Ericson, R.V., and P. Baranek. 1982. *The Ordering of Justice: A Study of Accused Persons as Dependants in the Criminal Process*. Toronto: University of Toronto Press

Finkel, A. 1977. Origins of the welfare state in Canada. In L. Panitch, ed., *The Canadian State*, 344–70. Toronto: University of Toronto Press

Fiser, V. 1966. Development of Services for the Juvenile Delinquent in Ontario, 1891–1921. MSW diss., University of Toronto

Fitz, J. 1981a. The child as a legal subject. In R. Dale et al., eds., *Education and the State*, vol. 2: *Politics, Patriarchy and Practice*. Milton Keynes: Open University Press

– 1981b. Welfare, the family and the child. In *Education, Welfare and Social Order*, Block 5, Unit 12. Milton Keynes: Open University Press

Foucault, M. 1977. *Discipline and Punish: The Birth of the Prison.* New York: Pantheon

– 1980a. *The History of Sexuality*, vol. 1. New York: Vintage Books

– 1980b. *Power/Knowledge*, edited by C. Gordon. New York: Pantheon

Friedman, M. 1927. Behaviour problems as related to family rehabilitation. *Social Welfare* 9 (7): 405–6

Garland, D. 1981. The birth of the welfare sanction. *British Journal of Law and Society* 8 (Summer): 29–45

– 1985. *Punishment and Welfare.* Brookfield, VT: Gower

Gavigan, S.A.M. 1988. Law, gender and ideology. In A. Bayefsky, ed., *Legal Theory Meets Legal Practice*, 283–95. Edmonton: Academic Printing & Publishing

Gaylin, W., et al. 1978. *Doing Good: The Limits of Benevolence.* New York: Pantheon

Gillis, J.R. 1975. The evolution of juvenile delinquency in England, 1890–1914. *Past and Present* (67/May): 96–126

Goff, C., and C. Reasons. 1978. *Corporate Crime in Canada.* Scarborough, ON: Prentice-Hall

Goheen, P.G. 1970. Currents of change in Toronto, 1850–1900. In R.D. Francis and D.B. Smith, eds., *Readings in Canadian History*, 217–47. Toronto: Holt, Rinehart & Winston

Gordon, Linda. 1988a. *Heroes of Their Own Lives.* New York: Penguin Books

– 1988b. What does welfare regulate? *Social Research* 55 (4): 609–29

Gordon, Lorraine. 1980. *Doctor Margaret Patterson: First Woman Police Magistrate in Eastern Canada.* sl: sn

– 1984. Doctor Margaret Norris Patterson: First woman police magistrate in Eastern Canada – Toronto – January 1922 to November 1934. *Atlantis* 10 (1): 95–109

Great Britain. Home Dept. 1936. *Report of Committee on Social Services in Courts of Summary Jurisdiction.* Chair: S.W. Harris (Cmd 5122). London: H.M.S.O.

Guest, D. 1980. *The Emergence of Social Security in Canada.* Vancouver: University of British Columbia Press

Gusfield, J. 1981. *The Culture of Public Problems.* Chicago: University of Chicago Press

Hagan, J., and J.S. Leon. 1977. Rediscovering delinquency: Social history, political ideology and the sociology of law. *American Sociological Review* 42: 587–98

– 1980. The rehabilitation of law: A social and historical comparison of the Canadian and American probation movements. *Canadian Journal of Sociology* 5 (3): 235–51

Hall, S. 1984. The rise of the representative/interventionist state 1880s-1920s. In G. McLennan et al., eds., *State and Society in Contemporary Britain*, 7–49. Cambridge: Polity Press

Hamilton, Ont., Probation Office. 1945. *Annual Report for the City of Hamilton and County of Wentworth.* Hamilton

Hareven, T.K. 1969. An ambiguous alliance: Some aspects of American influences on Canadian social welfare. *Social History* 3 (Apr.): 82–98

Harkness, D.B. 1924. *Courts of Domestic Relations: Duties, Methods and Services of Such Courts: Are They Needed in Canada?* (CCCW Pubn no. 11). Ottawa: Canadian Council on Child Welfare

Hay, J.R. 1978. *The Development of the British Welfare State, 1880–1975.* London: Edward Arnold Ltd

Held, F. 1927. Inter-relationship of family and children's agencies. *Social Welfare* 10 (2): 39–41

– 1959. *A Brief History of the Ontario Welfare Council, 1908–1959.* Toronto: Ontario Welfare Council

Herman, K. 1971. The emerging welfare state: Changing perspectives in Canadian welfare policies and programs, 1867–1960. In D.I. Davies and K. Herman, eds., *Social Space: Canadian Perspectives*, 131-41. Toronto: New Press

Hill, R. 1920. New objectives in family social work. *Social Welfare* 2 (10): 275–6

Hoffman, C.W. 1918. Courts of domestic relations: Report of the Committee of the N.P.A. *Journal of Criminal Law, Criminology and Police Science* 8: 745–48

Homel, G.H. 1981. Denison's law: Criminal justice and the Police Court in Toronto, 1877–1921. *Ontario History* 73 (3): 171–86

Honsberger, J. 1972. A history of legal education in Ontario. *Law Society of Upper Canada Gazette* 6: 35–54

Hosking, R.S. 1930. *The Family Court* (CCCFW Pubn no 53). Ottawa: Canadian Council on Child and Family Welfare

– 1932. The family court. *Child and Family Welfare* 8 (3/Sept.): 23–7, 35

Houston, S. 1972. Victorian origins of juvenile delinquency: A Canadian experience. *History of Education Quarterly* 12 (3): 254–80

– 1982. The 'waifs and strays' of a late Victorian city: Juvenile delinquents in Toronto. In J. Parr, ed., *Childhood and Family in Canadian History*, 129–42. Toronto: McClelland and Stewart

Hunt, A. 1978. *The Sociological Movement in Law.* London: Macmillan

Hunter, A.F. 1925. Historical note on finance in the Great War and afterwards. *Ontario History* 22: 125–43

Johnson, L.A. 1972. The development of class in Canada in the twentieth century. In G. Teeple, ed., *Capitalism and the National Question*, 141-83. Toronto: University of Toronto Press

Jones, A.E., and L. Rutman. 1981. *In the Children's Aid: J.J. Kelso and Child Welfare in Ontario.* Toronto: University of Toronto Press

Kanigsberg, R.A. 1936. The desirability of courts of domestic relations in Canada. *Fortnightly Law Journal* 5 (1 Feb.): 201–2

– 1937/8. Domestic quarrels in the law courts. *Dalhousie Review* 17: 61, 64

Katz, M.B., M.J. Stern, and M.J. Doucet. 1982. *The Social Organization of Early Industrial Capitalism*. Cambridge, MA: Harvard University Press

Kealey, G.S. 1972. Hogtown: Working class Toronto at the turn of the century. In R.D. Francis and D.B. Smith, eds., *Readings in Canadian History*, 175–95. Toronto: Holt, Rinehart & Winston

Kelso, J.J. c. 1894. Can slums be abolished or must we pay the penalty? In P. Rutherford, ed., *Saving the Canadian City: The first phase 1880–1920*, 165–70. Toronto: University of Toronto Press

– 1907. Delinquent children: Some improved methods whereby they may be prevented from following a criminal career. *Canadian Law Review* 6: 106–10

– 1908. Children's courts. *Canadian Law Times and Review* 28: 163–6

Kinsman, G. 1987. *The Regulation of Desire*. Montreal: Black Rose

Kirkpatrick-Strong, M. 1930. *Public Welfare Administration in Canada* (Social Service Monographs, No. 10). Chicago: University of Chicago Press

Klein, S.S. 1985. Individualism, liberalism, and the new family law. *University of Toronto Faculty of Law Review* 43 (8): 116–35

Komar, R.N. 1975. The enforcement of support arrears: A history of alimony, maintenance and the myth of the one-year rule. *Reports of Family Law* 19: 129–91

Krieger, L. 1963. The idea of the welfare state in Europe and the United States. *Journal of the History of Ideas* 24: 553–68

Lasch, C. 1979. *Haven in a Heartless World*. New York: Basic Books

Laycock, J.E. 1943. Juvenile courts in Canada. *Canadian Bar Review* 21 (1/Jan.): 1–22

Leacy, F.H., ed. 1983. *Historical Statistics of Canada*, 2d ed. Ottawa: Statistics Canada

Leon, J.S. 1977. The development of Canadian juvenile justice: A background for reform. *Osgoode Hall Law Journal* 15 (1): 71–106

– 1978. New and old themes in Canadian juvenile justice: The origins of delinquency legislation and the prospects for recognition of children's rights. In H. Berkeley et al, eds., *Children's Rights: Legal and Educational Issues*, 35–58. Toronto: Ontario Institute for Studies in Education

Lewis, J., ed. 1986. *Labour and Love: Women's Experience of Home and Family, 1850–1940*. Oxford: Basil Blackwell

Lowman, J., R. Menzies, and T. Palys, eds. 1987. *Transcarceration: Essays in the Sociology of Social Control*. Aldershot: Gower

Lubove, R. 1965. *The Professional Altruist: The Emergence of Social Work as a Career, 1880–1930*. Cambridge, MA: Harvard University Press

– 1968. *The Struggle for Social Security 1900–1935*. Cambridge, MA: Harvard University Press

McBarnet, D. 1981. Magistrates' courts and the ideology of justice. *British Journal of Law and Society* 8 (2): 181–97

McConnachie, K. 1983. A note on fertility rates among married women in Toronto, 1871. *Ontario History* 75 (1/Mar.): 87–97

McFarlane, G.G., A.H. Sumpter, and D.W.F. Coughlan. 1966. *The Development of Probation Services in Ontario.* Toronto: Queen's Printer

MacGill, E.G. 1955. *My Mother the Judge.* Toronto: Ryerson Press

McGrath, W.T. 1976. The juvenile and family courts. In W.T. McGrath, ed., *Crime and Its Treatment in Canada*, 237–48. Toronto: Macmillan

McKenty, N. 1967. *Mitch Hepburn.* Toronto: McClelland and Stewart

McKnight, J.R. 1963. Introductory Remarks by His Honour Judge John R. McKnight at the Official Opening of the Juvenile and Family Court Building of Ottawa and Carleton on 23 October 1963. Ottawa

McLaren, A. 1990. *Our Own Master Race.* Toronto: McClelland and Stewart

McLaren, A., and A.T. McLaren. 1986. *The Bedroom and the State.* Toronto: McClelland and Stewart

McLaren, J.P.S. 1986. Chasing the social evil: Moral fervour and the evolution of Canada's prostitution laws, 1867–1917. *Canadian Journal of Law and Society* 1: 125–65

MacMurchy, H. 1923. Child welfare in Canada. *Annals of the American Academy of Political and Social Science* 105: 267–76

McNaught, K. 1982. *The Pelican History of Canada.* rev. ed. Harmondsworth: Penguin

McPhedran, M. 1919. Domestic relations and the child. *Social Welfare* 2 (1): 14–15

Maines, J.A. 1959. Through the years in C.A.S.W. *The Social Worker* 27 (4/Oct.): 5–45

Manitoba Association of Women and the Law (MAWL). 1988. *Gender Equality in the Courts.* Winnipeg

Marchak, M.P. 1981. *Ideological Perspectives on Canada.* 2d ed. Toronto: McGraw-Hill Ryerson

Martin, S.L., and K.E. Mahoney, eds. 1987. *Equality and Judicial Neutrality.* Toronto: Carswell

May, M. 1973. 'Innocence and experience': The evolution of the concept of juvenile delinquency in the mid-nineteenth century. *Victorian Studies* 18 (1/Sept.): 7–29

Miller, P.J. 1982. Psychology and the child: Homer Lane and J.B. Watson. In P.T. Rooke and R.L. Schnell, eds., *Studies in Childhood History*, 57–80. Calgary: Detselig

Mohr, N.E. 1920. *A Study of Illegitimacy in Ontario* (SSCO Pamphlet No.8). Toronto: Social Service Council of Ontario

Mommsen, W.J., ed. 1981. *The Emergence of the Welfare State in Britain and Germany, 1850–1950.* London: Croom Helm

Morrison, T.R. 1976. Their proper sphere: Feminism, the family, and child-centred social reform in Ontario, 1875–1900. *Ontario History* 68 (1): 45–64, 68 (2): 65–74

Morton, M.E. 1988. Dividing the wealth, sharing the poverty: The (re)formation of 'family' in law in Ontario. *Canadian Review of Sociology and Anthropology* 25 (2): 254–75

Morton, W.L. 1950. *The Progressive Party in Canada.* Toronto: University of Toronto Press

Moscovitch, A., and J. Albert, eds. 1987. *The Benevolent State.* Toronto: Garamond Press

Moscovitch, A., and G. Drover. 1987. Social expenditures and the welfare state: The Canadian experience in historical perspective. In A. Moscovitch and J. Albert, eds., *The Benevolent State*, 13–43. Toronto: Garamond Press

Mossman, M.J., and M. MacLean. 1986. Family law and social welfare: Toward a new equality. *Canadian Journal of Family Law* 5 (1): 79–110

Mott, H.S. 1933. The juvenile court in crime prevention. *Child and Family Welfare* 9 (4/Nov.): 45–46

Muncie, J. 1981. Youth and the reforming zeal. In *Law and Disorder: Histories of Crime and Criminal Justice*, 1–28. Milton Keynes: The Open University

Neighbourhood Workers' Association. 1920. *Illegitimacy in Toronto.* Toronto

O'Donovan, K. 1985. *Sexual Divisions in Law.* London: Weidenfeld and Nicholson

Oliver, P.N. 1975. *Public and Private Persons: the Ontario Political Culture 1914–1934.* Toronto: Clarke, Irwin

– 1977. *G. Howard Ferguson: Ontario Tory.* Toronto: University of Toronto Press

Oliver, P.N., and M.D. Whittingham. 1987. Elitism, localism, and the emergence of adult probation services in Ontario, 1893–1972. *Canadian Historical Review* 68 (2): 225–58

Ontario. Dept. of Public Welfare. 1935. *Report of the Committee to Investigate the Present Reformatory School System of Ontario.* Chair: H.S. Mott. Toronto

– Inspector of Legal Offices. 1926–. *Annual Report* (Sessional Paper no. 5)

– Royal Commission of Inquiry into Civil Rights. 1968. *Report Number One*, vol. 2: *Juvenile and Family Courts.* Chair: J.C. McRuer. Toronto: Queen's Printer

– Royal Commission on Public Welfare. 1930. *Report.* Chair: P.D. Ross. Toronto: King's Printer

– Royal Commission on the Prison and Reformatory System. 1891. *Report* (Sessional Paper no. 18). Toronto: Queen's Printer

– Royal Commission to Inquire into, Consider and Report on the Best Mode of Selecting, Appointing and Remunerating Sheriffs, etc., etc. 1921. *Interim Report Respecting Police Magistrates.* Chair: W.D. Gregory (Sessional Paper no. 63). Toronto: King's Printer

– Superintendent of Neglected and Dependent Children. 1924–30. Annual *Report* (Sessional Paper no. 19). Toronto

Ontario Law Reform Commission. Family Law Project. 1974. *Report*, vol. 5: *Family Courts.* Toronto: Ministry of the Attorney General

Ottawa. Board of Control. 1928–46. *Minutes of Meetings.* Ottawa

– Family Court. 1940–50. *Annual Report.* Ottawa

Palmer, B.D. 1983. *Working-Class Experience: The Rise and Reconstitution of Canadian Labour, 1800–1980*. Toronto: Butterworths

Panitch, L. 1977. The role and nature of the Canadian state. In L. Panitch, ed., *The Canadian State*, 3–27. Toronto: University of Toronto Press

Parr, J. 1982. Introduction. In J. Parr, ed., *Childhood and Family in Canadian History*, 7–16. Toronto: McClelland and Stewart

– 1990. *The Gender of Breadwinners: Women, Men, and Change in Two Industrial Towns, 1880–1950*. Toronto: University of Toronto Press

Parsons, H. 1922. The National Council of Women. *Social Welfare* 5 (1): 4

Pateman, C. 1989a. Feminist critiques of the public/private dichotomy. In C. Pateman, *The Disorder of Women*, 118–40. Cambridge: Polity Press

– 1989b. The patriarchal state. In C. Pateman, *The Disorder of Women*, 179–209. Cambridge: Polity Press

Pitsula, J. 1979. The emergence of social work in Toronto 1879–1926. *Journal of Canadian Studies* 14: 35–42

Platt, A. 1969. *The Child Savers: The Invention of Delinquency*. Chicago: University of Chicago Press

Popple, A.B. 1921. Police court systems. *The Canadian Law Times* 41 (8–9)

– 1927. Magisterial courts: A plea for a re-adjustment of their legal machinery. *Canadian Bar Review* 5: 417–18

Poster, M. 1978. *Critical Theory of the Family*. New York: Seabury Press

Pound, R. 1916. Individual interests in the domestic relations court. *Michigan Law Review* 14: 177–96

– 1942. *Social Control through Law*. New Haven: Yale University Press

– 1943. The rise of socialized justice. In *National Probation Association Yearbook, 1942*, 3–24. New York

Price, W.H. 1934. Juvenile, family and domestic relations courts. In *Canadian Conference on Social Welfare Proceedings, 1934*, 16–17. s.l.: s.n

Pukacz, E., and G. Noble. 1965. *Report on the Organization and Operation of the Metropolitan Toronto Juvenile and Family Court*. Toronto: Ontario Dept. of the Attorney General and the Municipality of Metropolitan Toronto

Ramkhalawansingh, C. 1974. Women during the Great War. In *Women at Work: Ontario, 1850–1930*, 261–307. Toronto: Women's Press

Rankin, P. 1989. The politicization of Ontario farm women. In L. Kealey and J. Sangster, eds., *Beyond the Vote: Canadian Women and Politics*, 309–332. Toronto: University of Toronto Press

Roberts, W. 1979. 'Rocking the cradle for the world': The new woman and maternal feminism, Toronto, 1877–1914. In L. Kealey, ed., *A Not Unreasonable Claim*, 15–45. Toronto: Women's Press

Rooke, P.T., and R.L. Schnell. 1981a. Child welfare in English Canada, 1920–1948. *Social Service Review*, Sept.: 484–506

– 1981b. Women as Social Reformers: The Ambiguities of Charlotte Whitton's Social Philosophy (1920–48). Presented at the Fourth Bi-Annual Conference on Social Policy, Carleton University, April 1981

– 1982. Childhood and charity in nineteenth-century British North America. *Social History* 15 (29): 157–79

– 1983. *Discarding the Asylum*. Lanham, MD: University Press of America

– 1987. *No Bleeding Heart: Charlotte Whitton, a Feminist on the Right*. Vancouver: University of British Columbia Press

Ross, E.A. 1969. *Social Control*. Cleveland: Case Western Reserve University Press

Rothman, D.J. 1971. *The Discovery of the Asylum*. Boston: Little, Brown

– 1978. The state as parent: Social policy in the Progressive era. In W. Gaylin et al, eds., *Doing Good: The Limits of Benevolence*, 67–96. New York: Pantheon

– 1980. *Conscience and Convenience*. Boston: Little, Brown

– 1981. Social control: The uses and abuses of the concept in the history of incarceration. *Rice University Studies* 67 (1): 9–20

Russell, P.H. 1969. *The Supreme Court of Canada as a Bilingual and Bicultural Institution*. Ottawa: Queen's Printer

– 1987. *The Canadian Judiciary: The Third Branch of Government*. Toronto: Mc-Graw-Hill Ryerson

Rutherford, P. 1971. Tomorrow's metropolis: The urban reform movement in Canada, 1880–1920. *Canadian Historical Association Papers*, 203–24

– 1974. Introduction. In P. Rutherford, ed., *Saving the Canadian City: The First Phase 1880–1920*, ix–xxiii. Toronto: University of Toronto Press

Ryerson, E. 1978. *The Best-Laid Plans*. New York: Hill and Wang

Sangster, J. 1989. *Dreams of Equality: Women on the Canadian Left, 1920–1950*. Toronto: McClelland and Stewart

Schlossman, S.L. 1977. *Love and the American Delinquent*. Chicago: University of Chicago Press

Schnell, R. 1987. 'A Children's Bureau for Canada': The origins of the Canadian Council on Child Welfare, 1913–1921. In A. Moscovitch and J. Albert, eds., *The Benevolent State*, 95–110. Toronto: Garamond Press

Schull, J. 1978. *Ontario since 1867* (Ontario Historical Studies Series). Toronto: McClelland and Stewart

Schwendinger, H., and J. Schwendinger. 1974. *The Sociologists of the Chair*. New York: Basic Books

Scott, W.L. 1908. The Juvenile Delinquent Act. *The Canadian Law Times and Review* 28: 892–904

– 1927. *The Juvenile Court in Law and the Juvenile Court in Action* (CCCW Pubn. no. 34). Ottawa: Canadian Council on Child Welfare

– 1938a. *The Genesis of the Juvenile Delinquents Act 1888–1908* (mimeo). Ottawa

– 1938b. Jurisdiction of lower courts upheld. *Canadian Welfare Summary* 14 (2/July): 34–41

Scull, A.T. 1977. *Decarceration: Community Treatment and the Deviant – A Radical View*. Englewood Cliffs, NJ: Prentice-Hall

– 1981. Progressive dreams, Progressive nightmares: Social control in twentieth century America. *Stanford Law Review* 33: 575–90

– 1983. Community corrections: Panacea, progess or pretence? In D. Garland and P. Young, eds., *The Power to Punish*, 146–65. London: Heinemann

Smart, B. 1983. On discipline and social regulation: A review of Foucault's genealogical analysis. In D. Garland and P. Young, eds., *The Power to Punish*, 62–83. London: Heinemann

– 1985. *Michel Foucault*. London: Tavistock

Smart, C. 1982. Regulating families or legitimating patriarchy? Family law in Britain. *International Journal of the Sociology of Law* 10: 129–47

– 1984. *The Ties That Bind*. London: Routledge and Kegan Paul

– 1989. *Feminism and the Power of Law*. London: Routledge

Smart, C., and S. Sevenhuijsen, eds. 1989. *Child Custody and the Politics of Gender*. London: Routledge

Snell, J.G. 1983. 'The white life for two': The defence of marriage and sexual morality in Canada, 1890–1914. *Histoire Sociale* 16 (31): 111-28

– 1986a. Courts of domestic relations: A study of early twentieth century judicial reform in Canada. *Windsor Yearbook of Access to Justice* 6: 36–60

– 1986b. Marriage humour and its social functions, 1900–1939. *Atlantis* 11 (2): 70–85

Snell, J.G., and F. Vaughan. 1985. *The Supreme Court of Canada: History of the Institution*. Toronto: The Osgoode Society

Social Service Council of Canada. 1923. *Reports*. Ottawa

– Committee on the Family. 1923. Courts of domestic relations. *Social Welfare* 5 (5): 105–7

Social Service Council of Ontario & Neighbourhood Workers' Assn. 1921. *Report of Joint Committee to the Premier of Ontario and Cabinet Ministers*. Toronto

Speisman, S.A. 1973. Munificent parsons and municipal parsimony: Voluntary versus public poor relief in nineteenth century Toronto. *Ontario History* 65 (1): 33–49

Spettigue, C.O. 1957. *A Historical Review of Ontario Legislation on Child Welfare*. Toronto: Ontario Dept of Public Welfare

Splane, R.B. 1951. The Administration of the Children of Unmarried Parents Act of the Province of Ontario. MSW diss., University of Toronto

– 1965. *Social Welfare in Ontario 1791-1893*. Toronto: University of Toronto Press

Stapleford, F.N. 1938. *After Twenty Years: A Short History of the Neighbourhood Workers' Association, 1918–1938*. Toronto

Stewart, V.L. 1971. *The History of the Juvenile and Family Court of Toronto*. Toronto

Stewart-Hay, B. 1931. Family desertion. *Social Welfare* 13 (4): 84–5, 87

Strong-Boag, V. 1976. *The Parliament of Women: The National Council of Women of Canada, 1893–1929*. Ottawa: Museum of Man

– 1979. Wages for housework: Mothers' allowances and the beginnings of social security in Canada. *Journal of Canadian Studies* 14 (1): 24–34

– 1982. Intruders in the nursery: Childcare professionals reshape the years one to five, 1920–1940. In J. Parr, ed., *Childhood and Family in Canadian History*, 160–78. Toronto: McClelland and Stewart

– 1988. *The New Day Recalled: Lives of Girls and Women in English Canada, 1919–1939*. Toronto: Copp Clark Pitman

Struthers, J. 1983. *No Fault of Their Own: Unemployment and the Canadian Welfare State 1914–1941*. Toronto: University of Toronto Press

Sutherland, N. 1976. *Children in English-Canadian Society: Framing the Twentieth Century Consensus*. Toronto: University of Toronto Press

Taylor, J.H. 1987. Sources of political conflict in the Thirties: Welfare policy and the geography of need. In A. Moscovitch and J. Albert, eds., *The Benevolent State*, 144–54. Toronto: Garamond Press

Thorne, B., and M. Yalom, eds. 1982. *Rethinking the Family*. New York: Longman

Toronto. City Council. 1920–45. *Proceedings of the Corporation of the City of Toronto*. Toronto

– Family Court. 1912–52. *Annual Report*. Toronto

– Police Dept. 1901–35. *Annual Report of the Chief Constable*. Toronto

– 1935. Toronto Social Service Index celebrates twenty-first birthday. *Child and Family Welfare* 11 (1): 39

Torrance, C.V. 1967. The history of law enforcement in Hamilton from 1833 to 1967. *Wentworth Bygones* 7: 67–78

Traves, T. 1979. Security without regulation. In M.S. Cross and G.S. Kealey, eds., *The Consolidation of Capitalism 1896–1929*, 19–44. Toronto: McClelland and Stewart

Tudiver, N. 1987. Forestalling the welfare state: The establishment of programmes of corporate welfare. In A. Moscovitch and J. Albert, eds., *The Benevolent State*, 186–202. Toronto: Garamond Press

United Church of Canada. Board of Evangelism and Social Service. 1926–45. *Annual Report*. Toronto

Urquhart, M.C., and A.H. Buckley. 1965. *Historical Statistics of Canada*. Toronto: Macmillan

Ursel, J. 1986. The state and the maintenance of patriarchy: A case study of family, labour and welfare legislation in Canada. In J. Dickinson and B. Russell, eds., *Family, Economy, and State*, 150–91. Toronto: Garamond Press

Valverde, M. 1991. *The Age of Light, Soap and Water*. Toronto: McClelland and Stewart

Varcoe, F.H. 1954. *The Distribution of Legislative Power in Canada*. Toronto: Carswell

Vernon, C.W. 1929. Helping dependent families to help themselves. *Social Welfare II* (4): 80–2

Vipond, M. 1977. The image of women in mass circulation magazines in the 1920s. In S.M. Trofimenkoff and A. Prentice, eds., *Essays in Canadian Women's History*, vol. 1, 116–24. Toronto: McClelland and Stewart

Walker, C.J. 1943. The shape of things past. *The Social Worker* 12 (1): 4–11

Wallace, E. 1950. The origin of the welfare state in Canada, 1867–1900. *Canadian Journal of Economics and Political Science* 16: 383–93

Weaver, J. 1977. *Shaping the Canadian City: Essays on Urban Politics and Policy, 1890–1920*. Toronto: Institute of Public Administration of Canada

Weeks, J. 1986. *Sexuality*. London: Tavistock

Whitton, C.E. 1927. Ontario [Law Revision]. *Canadian Child Welfare News* 3 (2): 14–19

– 1931. Problems in delinquency treatment. *Social Welfare* 13 (5): 102–3, 108

– 1934. Some appreciations: Mr. J.J. Kelso. *Child and Family Welfare* 9 (6): 10–11

Wiebe, R. 1967. *The Search for Order, 1877–1920*. New York: Hill and Wang

Williams, D.R. 1984. *Duff: A Life in the Law*. Vancouver: University of British Columbia Press

Williams, T.D. 1928. Desertion and non-support: The importance of the problem. In *Proceedings of the First Annual Meeting of the Canadian Conference on Social Work, Montreal, 24–27 April 1928*, 49–52. Ottawa

Woodroofe, K. 1962. *From Charity to Social Work in England and the United States*. Toronto: University of Toronto Press

Zaretsky, E. 1976. *Capitalism, the Family and Personal Life*. New York: Harper & Row

– 1982. The place of the family in the origins of the welfare state. In B. Thorne and M. Yalom, eds., *Rethinking the Family*, 188–224. New York: Longman

– 1986. Rethinking the welfare state: Dependence, economic individualism and the family. In J. Dickinson and B. Russell, eds., *Family, Economy and State*, 85–109. Toronto: Garamond Press

Index